Downfall of the Templars

Downfall of the Templars

Guilty of Diabolic Magic?

Tony McMahon

First published in Great Britain in 2025 by
Pen & Sword History
An imprint of Pen & Sword Books Limited
Yorkshire – Philadelphia

ISBN 978 1 03611 358 2

A CIP catalogue record for this book is available from the British Library.

Typeset by Mac Style
Printed in the UK by CPI Group (UK) Ltd, Croydon, CR0 4YY.

The Publisher's authorised representative in the EU for product safety is Authorised Rep Compliance Ltd., Ground Floor, 71 Lower Baggot Street, Dublin D02 P593, Ireland.
www.arccompliance.com

For a complete list of Pen & Sword titles please contact:

PEN & SWORD BOOKS LIMITED
47 Church Street, Barnsley, South Yorkshire, S70 2AS, England
E-mail: enquiries@pen-and-sword.co.uk
Website: www.pen-and-sword.co.uk
or
PEN AND SWORD BOOKS
1950 Lawrence Road, Havertown, PA 19083, USA
E-mail: uspen-and-sword@casematepublishers.com
Website: www.penandswordbooks.com

To Joakim and Nikolai

Contents

List of Illustrations

Templar Timeline

1307 – Arrest warrants served on the Knights Templar, leading to mass arrests
1307 – Execution of the heretic, Fra Dolcino
1310 – Execution of the French mystic scholar, Marguerite Porete
1310 – Mass burning at the stake of fifty-four accused Templars
1313 – Death of Guillaume de Nogaret, chief minister of King Philip of France
1314 – Jacques de Molay burned at the stake in Paris
1314 – Death of King Philip IV of France
1314 – Death of Pope Clement V
1314 – Battle of Bannockburn
1315 – Execution of Enguerrand de Marigny
1317 – Death of Guichard, Bishop of Troyes, accused of heresy
1319 – The papal bull *Ordo Militae Jesu Christi* allows Knight Templar assets in Portugal to be transferred to the new Order of Christ
1334 – Death of Pope John XXII
1446 – Rosslyn Chapel founded in Scotland
1804 – Bernard-Raymond Fabré-Palaprat founds the Ordre du Temple and reveals the Larmenius Charter
1819 – Walter Scott's Templar-themed novel *Ivanhoe: A Romance* is published
1938 – Vladimir Bartol's novel *Alamut* is published, which will inspire the twenty-first century video game, *Assassin's Creed*
1939 – The body of Nazi medievalist, Otto Rahn, is discovered in a ravine at Söll, Austria
1947 – Death of the English occultist, Aleister Crowley
1972 – Under his nome de plume, Pierre Barbet, the French novelist Claude Avice, writes his sci-fi Templar fantasy, *L'Empire du Baphomet*
1977 – The movie *Star Wars* first shown in American cinemas
2003 – Dan Brown's Templar-themed novel *The Da Vinci Code* is published
2007 – The first version of the video game *Assassin's Creed* is launched by Ubisoft
2014 – The long-running TV historical drama *Diriliş: Ertuğrul* (Resurrection: Ertuğrul) first broadcasts on Turkish television before being distributed globally
2017 – The Templar-themed historical drama series *Knightfall* premiered on the History channel

The Templar Series

Downfall of the Templars is the second in a three-book series on the history and mystery surrounding the Knights Templar by author and TV historian, Tony McMahon.

The first instalment was *The Knights Templar: History & Mystery* and the third instalment will be, *The Knights Templar & Freemasonry*.

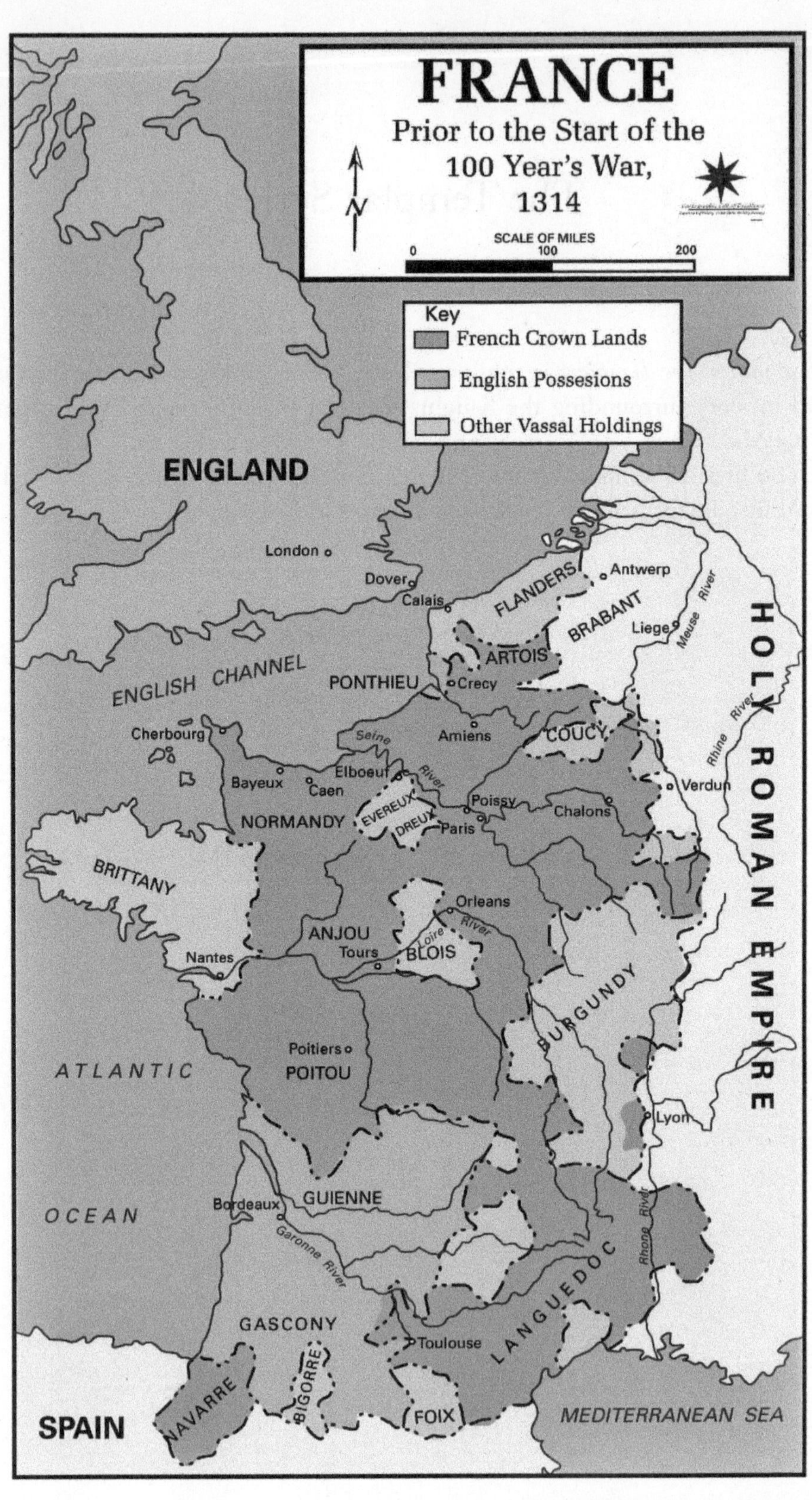
FRANCE
Prior to the Start of the
100 Year's War,
1314
N
SCALE OF MILES
0
100
200
Key
French Crown Lands
English Possesions
Other Vassal Holdings
ENGLAND
London
Dover
Calais
FLANDERS
Antwerp
BRABANT
Liege
Meuse River
ARTOIS
PONTHIEU
Crecy
ENGLISH CHANNEL
Cherbourg
Amiens
COUCY
Seine River
Rhine River
Bayeux
Caen
Elboeuf
Verdun
EVEREUX
DREUX
Poissy
Chalons
Paris
NORMANDY
BRITTANY
Orleans
Loire River
ANJOU
Tours
BLOIS
Nantes
BURGUNDY
HOLY ROMAN EMPIRE
Poitiers
POITOU
ATLANTIC
OCEAN
Lyon
Bordeaux
GUIENNE
Garonne River
Rhone River
LANGUEDOC
GASCONY
Toulouse
BIGORRE
NAVARRE
FOIX
SPAIN
MEDITERRANEAN SEA

Templar Grand Masters

(Dates indicate when they held the position)

Hugh de Payens – *c.*1119–1136
Robert de Craon – 1136–1147
Everard des Barres – 1147–1151
Bernard de Tremelay – 1151–1153
André de Montbard – 1153–1156
Bertrand de Blanchefort – 1156–1169
Philip de Milly – 1169–1171
Odo de St Amand – 1171–1179
Arnold of Torroja – 1181–1184
Gerard de Ridefort – 1185–1189
Robert de Sablé – 1191–1193
Gilbert Horal – 1193–1200
Philippe de Plessis – 1201–1208
William of Chartres – 1209–1218
Pierre de Montaigu – 1218–1232
Armand de Périgord – 1232–1244
Richard de Bures – 1245–1247
Guillaume de Sonnac – 1247–1250
Renaud de Vichiers – 1250–1256
Thomas Bérard – 1256–1273
Guillaume de Beaujeu – 1273–1291
Thibaud Gaudin – 1291–1292
Jacques de Molay – 1292–1312

List of Alleged Secret Templar Grand Masters in the Larmenius Charter

Jean-Marc Larmenius – 1313–1324
Theobald of Alexandria – 1324–1340
Arnaud de Braque, Lord of Chatillon sur Long – 1340–1349
Jean de Clermont-Nesles, Lord of Chantilly – 1349–1356
Bertrand du Guesclin, Count of Longueville – 1357–1381
Jean III d'Armagnac, Count of Armagnac – 1381–1392
Bernard VII d'Armagnac, Count of Armagnac – 1392–1419
Jean IV d'Armagnac, Count of Armagnac – 1419–1451
Jean de Croy, Count of Chimay – 1451–1472
Bernard Imbault – 1472–1478
Robert de Lenoncourt, Archbishop of Reims – 1478–1497
Galeas de Salazar, Lord of Lias – 1497–1516
Admiral Philippe Chabot, Count of Carny – 1516–1544
Gaspard de Saulx, Lord of Tavennes – 1544–1574
Henri Montmorency, Duke of Montmorency – 1574–1615
Charles de Valois, Duke of Angoulême – 1615–1651
Jacques Rouxel de Medavi, Count of Grancey – 1651–1681
Jacques Henri Durfort, Duke of Duras – 1681–1705
Philippe II de Bourbon, Duke of Orléans – 1705–1723
Louis-Auguste de Bourbon, Duke of Maine – 1724–1736
Louis-Henri de Bourbon, Prince of Conde – 1737–1740
Louis-François de Bourbon, Prince of Conti – 1741–1776
Louis Hercule Timoléon de Cossé, Duke of Brissac – 1776–1792
Claude Mathieu Radix de Chevillon, Lord of Chevillon – 1792–1804
Bernard-Raymond Fabré-Palaprat – 1804–1813 and 1827–1838

Introduction

Over 700 years ago, an order of knights sworn to defend Christ, and under the direct protection of the Pope, was destroyed – by the Pope. At his side, egging him on, stood the king of France. So shocking was this development that we are still reeling from it today, unable to fully comprehend what happened.

When a budding historian develops an interest in the Knights Templar, three key questions arise: Were the knights guilty as charged or wholly innocent of those terrible crimes? Did they possess treasure of incalculable value that they managed to hide before being arrested? And have they continued to exist, in some form, beyond the execution of the last grand master in 1314, even up to the present day?

This book sets out to answer all three questions.

In addressing the first question, we must grapple with the two main allegations against the knights: that they were guilty of both heresy and sodomy. These transgressions, terrifying to the medieval mind, were spiced up with claims of demonic worship, sorcery, and the rejection of Christ. An order of knights, once endorsed by the Pope, was described in legal hearings as corrupt and depraved. Those who refused to admit as much faced the ultimate penalty.

This was the first rumblings of the witchcraft mania that would grip Europe for over three centuries, leading to thousands of executions by burning. While the Templars were being cast as diabolists, others were being dragged before the courts on similar charges, both men and women. Heresy was now blended with magic and Satanism as part of a new, disturbing trend that would claim the lives of the knights.

The king of France, Philip IV, and Pope Clement V, spearheaded a purge of the Knights Templar that was unprecedented in its ferocity and cruelty. From being the heroes of the crusades in the Holy Land, they were now declared to be enemies of God and his church. Their continued existence posed a dire threat to the divinely ordained natural order. Arrests, imprisonment, torture, and executions followed as this order of holy warriors was annihilated.

The full force of the Papal Inquisition was wielded to extract confessions by any means necessary. Again, this foreshadowed a new development: the fanning out of inquisitors across Christendom, empowered to burn at the stake those who refused to accept the authority and truth of the Roman Catholic Church. The Christian world was entering a dark phase of its history.

Show trials of the Templars saw the knights, weakened by torture and starvation in dungeons, forced to answer claims that they spat on the crucifix, worshipped strange heads, conversed with demons, and engaged in disturbing, clandestine rituals. Sodomy was added to this toxic list of misdeeds. In their initiation rites, the Templars shared illicit kisses on the 'base of the spine'. These supposed holy men of God were nothing more than sordid necromancers whose many sins had somehow gone unnoticed for 200 years.

Before the trials of the Templars, belief in witches, magic spells, and sorcery had been confined to superstitious villagers, but it was now an elite obsession. By the mid-fourteenth century a pope would claim, in all seriousness, that his enemies were attempting an assassination via the medium of wax dolls sneaked into his palace. This would soon be followed by detailed manuals on how to identify and annihilate witches and others in league with Satan.

The French king, Philip IV, was a true believer when it came to these supernatural crimes. While moving in for the kill against the Templars, the superstitious monarch was pursuing multiple heresy and witchcraft cases. This included a bishop accused of poisoning the queen; a female preacher burned for her views; and a dead pope that the king wanted posthumously prosecuted for being in league with the devil. As for the Templars, Philip certainly coveted their wealth, but his actions also suggest a king who sincerely believed dark forces lurked in his realm. Therefore, the accusations made against the knights should not be breezily dismissed as just Machiavellian spin from a cash-strapped king.

Church and State saw heresy, sorcery, and treason everywhere. In the thirteenth century, a violent crusade had been launched by Pope Innocent III in southern France against the Cathar heretics with an unprecedented slaughter and slew of mass executions. This was a war fought by Christians against other Christians who rejected the need for a church, priesthood, sacraments, and the Pope. As papal power reached its peak, so did resistance to the Church's bejewelled bishops who seemed so remote from the original teachings of Christ. Many people, from all ranks of society, were fed up with ecclesiastical hypocrisy.

The popularity of heresies like the Cathars terrified the papacy. Rome feared that throughout Christendom, the faithful were being wooed by charismatic preachers and populist movements attempting to pull them away from their papal shepherd. The Pope was not about to let that happen. To keep the flock in line, the language and criminal charges deployed against heretics became more extreme, mixing in allegations of witchcraft and sodomy to heighten the sense of danger.

Once the Templars were placed outside the Church, they found themselves, like the Cathars, subjected to the most brutal treatment and appalling calumnies. Their past heroism on the battlefield counted for nothing as the torturers got to work. Some blurted out confessions that supported, and even further embellished, the astonishing charges made against them. But was every confession wrung from a Templar entirely false or were there germs of truth?

Which brings us to the second question about the Templars: what happened to their treasure? It's widely assumed that the knights possessed sacred artefacts like the Holy Grail, as well as vast amounts of gold and silver in the vaults of their preceptories. King Philip of France certainly hoped so. But was this wealth a mirage?

According to some sources, the Templars were tipped off in advance about the forthcoming arrest warrants, giving them time to ship their treasure in carts down to the port of La Rochelle, and from there to various safe havens overseas. Scotland and Portugal are often mentioned as likely locations. But is there any truth to this? A chapter in this book will seek to define what we mean by Templar 'treasure' before the next chapters follow the treasure trail up to Scotland and down to Portugal.

The third question being addressed here is whether the Knights Templar still exist today, and in what form. It may come as a surprise to discover that there is a plethora of organisations around the world that lay claim to being the direct continuation of the Templars. They range from Freemasons to Catholics and so-called neo-Templars. The latter emerged in the early nineteenth century when an associate of the French Emperor, Napoleon Bonaparte, made the startling claim that he was the latest in an unbroken line of clandestine Templar grand masters stretching all the way back to Jacques de Molay, burned at the stake in 1314. This neo-Templar movement has proven to be very fractious, with different groups vying for legitimacy, while fending off the rival claims of Freemasons and Roman Catholics to be today's genuine Templars.

In recent decades, the idea that the Templars were formed by a shadowy organisation, that pre-existed the order and continued afterwards, has gained traction. One name given to this mysterious organisation is the Priory of Sion, popularised by the American author, Dan Brown, in his novel (and subsequent movie) *The Da Vinci Code*. Sceptics argue that the Priory of Sion has been comprehensively debunked while others have posited their own version of the theory, claiming the Templars were set up by an ancient brotherhood known as Rex Deus. So, what has led an army of conspiracy theorists to insist that the Knights Templar was the external manifestation of a faceless secret society that still operates amongst us?

In popular culture, the Templars have lived on into the twenty-first century, wielding their swords in books, movies, and even video games. But they have alternated between being heroic defenders of truth to wicked and destructive villains. The Jedi order in the movie *Star Wars* fame was partly modelled on the Templars, projecting a positive image while, in sharp contrast, the Templars in the hugely popular video game *Assassin's Creed* are murderous control freaks.

Our relationship with this order of holy warriors is as conflicted today as it was for our medieval ancestors who lauded the knights for 200 years before tearing them down, consigning their leaders to the flames. Deep down, we still struggle with the question of their guilt or innocence. At one moment, they were self-sacrificing crusaders whose life of warfare and intense prayer was a shining example to Christendom. But then they were condemned as demon-worshipping necromancers, cavorting with each other behind closed doors, and plotting treason against Church and State.

Only one of these descriptions can be true. To uncover the facts, we must go back to the traumatic events of 1307, when the knights were arrested, and then follow their story, right up to the present day.

Chapter One

The Knights Templar – Heretics and Sorcerers?

In 1307, warrants were issued across France for the arrest of thousands of knights, chaplains, sergeants, and even labourers, who lived and worked on estates run by the Knights Templar. This dawn raid on the Templars was breathtaking in scale and intent. An order of holy warriors, protected by successive popes for two centuries, was now rounded up, imprisoned, tortured, and put on trial. Other military orders attached to the Church, such as the Hospitallers and Teutonic Knights, were spared, and continued to operate for centuries. The Templars, however, were singled out for brutal treatment. Nothing like this had ever been witnessed before.

Medieval Europe was stunned. Why had King Philip IV of France taken such drastic action? What did Pope Clement V have to say about it? How might the Knights Templar react? The legal proceedings dragged on for years, eventually culminating at the Papal Council of Vienne where the Templars were banned and their property confiscated. This was the end of a spectacular history that had begun in the year 1118.

The Crusades commenced in the year 1095 after Pope Urban II made an impassioned speech at Clermont in France calling for a new kind of religious war. He thundered to his audience that Christianity was under attack from new, previously unknown, Muslim forces that had burst out of the east. His Holiness was referring to the Seljuk Turks – a people of the steppe – who had overrun much of the Byzantine Empire. This previously formidable realm viewed itself as the continuation of the Eastern Roman Empire, once ruled by such mighty figures as Constantine and Justinian, but its territory had been massively reduced by the rise of the Islamic caliphate four centuries before. Now from the Islamic world came a new wave of warriors determined to snuff out the Byzantines altogether.

Although the Byzantines were Christians, they broke decisively with Rome to form what we now call the Eastern Orthodox Church. In the west, the Pope had long convinced most Christians that he was Christ's vicar on earth. But that was not the view in Constantinople, capital of the Byzantine Empire. They regarded the Pope as merely one of several Christian patriarchs and that the privileged position he claimed over the whole of Christendom was bogus. Things got so heated that the Patriarch of Constantinople and the Pope in Rome excommunicated each other in the year 1054. Yet despite the rancour between the western and eastern churches, by 1095 there was a common enemy that demanded a united response.

Urban's fiery words at Clermont must be among the most powerful uttered by any leader in world history. His call to arms was heeded, inspiring countless thousands to embark for places they had only read about in the Bible. These recruits to a new kind of war for Christ covered a wide social spectrum, from the dregs of medieval society to kings and emperors. In July 1099, they massed before the walls of Jerusalem and, despite a spirited defence by the inhabitants, overwhelmed the city engaging in a horrific slaughter of men, women, and children. Following this victory, the crusader kingdoms of Jerusalem, Tripoli, Edessa, and Antioch were carved out of lands ruled since the seventh century CE by Muslims, though still encompassing large Christian and Jewish populations.

Twenty years passed and the challenges of retaining control over these newly acquired territories became painfully obvious. Invasion, rebellion, and sedition were features of everyday life. European pilgrims who imagined it would be easier with the crusaders in charge to tread in the footsteps of Jesus, instead came to grief at the hands of murderous bandits on the roads into Jerusalem.

One large band of pilgrims was slaughtered on the banks of the river Jordan at Easter, 1119. It was in response to such atrocities that a group of nine knights, mainly from the Champagne region of modern France, resolved to form a new kind of military organisation. A band of warriors who would combine the piety of monks with the sword and lance. Every day marked by regular prayers interspersed with military drills. Theirs was to be a spartan existence of poverty, chastity, and obedience.

Young Christian men from all over medieval Europe aspired to join this new order: the Knights Templar. They rapidly became the poster boys of the crusades. Successive popes showered the knights with privileges, making them directly accountable solely to His Holiness, free from the control of local bishops and princes. In their first decades of existence, the order established an impressive network of wealth-creating hubs from England to the Balkans that funded their crusading activities in the Holy Land.

In military terms, they became a permanent standing army based in Jerusalem that Christian rulers could rely on to stay in place all year round, not returning home to manage their estates. In financial terms, their talent for managing money soon extended to running the State finances in England and France and operating the first global banking system. In political terms, Templar leaders were soon trusted advisers to monarchs and popes. This aroused intense jealousy and malicious rumour-mongering in the corridors of power as their enemies sought the order's destruction.

From their first years, the Templars were the subject of poison pen accounts of their origins, motives, and ultimate aims. These vindictive chroniclers, relentlessly bad mouthing the knights, were literate Church figures boiling with resentment at the papacy's special treatment of the Knights Templar. In hushed tones they whispered that the heroism of the Templars was nothing more than naked self-interest. When they charged into besieged cities ahead of everybody else, it was because they wanted to despoil them first, stripping any treasure for their own coffers.

Far from being selfless servants of the Christian kings of Outremer (the collective term for the crusader kingdoms), they operated to their own agenda like a state within a state. As for the wealth they had amassed, there had to be skullduggery involved. Worst of all, who knew what was going on in their secretive initiation rites and what dark forces had conjured them into existence and continued to protect them? The bile of these chroniclers fuelled conspiracy theories about the Templars that have persisted to the present day.

The crusades, pitching Christians against Muslims, were fought not only in the Middle East, but also on the Iberian Peninsula which had been invaded by the Islamic caliphate in the early eighth century CE. This spawned the glittering civilisation of Al-Andalus, governed from magnificent cities like Cordoba and Seville. But by the twelfth century, Christian kingdoms such as Castile and Aragon had emerged and expanded, pushing the Muslim emirs to the southern half of the peninsula. Together with the Knights Templar, the Christian monarchs scored incredible victories, taking Lisbon in 1147 followed by Seville and Cordoba in the thirteenth century. The Templar story in Iberia was one of unbridled success. Sadly, this was not matched in the Holy Land.

The first major setback for the Christian rulers in the Middle East was the loss of Edessa on Christmas Day, 1144. The Seljuk Turks spared most of the population but made a point of leading the Latin Christians, who were loyal to the Pope, off in chains to the slave markets. This shock sparked the Second Crusade with the Templar's main ecclesiastical ally, Saint Bernard of Clairvaux (1090–1153), tirelessly touring Europe to recruit young men for service in Outremer. The decades ahead would see stunning victories but also dramatic reversals of fortune, leading eventually to the capture of Jerusalem by the Saracen leader, Saladin (*c.*1137–1193), in 1187.

Despite losing their headquarters on the Temple Mount, the Templar mission endured with a succession of crusades. For a hundred years, their prestige grew, despite the constant carping at the margins. However, as Outremer slipped out of Christian hands at the end of the thirteenth century, the Templars were undermined by new political trends. The power of the papacy weakened, and this was a problem when the Pope was their main protector. Secular rulers wanted the right to govern their kingdoms without the Pope looking over their shoulder, threatening excommunication if they challenged his will. They especially wanted control over all armed forces in their realm, including the Templars.

It was under the leadership of the last grand master, Jacques de Molay, that things came to a head. In 1307, seemingly like a bolt out of the blue, arrest warrants were sent out to apprehend and imprison every Templar in France. This kicked off a process that led many knights, including De Molay, to be burned at the stake and the entire organisation to be dismantled with its assets redistributed to the Crown, nobility, and rival Hospitallers. It was a brutal end to a glorious story.

Jacques de Molay, grand master of the Knights Templar, had no idea what was about to hit him, and the order over which he presided. On 12 October 1307, he was a pallbearer at the funeral of Catherine of Courtenay (1274–1307), wife of Charles of Valois, the brother of King Philip IV of France. Given the honour of carrying the coffin of the king's sister-in-law must have assured De Molay that he was a trusted and valued member of the monarch's inner circle. Yet the very next day, De Molay and the leadership of the Knights Templar were rounded up in dawn raids, accused of heresy and sodomy, and cast into dank dungeons. All of this by order of the king himself.

On his last day of freedom, the ageing grand master dutifully played his role in the elaborate funeral ceremony conducted at the magnificent cathedral of Notre-Dame, located on an island in the river Seine: the Île de la Cité. There was no inkling of what was about to transpire. Within twenty-hour hours his life, and that of the entire Templar leadership, would be turned upside down. Seven years later, broken by torture and imprisonment, De Molay was burned to death in front of the very same cathedral. On the island today, there is a modest plaque marking the spot where his execution took place, ending the 200-year history of a remarkable order of holy warriors.

This was a catastrophic downfall that the Templars did not foresee. Yet the king and his chief minister, Guillaume de Nogaret (1260–1313), had been planning the mass arrest for weeks. Philip even flagged up his intention to deal with the knights to Pope Clement V (1264–1314), the Gascon-born leader of the Roman Catholic Church, often portrayed as a compliant, if occasionally grumbling, tool of the French king. Though his role and character were more complex, as will be seen.

Led in chains to dungeons, the once proud knights found themselves accused of blaspheming by spitting on crucifixes, engaging in obscene kissing on different parts of the body, and worshiping demonic idols. They were not warriors for Christ but agents of Satan. Contrast this with the previous two centuries when the Templars had been heralded as the very epitome of muscular Christianity, wielding their swords in the name of the one true Church. Brave warriors with the red cross of martyrdom emblazoned on their white mantles. Soldiers who lived a spartan, monastic existence with every day punctuated by prayer. Renowned for the simplicity of their attire and spirit of self-sacrifice in battle. Then, in a complete turnaround, the medieval public was informed that this was all a tissue of lies.

King Philip of France and Pope Clement clutched their respective pearls in horror as terrible revelations emerged from the lips of the knights, extracted under torture of course. Details of what had happened behind closed doors at Templar preceptories brought into the open at a series of legal hearings stretching for seven long years. Dishevelled, blood-stained knights hauled before commissions of senior Church officials to mumble their confessions. It was a pathetic and humiliating spectacle. Watching from the wings, the French king hoped this constant drip-drip of dreadful tales from within the order would demolish their credibility. He could then deal the final death blow to the Templars with little opposition from the public.[1]

For the last Templar grand master, Jacques de Molay, this was a terrible reversal of fortune. Events in recent years had moved against the order, but nothing signalled this terminal blow to his organisation. At times, De Molay could have been forgiven for thinking that a crusade as momentous as the First, Second, or Third Crusades of the past was on the cards. The Pope at one stage, not long before the arrests of the Templars, sent out very positive signals in November 1305. And yet, barely two years later, the knights found themselves chained up in dungeons.[2]

A decade and a half earlier, on 18 May 1291, the twenty-first grand master, Guillaume de Beaujeu (*c.*1230–1291), had been killed by an arrow as the city of Acre fell to the Saracens. One of the order's most senior figures, Thibaud Gaudin (*c.*1229–1292), then led a forlorn band of Templars with their treasure and most sacred relics from Acre, up the eastern Mediterranean coast, to Sidon, in modern Lebanon.

While there, Gaudin was elected as the new grand master. That city proved impossible to hold and Gaudin evacuated to Cyprus. Not long after, the last remaining Templar strongholds on the mainland of the Middle East fell: Tortosa and Athlit. At a chapter meeting in Cyprus, Gaudin was confirmed as grand master but several months later, he was dead. The burden of rebuilding the shattered order and convincing Europe to back another crusade would have overwhelmed anybody in his position. With Gaudin's passing, the spotlight fell on De Molay.

The exact point at which De Molay was elevated to grand master is a matter of conjecture among historians. It could have been 1291, 1292, or 1293, according to different sources. He may have been an interim leader of the order who then assumed pole position at some point. By whatever means he got the top job, it was not without opposition.[3] Some believe there was a split between pro-French and pro-Burgundian knights. De Molay was part of the Burgundian faction opposed by Hugh de Pairaud, who would have been the preferred choice of King Philip of France.[4]

From the outset, De Molay was painfully aware that he was picking up a poisoned chalice. The Templars were in a bad way and the knives were out. Marooned on Cyprus with no bases on the Middle Eastern mainland, the last grand master realised he had to do what Hugh de Payens (1070–1136), the first grand master, had undertaken two centuries before. De Molay needed to take the Templar case on the road, visiting what he hoped would be sympathetic audiences in England, France, and elsewhere. The Templar mission had to be restated.

In 1293 and 1294, De Molay was in England with his erstwhile rival Hugh de Pairaud, who was now the Templar Visitor-General, drumming up support and rebuilding the shattered morale of Templars at a series of chapter meetings. One can imagine that in preceptories all over Europe, knights, sergeants, and chaplains sought reassurances that the order still had a purpose, a reason to exist. Among the crowned heads of Europe, there was sympathy but no commitment to the level of crusading that would be required to get Christian forces back into Outremer.

England and France were far too busy fighting each other while Pope Boniface VIII was locked into an existential battle with Philip IV. The king wanted to finance his war against England by taxing the Church without the Pope's permission. Boniface thought differently. He believed Philip should seek Rome's approval first. The row escalated to the point where the French king accused the Pope of sodomy and heresy while Boniface threatened to excommunicate Philip.

A plot was even hatched in Paris to kidnap Boniface and bring him to Paris to stand trial for his alleged crimes. Meanwhile in Rome, the final preparations were made to throw Philip out of the Roman Catholic Church, thereby compelling his Christian subjects to reject his rule. They would be morally bound to revolt. As the political temperature reached boiling point, Philip's chief minister, De Nogaret, headed down to the Pope's summer palace in the Italian town of Anagni and roughed up the pontiff in an event dubbed 'The Outrage of Anagni'. Boniface died not long afterwards and was replaced, after the short reign of Benedict XI (1240–1304), by the more compliant Clement V.

De Molay was trying to make his voice heard while this drama was playing out. Unfortunately, his order was coming to be viewed as part of the problem in Philip's eyes. An armed body of men under papal control on French soil now looked like a potential threat to the king. In addition, the vast wealth that Philip believed the knights held at the Paris Temple, their imposing headquarters, was a piggy bank waiting to be raided. He had already fleeced France's Jews, Lombards, and monasteries, so why not the Templars?

But there was much more going on in the king's mind than balancing the books. As will be seen, he was convinced that his dynasty had a sacred purpose, ordained by God himself. The Capetian rulers of France had a direct line to the heavens. And Philip took his divine right to rule very seriously. He was haunted by the spectres of evil, which he saw all around him. Tragic misfortune that befell his family was blamed on sorcerers. Dissent within the realm evidenced the activity of heretics. It took little to convince him that the Knights Templar were engaged in heresy, sorcery, and treason.

The king's mindset was, of course, invisible to De Molay. What he sensed was that very little by way of concrete support for a crusade was coming from either Rome or the crowned heads of Christian Europe. Therefore, the Templars would have to fall back on their own resources. De Molay toured the preceptories encouraging these wealth-creating hives to re-commit to their core task of funding the frontline of crusading activity. At the same time, De Molay replenished the order's manpower in Cyprus. Older Templar knights, their bodies racked by war, were sent west into retirement while younger recruits headed east. Despite all the negative news flow from the Holy Land, medieval era youths were still applying to join the Templars.

Many historians have tended to portray the Templars under De Molay as an order in rapid decline. But Professor Malcolm Barber, who has researched the Templar trials in great depth, believes that the manpower and equipment under De Molay's control in 1307 was still impressive enough to undertake another crusade if required.

In 1300, fed up with festering in Cyprus, De Molay attempted to recapture the former Templar stronghold of Tortosa on the Syrian mainland as news came of defeats inflicted by the Mongol armies on the Muslim Mamluks. The grand master patched up his differences with King Henry II of Cyprus (1270–1324), who was also the last crowned king of Jerusalem, and together they conducted raids on Tortosa and other cities including Acre and even Alexandria in Egypt.

The Mongols sent their ambassador to Cyprus, the Italian-born Isol the Pisan, to accompany these expeditions. In November 1300, De Molay went for a full-scale invasion of Tortosa. He placed about 150 Templar knights on the nearby island fortress of Ru'ad as a stepping stone to their destination. The Templars, and hundreds of other crusaders, would mount a seaborne attack while the Mongols would bear down on the city from the other side. Faced with this pincer movement, the Mamluks would surely surrender.

However, the Mongols were delayed and De Molay lost patience. He charged ahead and the Templars entered Tortosa, ransacking the city they had once governed. But holding Tortosa was not feasible. Having trodden once more on familiar roads, the grand master reluctantly pulled the bulk of his forces back to Cyprus but left a significant garrison on Ru'ad island. Why then did he conduct this seemingly futile operation? Undoubtedly to give the Pope and Christian leaders across Europe an object lesson that the Templars could still hit out at the Saracen enemy. If only they had decent resources, Tortosa and other cities in the Holy Land could be retaken and, more importantly, retained.

While the Pope gave his consent to the Templars continuing to hold Ru'ad, no further assistance was forthcoming. The Mamluks, shaken by the assault on Tortosa, were painfully aware that Europe needed to be shown that a future crusade was not advisable. So, they advanced on Ru'ad. A Mamluk fleet besieged the Templar garrison which eventually surrendered after promises of safe conduct. But the moment the fortress gates were opened, the Mamluks reneged on the deal, massacring or imprisoning Templars and their auxiliaries. This grim incident marked the effective end of the crusades in the Middle East.

At least, that's how it looks in retrospect. But to De Molay, there was still hope. Tortosa and Ru'ad represented a setback and not a decisive defeat. The reason for De Molay's optimism was that a new Pope was sending some very encouraging smoke signals.

Shortly after his election in November 1305, Clement wrote to De Molay announcing that he was up for a new crusade. A delighted grand master began preparations for a monster chapter meeting in Cyprus, to be held in August 1306. It would be a council of war with knights from preceptories all over Europe mobilised and present.

But then, suddenly, on 6 June 1306, the Pope summoned both De Molay and the grand master of the Knights Hospitaller, Fulk de Villaret (died 1327), to meet him in the French city of Poitiers on All Saints Day that year (1 November). De Molay, still believing that a new crusade was in the offing, cancelled the chapter meeting and packed his bags. He had no inkling that a chain of events had now been set in motion that would culminate in his death by burning at the stake.

De Molay and De Villaret were asked what scale of crusade should be considered and whether the two men would consider merging their orders into one organisation. This merger idea had been floated before in the preceding decade and resisted by both the Templars and Hospitallers. The reasons given were that their internal cultures were very different, and that the outside world saw in the two orders very contrasting propositions. In truth, both organisations were deeply suspicious of each other and had no wish to lose their independence. Matters were not helped in this regard by the odious personality of the Hospitaller grand master, De Villaret.

This was a man so despised by his own knights that they attempted to assassinate him years later in 1317. Forced to flee to a Hospitaller castle on Rhodes, in the town of Lindos, he was then besieged by the rebel knights. Meanwhile they had informed the Pope that De Villaret had been replaced as grand master by Maurice de Pagnac although the Pope insisted on De Villaret's reinstatement – only so that he could fire him. It's unlikely then that De Molay in 1306 had any desire to develop a close working relationship with a man so loathed by his own troops.

With the calamity at Ru'ad fresh in his mind, De Molay pressed for a large-scale crusade 'to destroy the infidels and restore the blood-spattered Holy Land of Christ'. Only overwhelming force could be used against the Mamluks. Anything less, would result in an inevitable massacre and retreat. The Mamluk leader, Al-Malik al-Zahir Rukn al-Din Baybars al-Bunduqdari (*c.*1223–1277), known simply as Baybars, had once stated that faced with a force of 15,000 crusader knights, he would concede defeat. The Pope needed to rally the faithful to take the cross once more and head for Cyprus, which under Templar control would be a springboard into the Holy Land.

But De Molay's dreams of a new crusade would never come to pass. Instead, his order experienced the ignominy of mass arrests, imprisonment, and execution. The Templars would be extinguished while the Hospitallers endured. In hindsight, it seems as if De Molay sleepwalked into disaster, entirely unaware of the dire peril that lay immediately ahead.

The process of suppressing the Templars got underway on 13 October 1307. Secret arrest warrants had been sent out a month before and royal officials managed to keep the entire operation under wraps. The incendiary wording of the warrant described the knights as 'wolves in sheep's clothing, in the habit of a religious order vilely insulting our religious faith ... again crucifying Our Lord Jesus Christ'. The charges were set forth as 'a heinous crime, an execrable evil, an abominable deed, a hateful disgrace, a completely inhuman thing, indeed remote from all humanity'. The Templars had denied the very existence of the Messiah and spat on his cross; they organised bizarre initiation rituals that included obscene kisses; and they worshipped pagan idols, particularly the demon, Baphomet.

Accusations that had floated around the order for years were crystallised in the arrest warrant, repeating long aired grievances about their wealth, secrecy, and privileges. Despite being showered with gifts and bequests, they had shown nothing but ingratitude. Worse, they had mocked their benefactors and the Church behind closed doors. Theirs was a secret society governed by self-interest and an ungodly lust for riches.

About six weeks after the arrest warrants were served on the Templars, Pope Clement issued a document titled *Pastoralis praeeminentiae* (pastoral pre-eminence) that ordered all Christian monarchs and princes to 'prudently, discreetly, and secretly' arrest the Templars. Their property was to be seized and retained until granted to other parties. This was an important pastoral letter for Philip because it universalised his action against the order. Now, it was not only France clamping down on the knights but the whole of Christendom.[5]

The charges levelled against the Knights Templar coalesced around two themes: heresy and sodomy. These two heinous crimes were intertwined in the medieval mind as transgressions against nature and God's law, as set down in scripture and interpreted by the Roman Catholic Church.[6]

Heresy derives from the Greek word *aíresis* – meaning 'choice'. The heretic has chosen to reject the dogmas of the Church – the articles of faith. To qualify as a full-blown heretic meant being baptised as a Roman Catholic, then refusing to believe the truth God had revealed to his Church and persisting in that state of error.

The term 'sodomy' covered a range of non-procreative sex including homosexual intercourse, bestiality, masturbation, and other acts. This is sometimes cited as proof that gay men were not specifically targeted in the fourteenth century as the term 'homosexuality' did not arise until the nineteenth century.[7] But this argument does not stand up to scrutiny. There are plenty of medieval era legal codes, available to scholars online, that break down the crime of sodomy into sub-categories including the 'abominable' act, usually punishable by castration or death.

In the Byzantine Empire, Roman law was re-codified under Justinian and successive emperors, exercising a huge influence on legal frameworks in the west. The *Ecloga* of Leo III (717–741 CE) described sexual crimes and the appropriate measures in some detail. For example, a married man committing adultery should be flogged with six lashes. Carnal knowledge of a nun, thereby 'debauching the Church of God', led to the guilty party's nose being slit open. But the most severe penalties were for those who 'actively or passively' committed 'unnatural offences' and they were to be decapitated or 'emasculated'.[8]

Church councils, Church 'penitentials' (advice to priests on types of penance after hearing a confession) and guidance issued to inquisitors was quite specific about different types of sodomy and specified penetrative intercourse between men. In addition, from the late Roman Empire onwards, there were high profile cases of men who had engaged in same sex relations being severely punished by mutilation or death. Although some got off more lightly, just enduring years of salacious gossip and being ostracised from the community. They were the lucky ones.

The trials of the Templars featured a heady mix of alleged idol worship, homoerotic rituals and satanic initiation, cited by the prosecution to bring down an order that had been previously respected and venerated throughout Christendom. The knights were portrayed as sorcerers, inducting vulnerable initiates through immoral rites while taking orders from an embalmed head that spoke to them during these grotesque ceremonies.

This blending of Satanic practices with accusations of heresy was not entirely new. Even in the earliest centuries of Christian history, there had been a tendency in disputes between different groups of Christians to accuse each other of demonic practices. Claiming your opponents were in league with Satan immediately put them on the defensive.

In the second century CE, Saint Clement of Alexandria (*c.*150–*c.*215 CE) fired off such accusations at a preacher, Carpocrates, who was accused of having got his hands on a secret version of the gospel according to Mark, which differed substantially from the official version. Carpocrates was said to be working for demons and regularly held 'obscene banquets'.[9] In a similar vein, Saint Epiphanius (*c*.310–402) described the devilish Gnostics of the fourth century CE as 'fruits on a dung heap or scorpions and cobras from the egg of a snake'.[10]

In the century leading up to the Templar trials, magic and heresy were increasingly blended in a way that led directly to the witchcraft trials of the later Middle Ages. This disturbing trend was compared, by the historian Hugh Trevor-Roper (1914–2003), to the McCarthyite anti-communist witch hunts of the 1950s. Only that period of paranoia was of short duration compared to the centuries of witch-hunting that beckoned.

Trevor-Roper saw a link between the trials of the Templars in the early fourteenth century to those of Joan of Arc (died 1431) and Gilles de Rais (*c*.1405–1440) in the next century, forming part of a new horrific phenomenon that would soon engulf Europe. The trial of De Rais is especially noteworthy. Like the Templars a hundred years before, he was accused of both heresy and sodomy, as well as the murder of about 140 children, described as 'the savage baron more terrible than the ravening wolf'. Broken by his interrogators, De Rais confessed when faced with the threat of excommunication. At his execution at Nantes in 1440, a vast crowd of local people wept and prayed in the streets, unconvinced by the charges brought by the Church. To this day, there has been a sustained campaign by supporters of De Rais to rehabilitate his reputation.[11]

No rank in society would be spared accusations of sorcery as the anti-witch mania took hold. In England, both the Duchess of Gloucester, Eleanor Cobham, (*c*.1400–1452) and the Duchess of Bedford, Jacquetta of Luxembourg (*c*.1415–1472) were accused of witchcraft and put on trial. The former was imprisoned for life while the latter escaped the charges. These shocking assaults on women of rank were, in large part, made possible by the fate of the Templars. Their destruction set a precedent for tearing down the mightiest people and organisations in society with indictments blending heresy and sorcery.[12]

Accusing the Templars of heresy was a shocking moment. This was a crime that involved undermining the very theological foundations of the Church. Yet as the papacy grew ever more powerful, it provoked a rash of heresies across Europe attracting thousands who could not accept that the gilt trappings of the Roman Catholic Church had anything to do with the message of peace and poverty expounded by Jesus Christ in scripture. Pope John XXII (1244–1334), the longest serving of the popes based at Avignon in the fourteenth century, was so unnerved by this growing call to renounce worldly goods, that he issued a papal bull, *Cum Inter Nonnullos*, in 1322 declaring it a heretical sin to assert that Jesus and his apostles had no property whatsoever.

Some advocates of saintly poverty, like the Franciscan order, could be integrated into the Church and deployed to reinvigorate its evangelising efforts but others, like the Waldensians, resisted papal outreach and consequently fell victim to the merciless Inquisition. While the Cathars, who achieved a high degree of popularity in southern France in the early thirteenth century, were extinguished with a full-blown, bloody crusade where thousands of people, Cathar and non-Cathar, were massacred or executed.

Demonising the Church's opponents as heretics was enough to swing most of society behind efforts to crush the dissidents. Yet by the fourteenth century, allegations of heresy needed spicing up. It was not enough to condemn a group of people for having the wrong view on the trinity or the virgin birth; they were now accused of conjuring up demons and venerating pagan idols. Enrico de Corretto, Bishop of Lucca, was an adviser to Pope John XXII who argued that as all magic involves the intervention of the devil, then it must also be heresy.

The Church realised that magic was a powerful propaganda weapon against its enemies. Up until then, casting spells and necromancy had been a fringe interest, typically involving sociopathic, ageing widows in villages, subjected to the ducking stool by illiterate yokels to ascertain their guilt. Now, however, magic was brought into high politics and avidly discussed and investigated by highly educated elites.

In the years after the crushing of the Templars, Pope John exemplified the growing papal fixation with magic and sorcery. John decreed that witchcraft should be treated with the same severity as heresy by the Inquisition, after what he believed were several attempts on his own life by sorcerers. This was still a hundred years before the witch hunting mania that swept Europe from the late fifteenth to the seventeenth century. Yet it was the first rumblings of a satanic panic that would grip both Catholics and Protestants at the end of the Middle Ages.[13]

Pope John saw sorcery and demonic possession everywhere. He tasked Cardinal Bérenger Fredoli (1250–1323), who had interrogated De Molay during the Templar trials, with investigating senior clerics the Pope believed were trying to kill him using magical powers including the Bishop of Cahors, Hugues Géraud (died 1317). He was already suspected of embezzling Church funds and the story ran that to escape these charges Géraud resolved to murder the Pope using cursed wax dolls and a poisonous potion, both sold to him by the same sorcerer. In 1317, he hired three dubious characters in a tavern to smuggle the dolls into the papal palace on the assumption that if the dolls were in closer proximity to the intended targets, their magic would work more effectively. Those marked for death were the Pope, his nephew, and a couple of senior advisers.[14]

The plot was uncovered very quickly. The reprobates hired to smuggle in the dolls looked so shifty that papal guards arrested them almost immediately. Géraud was taken into custody and keen to avoid being tortured by the Inquisition, confessed everything. If he was hoping for leniency, then he was going to be disappointed. Even his ecclesiastical position offered no protection from the Pope's wrath. For his crime, he was burned to death on 30 August 1317. But that would not be the end of the matter.

Pope John was now gripped by a fit of paranoia comparable to the twentieth-century dictator Joseph Stalin. He saw demonic plots everywhere and in the papal palace drew up lists of those who should be arrested. In 1318, the Archbishop of Aix, Robert Mauvoisin, was arraigned on charges of performing magic but managed to escape prosecution. Others were not so lucky.

Every purge needs an enforcer. Stalin had Beria. Hitler had Himmler. Pope John could rely on some seasoned inquisitors who had spent years rooting out heretics. From 1307, when the Templars were arrested, the chief inquisitor of the French city of Toulouse was a man whose notoriety has travelled down the centuries: Bernard Gui (*c.*1261–1331). He became known to millions in the late twentieth century as the sinister inquisitor in the Umberto Eco novel, *The Name of the Rose*, made into a movie in 1986.

The real life Gui investigated a group of rebellious Franciscan friars led by Bernard Délicieux (*c.*1260–1320) who unwisely objected to the heavy-handed tactics of the Inquisition in the Languedoc region of France, which had been the epicentre of Catharism. If the friars hoped their status as men of God permitted them free speech, then they were about to be put right by Gui. Even babies in their cradles, he once said, were not safe from the Inquisition. Taken into custody, Délicieux was tortured and to justify imprisoning him for life, within the walls of Carcassonne, his interrogators claimed he owned books on sorcery. Whether this was true or not, we will never know, but once again, magic spiced up the prosecution case.[15]

It is thanks to Gui that we get a flavour of what the Templars would have experienced during an inquisitorial interrogation. He penned a manual for fellow inquisitors on techniques that would tease out the truth from a heretic. This bizarre document reveals a preoccupation with mind games, as opposed to the proper use of thumbscrews. Gui was more interested in drilling into the souls of those brought before him than stretching their tendons on the rack, though that was an option held in reserve.

One of his favoured tactics was to manoeuvre a suspected heretic into swearing an oath when they sincerely believed that lying would endanger their mortal soul, but telling the truth would lead to the execution scaffold. This was one scenario Gui demonstrated from his long experience in dungeons:

Inquisitor: Will you then swear that you have never learned anything contrary to the faith which we hold to be true?

Answer: (Growing pale) If I ought to swear, I will willingly swear.

I: I don't ask whether you ought, but whether you will swear.

A: If you order me to swear, I will swear.

I: I don't force you to swear, because as you believe oaths to be unlawful, you will transfer the sin to me who forced it; but if you swear, I will hear it.

A: Why should I swear if you do not order me to?

I: So that you may remove the suspicion of being a heretic.

A: Sir, I do not know how unless you teach me.

I: If I had to swear, I would raise my hand and spread my fingers and say, 'So help me God, I have never learned heresy or believed what is contrary to the true faith'.

Then trembling as if he cannot repeat the form, he will stumble along as though speaking for himself or for another, so that there is not an absolute form of oath and yet he may be thought to have sworn… But a vigorous inquisitor must not allow himself to be worked upon in this way but proceed firmly till he makes these people confess their error, or at least publicly abjure heresy, so that if they are subsequently found to have sworn falsely, he can without further hearing, abandon them to the secular arm.[16]

Gui's inquisition playbook reads like a multiple-choice questionnaire. This standardisation of inquisition tactics may explain why many interrogations yielded very similar confessions. In the same period that the Templars were being interrogated, there are several recorded cases that give some idea of the scope of the Inquisition at that time.

In 1319, a widow, Agnes Francou, was accused of heresy through membership of a banned sect: the Poor of Lyons. After refusing to swear any oaths to the bishop of Pamiers, she was burned to death. Women were increasingly the targets of inquisitorial activity, though sometimes displaying a streak of rebellion. In Bologna, in June 1299, three women voluntarily appeared before the local inquisitor to apologise for inflammatory remarks they had made about the conduct of the Inquisition. Domna Manina, and her neighbours Maria and

Bertholomea, had reacted angrily to the exhumation and public burning of a dead woman posthumously accused of heresy. They were excused along with an astonishing 320 other people who had reacted similarly.[17]

Women were already associated with witchcraft, but investigating it now became the regular business of the Inquisition. In 1321, Jaqueline den Carot successfully grovelled for absolution promising that in future 'she would no longer use witchcraft, sorcery, nor to frequent the caster of lots, sorcerers, and diviners, and if she knew any, she would denounce them to my said lord bishop'. How many women would eventually be executed as witches is hotly debated. Some argue that from the early fourteenth century to the mid-seventeenth century, anywhere between 200,000 and half a million people were judicially murdered for being witches, with 85% being women.[18] Others put the figure at a tenth of that, but it is nevertheless a shocking body count.[19]

As the religious frontiers of Europe changed, this impacted the work of the Inquisition and influenced the heresy charges against the Templars. Areas previously under Muslim rule on the Iberian Peninsula, and elsewhere, now came under Christian control. But there were still sizeable Muslim and Jewish communities in the urban centres. People might have agreed to convert to Christianity, but their sincerity was always in doubt. For example, in 1320, in the city of Pamiers, a Jew baptised into Christianity was accused of reverting to Judaism 'like a dog returning to his vomit'.

Unwisely he had stated out loud that the existence of the Holy Trinity was not supported by scripture in the Old Testament where it says in the book of Deuteronomy that the 'Lord your God is one'. His fate is unknown. Fear of such outwardly practising Christians harbouring secret religious convictions occupied the inquisitors. They were despised by Jews and Muslims who stayed loyal to their faith while being insulted and persecuted by their new co-religionists. King Jaume II of Aragon (1267–1327) even passed a law to stop Christians calling converted Jews insulting names but instead encourage them to be good Catholics.[20]

However, this fear of people lying about their new convictions meant that when the Templars were accused of a closet sympathy with the Muslim enemy, it chimed with contemporary anxieties. In fact, the allegiance of the knights to the Roman Catholic Church had been doubted from the very start. One leading Cistercian monk, Saint Bernard of Clairvaux (1090–1153) became their top advocate but another Cistercian, Isaac de Stella (1100–1178), cursed them as a 'monster' whose rule book was based on a condemned fifth gospel, written by the devil, that legitimised the spread of Christianity through murder, robbery, and the use of weapons.[21]

In the early nineteenth century, historians questioned whether the Templar method of warfare, ethos, and organisation had been borrowed from the Muslim world. Nothing in the New Testament supported the notion of anything like the Templars, so maybe its origins were in the Qur'an and hadiths (sayings) of Islam. Even the Templar commanderies, it was stated, were a version of the Muslim Ribāt – a fortified compound occupied by Islamic warrior monks.

The founders of the Knights Templar were crusaders who had gazed over the frontier at the Saracens and admired what they saw —then emulated it. They were westerners who had gone native in the Middle East. The idea was floated that the Templars may even have copied their erstwhile enemy: the Assassins. This was the fanatical Isma'ili (Shi'a Muslim) cult led by the so-called 'Man of the Mountain' who sent brainwashed followers on suicide missions, carrying out political assassinations of both Muslim and Christian political leaders.

The allegations of heresy against the Templars were based on testimonies alleging several misdemeanours: the knights were accused of denigrating the crucifix and denying Christ; new initiates were instructed that Jesus was not God but instead a false prophet (*quia falsus propheta erat, nec erat Deus*); the holy mass was corrupted; and individual Templars illegally assumed the role of priests.

The knights were said to omit the words of consecration in the Catholic mass. This is the moment in the Roman Catholic service where the bread and wine on the altar literally transform into the body and blood of Jesus – known as the Rite of Eucharist. The priest calls down the Holy Spirit by speaking the words of Christ at the Last Supper. He then holds up the consecrated bread and wine to the congregation and invites them to proclaim the mystery of the faith. If the Templars were altering this, then that miracle was not occurring – the spell was broken. This is still a subject of concern to the Vatican today with the Holy See issuing a 'disciplinary document' titled *Redemptionis Sacramentum* in 2004 ordering priests not to deviate from the texts of the Sacred Liturgy.[22]

The deeper significance of the Templars appearing to mock the Catholic doctrine of transubstantiation, where the bread and wine are transformed, might validate a widespread theory that the Templars became Gnostics in the east, imbibing a heretical account of Christ long forgotten in the west. Therefore, the Knights Templar believed Jesus was purely divine and did not have a corruptible human body. So, eating his body during the mass was a ludicrous proposition.

The problem is, there was not just one version of Gnosticism, but many, and there were Gnostics who thought Jesus was a false saviour, others who believed he was an enlightened human as opposed to a god, or that John the Baptist was the true messiah, usurped by Jesus and his sect. Which type of Gnostic were the Templars? Furthermore, we have nothing in writing from the knights to prove this assertion.

Another allegation was that secular members of the order, who were not ordained priests, were giving absolution, which was strictly forbidden by the Church. To the medieval Christian, the Sacrament of Penance was crucial to the salvation of their soul and hope of entering heaven. The penitent confessed to a priest in the hope of absolution, very often at the point of death. If a person had been especially sinful, a priest might withhold absolution and the inference in this charge against the Templars is that evildoers could then drop into their local Templar preceptory and get the absolution that a priest down the road had denied them.

But the most intriguing accusation was their worship of a demonic idol, referred to as Baphomet. While the crucifix was spat on and stamped underfoot, the knights venerated a head produced at their rituals. Under torture, the knights described a head with many faces; or a single face with a beard; a decaying and rotting head; a female head; a cat's head; and the head of an entity known as Baphomet. If they touched it with small cords bound around the waist of every knight, it would guarantee them wealth and victory. The head was either made of wood or silver or a mouldering human skull that some argue was that of the first grand master, Hugh de Payens.[23]

A Templar from Florence said that at clandestine chapter meetings, the idol was produced to the cry: 'Adore this head! This head is your God and your Mahomet!'

> *I was alone in a chamber with the person who received me: he drew out of a box a head, or idol, which appeared to me to have three faces, and said, thou shouldst adore it as thy Saviour and that of the order of the Temple. We then bent two knees, and I cried, Blessed be he who will save my soul, and I worshipped it.*[24]

At Carcassonne, a Templar brother, Jean de la Cassagne, was put through an experience he was unlikely to forget in a hurry. He entered a dark room in the middle of which the preceptor was lying naked, face down, on a bench. Everybody present was required to form a queue and kiss the preceptor's backside after which he turned over for a kiss on the navel. The preceptor then rose from the bench and opened a box, from which he produced a large idol in the shape of a man. From the trial description, this seems to have been a small mannequin clothed in liturgical vestments. It was then placed on a chest and the preceptor addressed the group:

> *Here is a friend of God, who speaks with God, when he wishes, to whom you must bring thanks, since he has led you to this state, which you desire greatly, and he fulfils that desire.*[25]

Gauserand de Montpesant, a Templar from Provence, described 'an idol made in the form of Baffomet'. Another knight from the same region, Raymond Rubei, confessed to being presented with a wooden head upon which was painted the word 'Baphomet'. He prostrated himself before the idol, exclaiming 'yalla, a word taken from the Muslims'. Presumably this was a corruption of Allah, although portraits of God or his Prophet are strictly prohibited in Islam. Nevertheless, a Templar from Florence claimed the head he witnessed was referred to as 'Mahomet', which is why many contend that Baphomet was a corruption of Muhammad, the Muslim prophet. Despite these many testimonies, no actual head was ever produced in a trial hearing to support the existence of such a lurid idol.

The word 'Baphomet' first emerges in correspondence during the First Crusade between a crusader noble, Anselm of Ribemont (died 1099), and Archbishop Manasses II of Reims (died 1106). Anselm was an eyewitness to the Siege of Antioch from 1097 to 1098 – a major clash between the Muslim Seljuks and the Christian crusader forces. The resulting victory opened the way to Jerusalem. Anselm mentioned a point in the siege during which the city's defenders 'called loudly upon Baphometh'.

Another chronicler of the First Crusade, Raymond of Aguilers, reported that he had heard the term 'Bafomet' used for Muhammad, and 'Bafumariae' for a mosque. It also pops up in the songs of troubadours, including an almost treacherous poem by a troubadour from the Auvergne, Austorc d'Aorlhac. After the defeat of the Seventh Crusade in 1250, he penned a lament in the Occitan language, where he expressed sympathy for those Christians who had converted to Islam, believing that was the one true faith. In the poem, he used the word 'Bafomet'.[26]

> *...and it is therefore reasonable that we from now on abandon our belief in God and instead worship Muhammad (Per qu'es razos qu'hom hueymais Dieu descreza e qu'azorem Bafomet...).*[27]

Based on Templar trial records, one could assume that the knights worshipped a strange head, associated with Islamic religious practice, resulting in a corruption of the Muslim prophet's name to Baphomet. However, Muslims do not venerate graven images of God or the prophet Muhammad. The reason for linking the Templars to Islam was a means of discrediting the order. The veneration of

Baphomet proved they had gone native in the east and worse, consorted in treacherous ways with the Muslim Saracens.

Over the centuries since their downfall, commentators have rejected the link to Islam but still maintain the knights prayed to an entity called Baphomet. But what was it then? The emergence of Freemasonry in the eighteenth century led to the knights being recast as heretical Gnostics, worshipping a supreme being. This became the identity of the idol produced at their secret rites. As for the name Baphomet, according to the Masonic writer Christoph Friedrich Nicolai (1733–1811), it derived from the Greek βαφη μητ8ς meaning Baptism of Wisdom (*baphe metous*).

By the turn of the nineteenth century, the idea that the Knights Templar were part of a secret society stretching back millennia, and still operating amongst us, was taking root. A leading light in this development was the Austrian historian, Joseph Hammer, who later styled himself, in much grander terms, as Joseph Freiherr von Hammer-Purgstall (1774–1856).

Hammer was involved in the Napoleonic Wars as an Austrian diplomat, taking part in an expedition under the command of Admiral Sir Sidney Smith (1764–1840) who was a leading figure in the neo-Templar movement that arose at this time, and which will be dealt with more fully in a later chapter. Smith adorned his uniform with a Templar Cross he believed had been owned by Richard the Lionheart during the crusades. The admiral can be seen wearing the cross in a miniature owned by the present British king, Charles III (born 1948), in the Royal Collection.

While Smith had a romantic attachment to the Templars, Hammer took a far dimmer view of the knights that would have chimed with the prosecutors at their trials. The Templars were 'guilty of apostasy, idolatry, and impurity'. They were clandestine Ophites – a type of Gnosticism originating in the Roman Empire. The word Ophite comes from the Greek 'ophis' meaning serpent, but this was seen as a compliment and not an insult by the cult followers. To them, the serpent was not a symbol of evil, but the creature that unlocked wisdom in the Garden of Eden. Hammer, though, shared the negative view of their mainstream Christian enemies.[28]

Hammer's view of the Templars, and their alleged worship of Baphomet, must be seen in the context of the time in which he wrote. Here was a senior diplomat working for the Austrian Empire, which had been shaken by the invasions of the French Emperor, Napoleon, who had overturned the medieval dynasties that for so long ruled the continent.

Men like Hammer were out to restore the old order and they saw dangerous, radical conspiracies everywhere. So, when it came to writing the history of the Templars, he was convinced there were clandestine connections between the knights, the Gnostics, and the Cathars. They were even, in his mind, in league with the Assassins – and together they formed a medieval axis of evil. All of this was set forth in a book, written in Latin, titled *Mystery of Baphomet Revealed*, which was published in 1818.[29]

Many of his arguments about the beliefs of the Templars have been taken up, in recent decades, by Templar theorists who view the order in a positive light. But Hammer was not a supporter. Associating the Templars with Baphomet and a long line of heretics was intended to damn the knights, not praise them. Like other deeply conservative and reactionary writers of the time, he loathed Freemasonry and wanted to prove that they were the latest manifestation of a secret, ungodly movement that, he claimed, cursed Jesus and worshipped phalluses. He cited as evidence, ancient hermaphroditic stone figures held in the Austrian imperial art collection, which he believed were versions of Baphomet. The Templars had been temporary guardians of an ancient Satanic creed, stretching back to the dawn of civilisation, now passed on to the Freemasons.

Hammer's theories about the Templars were very influential and would be further developed in the 1930s by the Nazi archaeologist Otto Rahn (1904–1939) during his fill-fated quest for the Grail, detailed further on. Like Hammer, Rahn would try to shore up his ideas about the Templars with an appeal to the Grail myths, especially the medieval Arthurian legend *Parzival* by the poet-cum-knight Wolfram von Eschenbach (*c.*1160/80–*c.*1220). But in Rahn's case, the supposed anti-Catholic, Gnostic rituals and beliefs of the Templars became a positive feature.

The question that vexes many who study the Templars, and the conspiracy theories that swirl around them, is how could the knights have projected themselves as the military vanguard of the Roman Catholic Church and loyal sons of the Pope while at the same time worshipping a demonic head and spitting on the crucifix? Hammer dismisses this concern stating that plenty of people divide their external conduct from their internal beliefs.

However, while it's easy to believe that assertion on an individual basis, it's harder when it comes to an entire institution over a 200-year period. We are being asked to imagine that, between 1118 and 1307, the Templars perpetrated a hoax on the whole of Christendom, yet nobody noticed. Publicly, they fought and died for Christ in the Holy Land, while in private they mocked Jesus, throwing themselves down before a demon. Yet not a single person went to the authorities to report this heretical activity. This stretches credulity.

When it comes to the physical appearance of Baphomet, there is a well-recognised image circulating today. It features a humanoid goat with a flaming torch between its horns and its crossed legs covered in shaggy hair. Great black wings grow from its back while engraved on its arms are the words 'solve' (separate) and 'coagula' (joining together). On its forehead is a pentagram while carved on to its stomach is the Caduceus – two serpents intertwined around the staff carried by the Greek god, Hermes. Baphomet encompasses seemingly opposing binaries: it is a hermaphrodite; one arm is raised in benediction while the other points downwards meaning 'as above, so below'; and it is both animal and human.[30] But this image of Baphomet, so often associated with the Knights Templar, is only about 150 years old.

It was the creation of a French ex-Catholic priest turned occultist, Alphone Louis Constant, who adopted the nom de plume, Éliphas Lévi (1810–1875). Having quit Catholicism, he later exited the Freemasons while dabbling in socialist politics and the neo-Templar movement. Examining the charges of heresy levelled against the Templars, he deduced that while crusading in the east, they had absorbed the teachings of the Ancient Egyptian priests of the god Osiris, transmitted to the knights via the Gnostics and the Jewish mystical creed, the Kabbalah. He peppered his book, *Transcendental Magic: Its Doctrine and Ritual*, with mystical and occult illustrations, penned by his own hand, including the classic representation of Baphomet.

In this comprehensive, if confusing, tour of mystical beliefs, which heavily influenced the notorious English occultist Aleister Crowley (1875–1947), Lévi claimed that the word 'Baphomet' was a secret code used by the Knights Templar:

> *The name of the Templar Baphomet, which should be spelt Kabbalistically backwards, is composed of three abbreviations: TEM. OHP. AB. Templi omnium nominum pacis abbas – the father of the temple of universal peace among men.*[31]

Were the Templars guilty of venerating the demon Baphomet? Lévi thought they were:

> *Did the Templars really adore Baphomet? Did they offer a shameful salutation to the buttocks of the goat of Mendes? What was this secret and potent association which imperilled Church and State, and was thus destroyed unheard? Judge nothing lightly; they are guilty of a great crime; they have exposed to profane eyes the sanctuary of antique initiation. They have gathered again and have shared the fruits of the tree of knowledge, so that they might become masters of the world.*

By the 1890s, a Satanic panic swept Paris with reports of diabolists attacking the Roman Catholic Church. In 1895, there was an audacious robbery at Notre-Dame cathedral of two chalices containing fifty communion hosts. The perpetrator was an elderly woman who shuffled in and walked off with the holy vessels. Similar thefts had been reported in Rome, Italy. Journalists concluded that as the chalices, made of aluminium or 'washed gold', were worth little on the black market, they were being taken for their contents: the communion hosts.[32]

Why? One newspaper reported that among the French, there were beliefs and rites 'almost inconceivable in depravity and sacrilege' with 'demoniacal exorcisms with indescribable and shameful scenes'. The robbers were neither Roman Catholics nor atheists, who would not have attached any significance to the hosts, but those who wanted to use the body and blood of Christ for 'acts of desecration'. A reversing of the holy mass into something Satanic.

> *The thefts point to the Luciferians, as they have adopted as their emblem a transpierced eucharist and an overturned chalice.*

Whether or not the Templars were diabolists who worshipped an idol called Baphomet to achieve global power, as Lévi thought, this charge of supernatural idolatry has captured the popular imagination ever since. After nineteenth century mystics like Hammer and Lévi had speculated wildly in their books, the twentieth century saw the demon Baphomet embraced by mid-century Satanists, most prolifically Anton LaVey (1930–1997), founder of the Church of Satan. Since the 1960s, the heavy metal music scene has dabbled with devil worship and paganism with Baphomet featured on albums and T-shirts.

In recent years, huge statues of Baphomet have been unveiled in several American towns and cities by the Satanic Temple as part of their campaign against increasing displays of Christian worship in public institutions, promoted by politicians sympathetic to evangelical Christians. Wherever a crucifix has been installed, or a stone carving of the Ten Commandments, a Satanic Temple lorry turns up with a statue of Baphomet. Proving that this symbol is still incredibly potent, its mere appearance has sparked anti-Satanic protests with one statue in New Hampshire vandalised to such an extent that only its legs remained standing.[33]

Interwoven with the heresy charges against the Templars was the accusation of sodomy. Throughout history, what has been construed as sexual deviance has often been seen as a precursor to treason and sacrilege. The demonising of homosexuals as untrustworthy, because they violate natural law, extends from ancient times down to 1950s McCarthyite America.[34] It's often forgotten that not only did Senator Joseph McCarthy (1908–1957) purge suspected Communists from government posts, but also gay men, in what was termed the Lavender

Scare. In 1952, President Dwight D. Eisenhower signed Executive Order 10450 prohibiting gays and lesbians from working for the federal government.[35]

In the early medieval period, the papacy was relatively relaxed about sodomy, especially so during the reign of Benedict IX (*c.*1012–1056) who was crowned Pope aged just 20 (some scholars believe he was 12). Between 1032 and 1048, he held the papacy for three separate periods, selling it to his godfather at the end of his second pontificate.

Saint Peter Damian (1007–1072), a contemporary, said his election 'seemed as if a demon from hell, in the disguise of a priest, occupied the chair of Peter and profaned the sacred mysteries of religion'.[36] After Benedict was removed for the last time, Peter Damian put pen to paper, publishing a blistering attack on sexual licentiousness: *Liber Gomorrhianus* (The Book of Gomorrah). He urged Rome to enforce the death penalty on all acts of sodomy. However, even as the Church cleaned up its act, Pope Leo IX (1002–1054) still urged penance for sodomites and refused to endorse Peter Damian's more draconian approach.

But things began to change in the twelfth and thirteenth centuries. Alongside an increasing obsession with heresy (mixed with magic) was a growing conviction that sodomy, the handmaiden of heresy, had to be stamped out. Specifically, the sub-category of sodomy where men were getting into bed with each other. Same sex activity was condemned at the Council of London (1102), the Council of Nablus (1120), and the Third Lateran Council (1179). Abbess Hildegard of Bingen (*c.*1098–1179), a formidable female figure in the twelfth century Church, stated that 'a man who sins with another man as if with a woman, sins bitterly against God' leaving both 'polluted' and deserving only of death.[37]

In 1203, Pope Innocent III (1160–1216) ordered an inquiry into sexual malpractice among the clergy at Mâcon while a similar investigation was conducted among German priests in 1231. In 1290, a man was executed in Navarre for 'committing heresy with his body'. What form of sexual act had taken place is unclear, but here was a clear example of the blending of heresy and sodomy in the medieval mind.[38]

Even more damaging for the Templars was the association of sodomy with the Muslim world. Today, we think of the west as being broadly tolerant towards LGBTQ people, while Muslim majority countries tend to be intolerant. However, in the medieval period, quite the reverse was true. Medieval Islamic poetry could be very homoerotic, especially 'Mujun' literature, exemplified by poets like Ibn Sara as-Santarini (1043–1123) and Ahmad al-Tifashi (1184–1253). The word 'mujun' translates as 'shameless', describing behaviour intended to shock, using explicit vocabulary.[39] What is clear from their verses is that among the elite, same sex attraction was very much recognised. The implication with regards to the

Templars is that they had succumbed to this vice on account of their closeness to the Muslim enemy, offering further proof of their guilt.

In Muslim Al-Andalus (modern Spain and Portugal) gender identity was remarkably fluid. There were eunuchs, homosexuals, and 'ghumaliyyat', enslaved women who cross-dressed to look more masculine to appeal to gay men. There are stories of high-ranking mothers despairing of their obviously homosexual sons ever getting married, so they convinced a desirable woman to dress more manly, like a ghumaliyyat, and make their move. Apparently, this strategy occasionally worked.[40]

Poets like Abu Nuwas (756–*c.*814), during the golden age of Islamic civilisation, wrote with breathtaking candour about his sexual relations with young men. In his youth he had honed his talents working as a male prostitute. He and other poets offered advice on seducing young men, even involving coercion on occasions in a way we would now find unacceptable and illegal.

Al-Tifashi described Nuwas as 'gifted with the fairest appearance … the perfection of his shapes and his grace fulfilled the eyes of those who looked upon him … all the young men were enticed by him, attracted by both excitement and the pleasure of his company'. Describing a very popular young man, Al-Tifashi was so direct that some of the lines are unquotable. He wrote that 'Abu Ahmad is so proud of his origin, that he wriggles when he walks, like a swimming fish …what a beautiful gazelle you make, useful for the sodomite, who is active and the sodomite who is passive'.[41] Medieval Arabic had distinct terms for the active and passive male.

The court poet to the most powerful ruler of Al-Andalus, Abd al-Rahman III (891–961 CE), was Ibn 'Abd Rabbihi (858–940) who described a male cup bearer declaring 'it was from his eyes that I drank'. While a youth who had grown a beard had 'drawn two lines arousing passion and frustration, I never knew your glance could be a sword until you put on the sword belt of your new beard'. The poet Muhammad ibn Ammar (1031–1086) experienced a stormy love affair with the ruler of Seville, Al-Mu'tamid ibn Abbad (*c.*1069–1091) describing their 'night of union' where 'there was wafted, to me, in his caresses, the perfume of its dawns'. Al-Mu'tamid made Ibn Ammar his vizier but inadvisably the ungrateful lover rebelled and was not only imprisoned but killed in person by the man with whom he had shared a bed.[42]

Christian concern at perceived Muslim licentiousness was a theme that continued through the Middle Ages, especially with the advance into Europe of the Ottoman Turks. The Archbishop of Thessalonica, Gregory Palamas (1294–1359) spent a year at the Ottoman court and wrote that 'they live by their bows and swords, rejoicing in enslavement, murder, raiding, looting, wantonness, adultery, sodomy. And not only do they indulge in such practices, but they think that God approves them'. The Byzantine chronicler, Laonikos Chalkokondyles (1423–1470) claimed that sultan Mehmed II forced himself on to the younger brother of the Christian ruler Vlad III, Voivode of Wallachia, better known as Vlad the Impaler – who inspired the literary vampire created by the Irish novelist Bram Stoker (1847–1912): Count Dracula. His brother was nicknamed Radu the Handsome and Mehmed helped him overthrow Vlad to become the new Voivode.

The Christian medieval world was not immune to same-sex love, but it was convenient to claim it was an undesirable import from the opulent and corrupt Islamic caliphate. By accusing the Templars of 'sodomy', it played to an implicit narrative that the knights had 'gone native' in the Holy Land, adopted the manners of the infidel, and worse, might be in league with the Muslims.

So, were the Templars guilty of sodomy? Either the charges were a fabrication, or abuse was widespread, as claimed. How else to explain those Templar knights who confessed (normally after torture) to the lewd behaviour of their superiors at initiation rituals, where they were forced to submit to kisses on different parts of their body including the 'base of the spine'. The young men experiencing this felt compelled to comply. Yet it distressed them to be treated in this way. It was said that rumours about such salacious activity had been circulating for years. The Templars, people whispered, were a nest of sodomites. Though in truth, the same kind of malicious gossip swirled around other monastic orders and the Church in general.

Allegations of sexual abuse against initiates at their initiation were hard to verify because only fully inducted Templars were present – as opposed to the non-Templar servants and peasants who might have spoken more freely if they had witnessed anything untoward. Those being initiated claimed they were too frightened to speak out at the time. They feared being thrown out of the order or disciplined by the other brothers. Instead, long before the mass arrests in 1307, some confessed privately to a priest or a friar about what was happening within the order. Very few shared their misgivings to Templar chaplains who might have informed on them to their superiors.[43]

There is, however, another explanation for the sodomy charges faced by the Templars: that they were being accused, in effect, of witchcraft. Their initiation rituals, as described in the trials, included elements that would become recurring features in proceedings against witches in the centuries that followed. The kissing on the base of the spine, for example, is very similar to the 'osculum infame', the shameful kiss, that witches were said to give the devil on his anus. One Templar was said to have a tattoo of an upside-down crucifix close to his buttocks.

Some Templars confessed to kissing the anus of a Satanic cat and demonically possessed felines often featured in later witch trials.[44] Go back a century before the arrest of the Templars and the chronicler, Walter Map (1130–*c.*1209/10), who disliked the Templars intensely, described a feline-focused heresy called the Paterines. Male and female members of this movement lived together in communal houses and venerated a large cat that they kissed very inappropriately:

> *Then there cometh down by a rope, which hangeth in their midst, a black cat of marvellous size. At the appearance of this creature, they put out all the lights. They neither sing hymns nor even speak articulately, but they gnash with clenched teeth, and they approach, feeling their way, to the spot where they have seen their lord, and, when they find him, they kiss him, each with a measure of humility proportioned to the heat of his frenzy, some his feet, many under the tail, and very many his private parts…*[45]

After kissing their large cat, the Paterines cavorted with each other in an unbridled orgy. The Templars were similarly aroused. At the turn of the twentieth century, the German historian Heinrich Finke (1855–1938) combed through the Vatican Archives and found accounts of Templars admitting to the worship of a cat, variously described as black, brown, white, or red, which they kissed on the anus or buttocks. All of this confirmed to the inquisitors that they were dealing with sorcerers in league with the Lord of Darkness.

The knights' kisses, planted on each other and cats, mocked the Christian kisses during the Catholic mass: when the priest kisses the altar, when parishioners exchange the sign of peace or when on Good Friday, the feet of Jesus on the crucifix are kissed in an act of humility. Instead of kissing the crucifix, the Templars spat on it. And here we can see how the sodomite kissing and heretical spitting combine to paint a picture of witchcraft, sorcery, and devil worship.

Church and State were gearing up for a purge of Europe's dark magical forces, and it was the ill fortune of the Templars to find themselves picked as the first targets for prosecution.

Chapter Two

King Philip of France Versus the Templars

King Philip IV of France arrested and imprisoned the Knights Templar in 1307, subjecting them to seven years of torture and trials on charges of heresy and sodomy. However, it's an overlooked fact that Philip was at war against sorcery and necromancy on multiple fronts during this period.

Between 1307 and 1314, the Templars were accused of secret nocturnal rituals where Christ's divinity was denied, and a Satanic head was worshipped. Soon, others faced similar allegations. From 1308, the Bishop of Troyes was on trial for his life charged with murder, and the attempted murder, of members of the royal family as well as being a half-demon and doing homage to Satan. In 1310, the female mystic and scholar, Marguerite Porete, was burned at the stake for writing a book, *The Mirror of Simple Souls*, where she claimed that once an individual's soul is united with God, there is no need for the Church's sacraments. This was part of an assault on the all-female lay preachers known as the Beguines, previously encouraged and supported by the king. Many leading members of the Church had once claimed that the Beguines had inspired them to dedicate their lives to Christ. Now, however, the Beguines were witches.

And while all this unfolded, Philip pressed ahead with charges of devil worship against Pope Boniface VIII, even though the pontiff had died in 1303. Ignoring this inconvenient truth, Philip set his top advisers to work on a dossier proving that Boniface was guilty of heresy, simony, fraud, and was an irreligious impostor, falsely elected as pope. No expense was spared pursuing this legal action against a dead man. Nothing Pope Clement could say or do would deflect the king from this vendetta against a corpse.

With a keen sense of papal history, Clement shuddered at the thought of his predecessor, Boniface, being arraigned on trumped up charges. This all had echoes of the grisly proceedings against Pope Formosus (*c.*816–896) in the ninth century who was exhumed and tried in the 'Cadaver Synod' a year after his death. Formosus was found guilty and his successor, Stephen VI (died 897), took it upon himself to remove the papal vestments from the mouldering corpse, cut off the three right-hand fingers used for benediction, and order that the body be thrown in the River Tiber.[1] However, Clement may have recalled that

Stephen was subsequently overthrown in a popular uprising, then strangled in prison. Measures had been enacted by the papal curia to forbid the trial of any dead popes in future. Philip ignored papal law and pursued the matter like a dog furiously chewing on a bone.

The king was not in his right mind. For two years he had been in a state of intense grief after the death of his queen, Joan of Navarre (1273–1305), in childbirth. The shock of her sudden demise led Philip to contemplate giving up the crown and, according to one account, he even requested to join the Templars.[2] The knights held a chapter meeting to consider this unexpected application for membership and turned it down. No reason was given for this snub, though it's possible that the Templars suspected a ruse to exert more royal control over them. Yet it's arguably a decision they came to regret. Unable to assuage his grief, Philip went on to accuse a high-ranking bishop of having murdered his wife by poison obtained from a sorcerer, and his trial ran for years alongside that of the Templars.

Everything Philip did in these years constituted a grim foreshadowing of two upcoming phenomena that would cause so much pain and death over the next three centuries: the witch hunting mania that swept across Europe until the eighteenth century and the unleashing of the Inquisition that would only finally be abolished in Spain and Portugal in the early nineteenth century. Both these phenomena witnessed the melding of heresy, sorcery, and necromancy to deadly effect. Philip was a trail blazer in this regard. Not just regarding the Templars, but all the other legal proceedings he had running in parallel.

But surely, as many historians contend, crushing the Templars was just about money? France was mired in debt from its wars with England and Philip had form when it came to shaking down different sections of society (Jews, Lombards, monasteries) for ready cash. His financial woes were undoubtedly a motive. But reality is many-sided and while it's true that Philip's desire to balance the kingdom's books accounted for his action against the Templars, he simultaneously had other things going on in his head. This was a king who believed his dynasty, the Capetians, had a divine mission, ordained by God, to defend Christendom. And he also seems to have nurtured a sincere belief in the growing prevalence of Satanic forces in his realm.

On 2 April 1305, the queen of France died in childbirth, aged 32. This tragic event was just over two years before her husband, Philip IV, ordered the mass arrest of the Templars. The aftermath of the queen's death affords an insight into the king's mental state in the lead up to the trial of the knights. There is no doubt that the loss of Joan of Navarre was an enormous emotional blow to a devoted husband who, according to contemporary accounts, constantly needed Joan by his side. However, while the relationship was undoubtedly loving, it also had a suffocating and controlling quality.[3] Philip did not regard Joan as his equal and on occasions publicly slapped her down, for example, forcing the return of gifts to Joan from the burghers of Carcassonne whom, he suspected, still harboured residual Cathar sympathies.

Joan had worn a crown all her life. She became Queen of Navarre at the age of one after her brother, Theobald, was killed, having fallen headlong from a castle battlement at Estella in 1273. He was accidentally dropped by his nurse whose subsequent fate is unknown.[4] Joan's father, known unkindly as Henry the Fat (*c*.1244–1274), passed away the following year, leaving the infant Joan as queen.

In Navarre, the daughter of a dead king had a stronger claim to the throne than a male cousin. This explains why so many women became queens of Navarre compared to other kingdoms in the Middle Ages. Basque and Visigoth laws still applied, with the former ruling that a child could inherit a family fortune regardless of sex, while the latter required property to be divided equally between males and females when parents died intestate. This was all remarkably progressive for the time.[5]

However, despite the favourable legal situation, Joan was forced to flee Navarre while still a toddler, with her mother, Blanche of Artois (*c*.1248–1302). Blanche was the widow of Henry the Fat who had been both King of Navarre and Count of Champagne. She now assumed the regency in both those realms for her infant daughter.

But Navarre was coveted by the two neighbouring Iberian kingdoms of Castile and Aragon, and sensing a power vacuum, the Castilians invaded. While they were repulsed, Blanche lost her nerve and fled for Paris with Joan in her arms. She told courtiers in Navarre that this was a quick visit to her cousin King Philip III of France (1245–1285) to seek military assistance, but she never returned. The infant Joan grew up at the French court where she received offers of marriage from Castile, Aragon, and England. It was the French, though, who clinched a wedding between Philip's son, the future Philip IV, and Joan.

The logic for the union was indisputable. It gave France a presence in the Iberian Peninsula and cleared the path to fully integrating Champagne into the kingdom of France. The county of Champagne was both extremely wealthy and fiercely independent. It had been the homeland of the first Knights Templar and the site of the Cistercian abbey of Clairvaux led by Saint Bernard, the ecclesiastical champion of the Templars. One of Champagne's most famous sons was the writer Chrétien de Troyes (*c.*1160–1191) who largely created the legend of King Arthur. Its leading city, Troyes, played host to booming merchant fairs that undoubtedly influenced the Templar flair for finance.

When the Templars were founded by Hugh de Payens, a vassal of the Count of Champagne, the county exceeded in size the kingdom of France in the twelfth century. The Angevin kings of England dominated the north, centre and southwest of what is now France, while independent Champagne and Burgundy dominated the east. But throughout the thirteenth century, the balance of power shifted. By the early fourteenth century, the kings of France had extended their reach in all directions. England still had a French presence but was officially a vassal to Paris. The crushing of the Cathar heresy had also brought the south more firmly under French control.

Yet Champagne, heartland of the Templars, still needed to be brought decisively into the fold. The marriage of Philip to Joan brought this a step closer. Even her mother's decision to take an English prince, Edmund 'Crouchback' (1245–1296), brother of King Edward I of England (1239–1307), as her second husband, only delayed the integration of Champagne. Edmund exercised his wife's regency powers in Champagne to the full, giving it a last taste of independence before it was absorbed into France. His nickname, Crouchback, is a source of confusion. It referred to the cross sewn on to the back of his mantle while on crusade in the Holy Land.

Once Philip and Joan were crowned king and queen of France in 1285, they assumed a clear division of roles. Philip ran France and Navarre while Joan managed Champagne alongside Blanche, the dowager countess. They needed trustworthy advisers and alighted on an ambitious priest, Guichard (*c.*1250–1317), born in Villemaur, from a relatively humble background. By 1273, still a young man, he was appointed Prior of Saint-Ayoul de Provins then Abbot of Montier-la-Celle in 1284. His talent was spotted by Blanche who supported his elevation to the bishopric of Troyes, and he became, as one historian put it, 'a creature of two queens': Blanche and her daughter Joan.[6] From 1296 to 1299, Guichard sat on the Grand Jours of Troyes, which was the parliament of the county of Champagne, and used his new secular power to enrich himself and his diocese. As with the Templars, his very evident business acumen led him to being heavily involved in the financial administration of Champagne, including tax gathering. Certain irregularities were spotted by advisers to Blanche, but she accused the Canon of Troyes, Jean de Calais, of being the culprit. He was arrested and put under lock and key by Guichard in his episcopal prison, pending an investigation, but then escaped. Furious, Blanche now accused her protégé, the bishop, of having deliberately let Jean slip away in return for a bribe. Guichard found himself the main target of her suspicion.

Having fled justice, Jean de Calais attempted to save his skin by becoming one of the main accusers against Guichard. Another prosecution witness was a shadowy figure: Noffo Dei, also known as Arnoldo Deghi. Intriguingly, a contemporary chronicler, Giovanni Villani (*c.*1276–1348), links the Guichard case and the trials of the Templars through this man who was 'full of all the vices'.[7] Though as a reliable source of information, Villani needs to be taken with a pinch of salt having spent time in prison himself, before succumbing to the Black Death.

According to Villani, Noffo was imprisoned in a dungeon with a renegade Templar, the former prior of Montfaucon near Toulouse, who had been condemned to life imprisonment by the grand master, Jacques de Molay. The two men conspired to make a series of allegations against the Knights Templar to the French king, in the hope of both securing their release and making some money. This disgraced Templar prior, Esquin of Floyran, is said to have been the first member of the order to raise allegations against his fellow brothers of heresy and sodomy. He first approached the King of Aragon who rebuffed him, but then made a beeline for Philip IV, who gave the prior a far more favourable reception.

Floyran later wrote to the King of Aragon reminding him that 3000 livres had been offered by his majesty if what Floyran said about the Templars turned out to be true. When Philip kicked off the trials, Floyran demanded that large payout from Aragon, but was ignored. It has been conjectured that these two scoundrels, Noffo Dei and Esquin, were one and the same person but this seems a little far-fetched.[8] If Villani's account is accurate, then Noffo Dei was heavily involved in both the Templar and Guichard trials as a prosecution witness.

Bishop Guichard's legal woes began with accusations of fraud by Blanche and Joan at the turn of the thirteenth century. Mother and daughter were convinced he had diverted tax revenues from the people of Champagne into his own pockets, and they wanted the money back. In 1302, fortune seemed to smile a little when Blanche died, though Joan soon made an eye-watering demand for the repayment of 40,000 livre tournois. His fraud was not going to be forgiven or forgotten.

Then fortune smiled again when Joan passed away during childbirth. With the queen and dowager queen gone, Guichard was confident the charges would be quietly dropped. His allies were convinced that rumours of his financial impropriety had originated with a rival, Simon Festu, Archdeacon of Vendôme, who had ambitions to be Treasurer of France, which he soon achieved. It's likely that Clement V thought that Festu had been mischief making because in 1307, he dismissed the corruption charges against Guichard. The matter appeared to be closed.

By the end of that year, the Pope and king were fully immersed in arresting the entire Templar order. But in February 1308, events moved decisively against Guichard. A ragged hermit, Regnaud de Langres, emerged from his cell at Saint-Flavit de Villemaur, in the diocese of Troyes, to make the most astonishing claims about Guichard. The most damning was that through sorcery, the bishop was responsible for the death of the late queen. He told a royal official, Guillaume de Hangest, that Guichard created a wax figure of the queen, baptised it with the name Joan and pricked it with a needle. He then melted it by a fire. Once the figure was reduced to an unrecognisable lump, the queen was dead.

To ensure the spells worked, the bishop turned to a rogue Dominican friar, Jean de Fay, who was experienced in summoning up demons, and a witch, Margueronne de Bellevillette.[9] Guichard asked the hermit to help him brew a poison that would be used on the king's brother, Louis, and his son Charles (1294–1328). In happier times, the queen had made Guichard godson to Charles but now he plotted his murder.[10] The toxic substance was a heady mix of scorpions, toads, and venomous spiders – familiar ingredients in many Satanic potions.

As these details seeped out, Guichard's accusers became legion. Monks from Saint-Ayoul declared that Guichard had told them in confidence that his mother had given birth to him after intercourse with a devil that frequented the family home. Local people were so terrified of it that they refused to work there as servants. As for becoming prior of Saint-Ayoul, that only happened because he poisoned the previous prior, according to thirty-three witnesses. A further eight witnesses claimed that demons in the form of ashes ('cendres' in the original French) continuously fell from Guichard's hair and hood in what sounds like a severe case of dandruff.

All of this was deemed grave enough for Guichard to be put on trial for multiple capital offences, each backed up by tens of witnesses. As the bishop was accused of killing the queen, Philip took a keen interest. Guichard had defrauded his wife as countess of Champagne and then murdered her. The king was busily prosecuting the Templars, a dead pope, and a leading voice of the Beguines but he was prepared to initiate another heresy proceeding. Especially if he could uncover the diabolical truth about his wife's death.[11]

Clement was badgered by Philip into setting up a commission of bishops to investigate Guichard's crimes. Among its members were Raoul Grosparmi, Bishop of Orléans; Robert de Fouilloy, Bishop of Amiens; Richard Le Neveu, Bishop of Béziers; and Pierre le Grez, Bishop of Auxerre. Initially, Guichard was held in the prison of the Archbishop of Sens, but he was then transferred, by order of the king, to the Louvre, a secular jail. This undoubtedly reflected the king's mistrust in the Church's ability to judge its own, bolstered by his experience of the Pope's vacillations over the Templar trials. Noffo Dei, a trained notary as well as a convicted criminal and scheming liar, drafted many of the charges, passing them on to the king's chief minister, De Nogaret, who put a stronger emphasis on heresy, but he was not responsible for the ceaseless reference to imps and devils.

It seems incredible that somebody of Noffo's base character could have been rubbing shoulders with the greatest figures in the kingdom, working together to bring down Guichard. What were Noffo's motives, other than retaining his liberty and filling his purse? One theory is that as a Lombard money lender, he resented Guichard squeezing the Lombards to fill his coffers. However, the king had also raided Lombard accounts, arresting anybody who resisted. Indeed, he shook down the Italian financiers, Jewish money lenders, and monastery abbots, before turning his attention to the Templars. If, as has been claimed, Noffo was the same person as Esquin of Floyran, then he was on a revenge mission for having been imprisoned by his superiors in the Templar order. But to avoid confusion, we will assume they were two different people, but equally roguish, and associated with each other.

Guichard was in a perilous position. He had committed 'sacrilegious crimes', which continued to multiply. New allegations were made that he lived with a nun as a concubine, as well as being a sodomite and adulterer. When one accuser journeyed to tell the Pope of the bishop's misdeeds, he was mysteriously poisoned before reaching the papal palace. A total of twenty-one witnesses swore that the bishop created counterfeit coins by means of alchemy. Guichard also abused his position as bishop to falsely accuse others of heresy before extorting huge sums from his victims in return for waiving the charges and releasing them from prison. But most heinous of all was his alleged murder of the queen, for which he earned the king's undying wrath.

The odds were against Guichard and anybody gambling on his future would have bet on him being burned at the stake. Yet of all the heresy related trials that ran concurrently in those years, this was the one that ended most inconclusively. After Clement V formally banned the Templars at the Council of Vienne, held between 1311 and 1312, Philip's interest in the Guichard case waned. The commission of bishops sent him a report that fell way short of condemning Guichard as a heretic and sorcerer. Then the two original key prosecution witnesses withdrew their statements.

While still in exile and on his deathbed, Jean de Calais retracted every word of his testimony against Guichard. Noffo, meanwhile, met a fitting end for a scoundrel. The mendacious Lombard had run up huge debts with traders at the biannual Troyes fairs and they pursued him with the same vigour that he expended trying to destroy their bishop. Cash strapped and friendless, Noffo was sentenced to death and hanged in Paris in 1313. But not before confessing that everything he had ever said about Guichard was a tissue of lies. Right back to the testimony he had given to Blanche claiming that the bishop had let Jean de Calais escape from his prison. All his words were false.

Clement had heard enough. Guichard was permitted to join the Pope at Avignon where he was ordered to relinquish the bishopric of Troyes in return for Bosnia, in the Balkans, with his new episcopal seat in the city of Diakovar (modern Djakovo in Croatia). He had faced charges and a process very similar to that of the Templars but, unlike them, was a free man. The evidence suggests that he never set foot in his new, remote diocese and most likely died peacefully in France in January 1317.

Guichard's trial contained many of the sordid elements found in the Templar hearings, which were being conducted at the same time. It was almost as if the king had developed a playbook for dealing with perceived enemies – a template in which charges of heresy and sodomy were guaranteed to destroy the accused. The Templars were lambasted for inappropriate kissing and speaking to a demon's head, while Guichard was labelled a sodomite, adulterer and sorcerer. It was almost impossible to defend oneself against this torrent of lurid indictments. Guichard struggled to bat away charges of financial impropriety, murder by poisoning, murder through magic, heresy, and being an illegitimate semi-demon. By sheer luck, he wriggled off the hook.

Prosecutions such as this began the process of normalising witch hunting, drawing in elite figures as both accusers and accused. Joan of Navarre had pursued Guichard as a sorcerer yet one of her descendants would be ensnared by what she was helping to unleash. Joan's great-great-granddaughter, also called Joan of Navarre, went down in infamy as the only queen of England ever to be charged with witchcraft. She was the consort of Henry IV (*c.*1367–1413) who had seized the throne of England in a rebellion in 1399 that saw the previous monarch die in highly suspicious circumstances. When Henry passed away in 1413, the widowed queen strove to continue good relations with her stepson, the new king, Henry V (1386–1422). But by 1419, things had soured between the two to such an extent that the huge dowry she was still receiving from her marriage to Henry IV was redirected to her stepson's war chest, her castles were seized, and she was placed under house arrest.

Joan's confessor, a Franciscan friar, John Randolf of Shrewsbury, went before parliament to claim the queen had been working for 'the death and destruction of our lord the king in the most treasonable and horrible manner that could be devised'. Contemporary chroniclers were more specific, claiming she had tried 'by sorcery and necromancy for to have destroyed the king'. This was at the dawn of the witch hunting craze that would crash through Europe for nearly three centuries. Fortunately for Joan, her stepson relented a year later, and she was released.[12]

The trial and execution of Jacques de Molay revealed a king prepared to destroy those who had once been his closest confidantes, if he suspected them of heresy and sorcery. Just twenty-four hours before his arrest, the Templar grand master had been an honoured guest at the funeral of the king's sister-in-law but that counted for nothing. Already, Philip knew that the old Templar would be rotting in a dungeon cell the very next evening. This willingness to betray friends, displaying a hideous level of paranoia, has been the hallmark of authoritarian monarchs from England's Henry VIII to a twentieth-century dictator like Joseph Stalin. In the Templar trials, like the show trials of the Soviet Union in the 1930s, the knights so often appear dazed and unable to process the horror unleashed against them by a king who was once their staunchest defender.

Similarly, Philip had once championed a group of women lay preachers: the Beguines. He had ignored Church critics who disliked these assertive female communities, based mainly in Paris, who combined involvement in business and trade with an intense piety.[13] The saint king and crusader Louis IX (1214–1270) had been a fervent supporter, funding their houses and placing them under the protection of the Dominican order, renowned for its preaching.

The Beguines were not nuns and were able to pursue professions like silk weaving and managing shops while leading an especially prayerful existence. Their combination of industriousness with religiosity was comparable to the Templars and attracted many wealthy, female nobles. Yet when the Council of Vienne met in 1311 to ban the Templars, the Pope and his bishops also shut down the Beguines with these blistering words:

> *These Beguines thus ensnare many simple people, leading them into various errors. They generate numerous other dangers to souls under the cloak of sanctity. We have frequently received unfavourable reports of their teaching and justly regard them with suspicion. With the approval of the sacred council, we perpetually forbid their mode of life and remove it completely from the church of God. We expressly enjoin on these and other women, under pain of excommunication to be incurred automatically, that they no longer follow this way of life under any form, even if they adopted it long ago, or take it up anew.*[14]

Far from being faithful daughters of the Church, these women expressed opinions contrary to the Catholic faith. By the time the council made this ruling, one Beguine had paid the ultimate price for her involvement in this movement. In 1310, Marguerite Porete (*c.*1260–1310) was burned at the stake along with a copy of her book, *The Mirror of Simple Souls*. It was even jested, in rather poor taste, that her legacy on the day of execution was 'two plumes of smoke', one for her and another for her book.

The Mirror was an accessible religious tract featuring a lively discussion between the allegorical figures of Love, Reason, and the Soul. The main gist was that by reaching out to God, the individual soul could become subsumed into the divine. This idea was an echo of the Gnostic beliefs that influenced the Cathars and may have been imbibed by the Templars. The mystical saint, Catherine of Siena (1347–1380) had views that were not entirely dissimilar to Marguerite but unlike the renowned beguine, Catherine adopted a servile posture towards the Church with an unquestioning obedience to the Pope and male, priestly authority.[15]

From 1308, Marguerite Porete was one of two women at the receiving end of an aggressive, ecclesiastical inquiry; the other was Margueronne de Bellevillette, the alleged witch with whom Guichard had allegedly consorted in the woods.[16] Porete's troubles began when her book was condemned to be burned in public by Guy of Colmieu, Bishop of Cambrai (died 1306). Initially, she feigned contrition but then changed her mind.

Determined to defend her work, she got an endorsement from the head of theology at the University of Paris, Godfrey of Fontaines (died 1306) and received guarded praise from John of Querayn, a Franciscan friar, as well as the Cistercian cantor of Villiers abbey. With these positive reviews in the bag, Marguerite decided to ignore the Bishop of Cambrai and hit the road to promote her book. Her timing could not have been worse. Both the royal and papal appetite for heresy hunting was increasing and her strident activity was almost bound to attract the attention of the Inquisition.

Two years later, Marguerite Porete found herself surrounded by uniformly hostile voices as her trial got underway.[17] The inquisitor in charge of Porete's interrogation was William of Paris (died 1314), a leading Dominican and the king's own personal confessor. He was a busy man, involved at the same time with the prosecution of the Knights Templar. Despite being thrown in prison, Marguerite refused to answer William's questions and displayed a marked degree of contempt for what she clearly felt was his inferior intellect. This only made the verdict even more of a certainty.

The legal process took just under two years with William confirming her guilt and Marguerite sentenced to die by burning. On the Sunday after the

Feast of the Ascension, a large crowd gathered in what was then the field of La Grève in Paris (later a public square) where she arrived in a procession led by her inquisitors. William of Paris declared that Marguerite bore 'the stain of heretical depravity' and that her demeanour was that of 'a rebel and obstinate person'. He expressed his exasperation at her conduct throughout the proceedings:

> *Until now, however, you have disdained to seek absolution, and you have thus far wanted neither to swear nor respond to us concerning the aforesaid matters. On account of your refusal to do these things, and according to the holy canons, we hold you, as indeed we ought to hold you, both as convicted and confessed and as one lapsed into heresy; that is, we hold you to be a heretic… This inquisition and hearing made it clear to us that you had at one point composed a pestiferous book containing heresy and errors; because of its errors, this book had been condemned… Inasmuch as your erroneous and heretical book contains heresy and errors, by the judgment of and advice of the masters in theology residing in Paris, we finally condemn you and now want you to be excommunicated and burned.*[18]

Philip did not lift a finger to save Marguerite from the flames. While she endured the ultimate penalty, Guichard's witch, Margueronne de Bellevillette, was incarcerated but then freed after eleven years behind bars, when the case against the bishop was shelved. The reason she survived was that her claims to holy power were rustic and illiterate, covering such trivial issues as finding lost animals. Whereas Marguerite Porete posed a more intellectually based theological challenge to the Church that could not be ignored or unpunished. She was no wizened, fortune telling village sorcerer, but a recognised face in elite religious and political circles. In the eyes of the authorities, Marguerite's pen was way mightier than Margueronne's wand.

The execution of Marguerite Porete took place on 31 May 1310. Nearly three weeks before, on 12 May, fifty-four Templars were burned at the stake as heretics. Even by the standards of the time, this was an exceptionally high body count for heresy-related executions in a single month. Philip was acting like a blood-soaked zealot. But far from slowing the pace, the king was relentless in his prosecution of the knights, the beguines, and a dead pope.

The instrument of the king's campaign against the Templars was his chief minister: Guillaume de Nogaret. Born into the minor nobility, he was a clever and articulate individual who worked as a professor of law at the universities of Montpellier and Orléans, before becoming a leading figure in Philip's royal administration. While De Nogaret had a thorough grounding in the law, he was not averse to reaching for the knuckle dusters when the situation demanded an unorthodox approach.

He skilfully combined an ability to draft watertight legal documents with brute force when it came to dealing with Church power. The end truly justified the means. Hence his expedition in 1303 to the papal palace of Pope Boniface VIII to ram home the point that King Philip of France would tax the Church within his realm with or without the Pope's consent. De Nogaret descended on the Italian town of Anagni with a band of French soldiers, which had long been a retreat for the popes, escaping the malaria and poisonous politics of Rome.

On the way, De Nogaret hooked up with Giacomo 'Sciarra' Colonna (1270–1329), an aggrieved member of a powerful family who felt one of its members should have been elected Pope and not an upstart like Boniface, coming from the relatively modest Caetani family. Barging their way into the palace, it's alleged that Sciarra slapped the Pope around the face. More accurately, he planted his heavily mailed fist into the head of a 68-year-old Pope and then locked Boniface up for two days without food or water. Little wonder that His Holiness died just a few weeks later, most likely of bleeding on the brain (subdural haematoma).[19]

He was succeeded by a very short-lived Pope, Benedict XI, who lifted Boniface's excommunication of King Philip but left everybody else involved in the Anagni outrage out of the Church. Benedict had been present when his predecessor had been punched to the ground and saw no reason to forgive De Nogaret. However, Benedict expired barely nine months into his reign with wagging tongues accusing De Nogaret of poisoning him. The Pope's death led to the election of Clement and the papacy being relocated out of Italy to the city of Avignon, today in modern France, but then in the Holy Roman Empire.

De Nogaret is usually cast as the evil, amoral, and compliant tool of a capricious king. But others have seen De Nogaret as a radical reformer – a medieval Robespierre even. Far from being mindlessly cruel and vindictive, this highly intelligent and resourceful individual was a French patriot seeking to remove the yoke of Rome, giving his country complete control over its own affairs. This was a view advanced in the nineteenth century by the French writer Ernest Renan (1823–1892), at a time when nationalist fervour was sweeping Europe. In Renan's view, De Nogaret was an almost heroic figure sticking it to the papacy.

To emancipate the French State from clerical control, the Knights Templar, a large body of armed men under papal control, had to be disarmed and rendered harmless. Achieving this meant a series of show trials in which the Templars were depicted as an organisation operating to an agenda that was both hostile to France's interests and its morals, a secret society with no allegiance to the king or God.

Even though Clement eventually absolved De Nogaret in 1311, Philip was constantly haunted by the ghost of Boniface. Their long running feud over clerical power in France played on his mind, even though Boniface now lay mouldering in his tomb. Philip had been unable to kidnap and bring the Pope to trial in France while he was still alive, but death would not be an obstacle. De Nogaret was ordered to draw up legal papers for posthumous proceedings. The minister obliged, accusing the dead pontiff of being a false pope whose name was 'Bonifacius' when it should have been 'maleficus'.[20] The documents continued in this rather vindictive vein.

De Nogaret was adept at combining biblical and legal terminology as can be seen in the wording of the Templar arrest warrants. He elaborated further that Boniface was an impostor, had no God-given authority and had usurped the apostolic see. In life, he denied the immortality of the soul, the doctrine of transubstantiation (the communion bread literally becoming the body of Christ in the Catholic mass), and the forgiveness of sins.

On what basis did the king of France imagine that he could sit in judgement on a pope and the Knights Templar? Up until Philip's reign, an assertive pope like Boniface represented the norm, demanding that secular rulers be obedient to Christ's vicar on earth. As for the Templars, they enjoyed papal protection that gave them two centuries of independence from the whims of kings, princes and dukes. Their only line manager beyond the grand master was the Pope himself.

Yet Philip dared to put himself above the Pope, adopting what one historian called a 'Christlike function', while another termed his actions the 'pontificalisation' of the French monarchy.[21] He took it upon himself to arbitrate on what made a good pope while bringing the Templars to heel. What made Philip so audacious? It helped to know he was the grandson of a saint.

Decades before the Templar trials, on August 25, 1270, King Louis IX of France, grandfather of Philip IV, died on crusade near the ancient city of Carthage on the north African coast.

He had succumbed to dysentery, an unpleasant bacterial infection that had swept through his army, often referred to as the 'bloody flux'. It is a debilitating form of gastroenteritis, and the last days of the future Saint Louis were full of pain and indignity. But nothing compared to what his body would experience in death. The king's corpse was de-fleshed by being boiled in water or wine. This isolated his skeleton for the long journey back home, while the discarded human tissue was either buried or placed in an urn. The macabre process of excarnation was referred to as 'mos teutonicus', possibly because it originated among German crusaders.

Louis had experienced a rather torrid time on crusade. Initially full of optimism, he had embarked on the full-scale invasion of Egypt, taking advantage of divisions and intrigue within the ruling dynasty in Cairo. The rule of the Ayyubids, the dynasty of Saladin, was ending and the Mamluks were taking control. Fighting alongside Louis were the Knights Templar who threw themselves into a series of bloody battles in the Nile Delta, losing one of their grand masters who was cut down by Egyptian scimitars. This unfortunate Templar leader had lost an eye in one battle then the remaining one in the next battle leaving him staggering around, an easy target for the Egyptians.[22]

The Seventh Crusade saw Louis defeated at the Battle of Fariskur in 1250 and captured, requiring a hefty ransom of some 400,000 livres tournois for his release. Undeterred he spent another four years in the Holy Land refortifying Acre, Caesarea, and Jaffa in the hope of retaking Jerusalem, which Saladin had seized from the crusaders in 1187. But events forced his return to France from where he made a series of overtures to the Mongol Emperors in the hope that they would ally with him against the Saracens. But nothing very tangible was forthcoming. Then in 1267, he took three of his sons on the Eighth Crusade and headed for Tunis. While there, he died of dysentery.

Philip, Count of Orléans, the oldest son of the dead king, was also stricken with the bloody flux but survived to be proclaimed the new monarch. Back in France, his eldest son and heir, Louis, was 4 years old while his second, Philip, was just 2. It was the second son who would end up taking the throne, becoming the nemesis of the Knights Templar. He would decimate the very knights who had fought with such courage and determination alongside his grandfather.

King Louis IX had been renowned throughout Europe for his piety. Privately he spent many hours praying, fasting, and doing penance. He commissioned the opulent Sainte-Chappelle, a Gothic masterpiece, to house the Crown of Thorns and a piece of the True Cross bought from the Byzantine Emperor for an astronomic sum that crippled the kingdom's finances.

Reportedly, Louis also allowed beggars to eat at his table, washed their feet and ministered to lepers. As regards his relationship with Rome, the king went out of his way to placate the popes, portraying himself as a faithful son of the Church. Quite a contrast with his grandson Philip who almost delighted in being at constant loggerheads with Boniface VIII. Louis extracted a considerable amount of money from the Church in his realm but avoided the kind of acrimony Philip provoked, as the money was used to fund the crusades in the Holy Land, which had the full support of the Pope, as opposed to funding a war with England, which did not.

At his death, the body of Louis was treated like that of a saint, even though his canonisation was still some years away. His skeleton was transported back to Paris to be interred at the Basilica of Saint Denis while his viscera ended up in an urn at Monreale Cathedral, just outside Palermo in Sicily. Later his bones were distributed more widely, with the jawbone ending up at Notre-Dame cathedral. So dispersed were the relics of King Louis IX that they sometimes end up in auction rooms today. One tiny piece of bone was up for grabs in 2024 at an asking price of 800 Euros.[23]

Louis cast a long shadow down the generations.[24] Boniface canonised Louis as a saint on 6 August 1297, in a futile attempt to de-escalate the row between himself and Philip over taxation of the Church in France. Far from calming things down, it bolstered the king's own self-belief as he was now the grandson of a saint-king. Two years later, Boniface ruled that the practice of 'mos teutonicus' was in fact 'mos horribilis' and ordered it to stop immediately. Dead kings, such as the late Louis IX, were no longer to be boiled and de-fleshed.[25]

But that was too late to prevent the royal cult of Louis the saint from being promoted, full throttle, by Philip. The Capetian dynasty, of which Philip was a part, had long termed themselves 'the most Christian of kings', but now they had a saint in the family.[26] The royal propaganda machine fostered a series of legends about his life, emphasising his goodly deeds. He fed monks afflicted with leprosy and fed sick people, emaciated and unable to rise from their beds. Ignoring the smell of death, he collected the bones of Christian martyrs in the Holy Land and brought them back to Europe. When he died, two angels appeared and transported his body upwards to heaven.

On 17 May 1306, Philip removed his grandfather's skull from the Basilica of Saint Denis, transferring it amidst much pomp and circumstance to Sainte-Chappelle. Power was ebbing gradually from the papacy to secular rulers, but that power still needed a sacred quality to be legitimate. Philip presented himself as doing God's work as he put the Templars on trial and pursued Boniface beyond the grave. He still needed a papal rubber stamp of approval, but the king was calling the shots.[27]

Philip's relentless display of sanctity was punctured by a sex scandal that engulfed the royal family. In March 1314, Jacques de Molay was executed. A month later, Pope Clement died and by November, Philip had also gone to the grave. But not before the closing months of his reign were clouded by the Tour de Nesle affair. From a modern perspective, it has the ring of a tabloid newspaper scandal or social media generated sleaze. As with audiences today, the medieval public lapped up the salacious details.

The king had married off his three sons to noble ladies. Louis (1289–1316) was paired with Margaret (1290–1315), daughter of Robert II of Burgundy (1248–1306), while another of Robert's daughters, Joan (1293–1348) was wedded to prince Philip (1293–1350). The king's youngest son Charles (1294–1328), whose godfather had been the disgraced Guichard, married Blanche of Burgundy (*c.*1296–*c.*1326), daughter of Otto IV, count of Burgundy (1248–1303).

The king's daughter, Isabella (*c.*1295–1358), became queen of England through her marriage with Edward II. Often referred to as the 'she-wolf of France', this formidable woman shared many of her father's ruthless character traits. She joined Edward in battles against the Scots but after becoming disenchanted with the power exercised at court by his male favourites, she plotted successfully to overthrow and murder her own husband. Years before that, in a state visit to France with her still living husband King Edward, she informed her father, Philip, that her three sisters-in-law were involved in adulterous relationships.

What emerged during the subsequent investigations were tales of orgies at the Tour de Nesle, an imposing thirteenth-century tower, across the river Seine from the Louvre. The king's equerry, Philip of Aunay (*c.*1290–1314) was accused of adultery with Margaret while his brother, Gautier, was linked amorously to Blanche.

The king had shown his disregard for human rights in his treatment of the Templars over a seven-year period, ignoring the protests of the Pope over their torture. When it came to dealing with Philip and Gautier, his sadism reached new highs. Having confessed to their crimes, the pair were castrated in public, skinned alive, covered in boiling lead, decapitated, dragged through the streets, and finally hanged on the gallows.

Philip's tempestuous reign reached a climax in the year that he died. In November 1314, he breathed his last, having sent the last Templar grand master to the flames six months earlier. If the motive for destroying the Templars had been financial gain, was he successful? Were the Capetian coffers now brimming with the knights' gold and silver?

An important fact that needs to be stated is that much of the wealth held in the Paris Temple – the order's headquarters that dominated the city skyline – was already the king's property. The Templars managed the State finances with Crown revenues deposited at the heavily fortified Temple by royal officials from all over France. Detailed records were kept of all these deposits and the king was then credited with the full amount minus a handling fee for their time and effort. In terms of monitoring local officials to ensure they had submitted the correct amounts, that was a task undertaken by a special council of royal advisers who often met at the Temple. The king often ran up debts with the Templars but paid them promptly, and there were even rare occasions when the Templars owed Philip money.

Other sources of Templar income included the agricultural and trading activities in their network of preceptories across Europe, holding money and valuables for wealthy clients and lending. But in Paris, the vaults of the Temple were primarily filled with the tax revenue of France, which Philip owned already. When he shut down the order and seized its assets, the total gain to the royal treasury was about 260,000 livres tournois, which was a sizeable sum but, like a modern windfall tax, it was a one-off that could not be repeated.

If Philip was expecting a bigger payout from crushing the Templars, then either he was deluded or the knights managed to hide their assets from his officials, before or after the mass arrests in October 1307. The various claims of the Templars spiriting their treasure away in the dead of night will be explored in the following chapters, examining where they may have hidden their fantastic wealth.

The king undoubtedly had major financial headaches, not least from the cost of his wars with England, Aragon and Flanders. Philip tried to tackle his debts by debasing the silver coinage, which sparked inflation that in turn provoked riots and widespread discontent. In the two decades before he moved against the Templars, Philip was nervously casting around for ways to plug the State deficit. This led him into conflict with the Pope over his wish to extract more from the Church and resulted in the arrest and mass fleecing of Lombard merchants in 1292. The Lombards were forced to buy French nationality, yielding an amount comparable to what would later be derived from Templar assets. But still the deficit climbed.

The king was wrestling with ways to revive the currency amidst a growing shortage of silver in Europe as mines became depleted. This 'bullion famine' continued across Europe and the Middle East into the next century and some historians believe it was this that drove the Spanish and Portuguese into the New World (the Americas) and Africa, in a desperate bid to find new sources of gold and silver.[28] Philip looked to raid those he believed had stores of silver to spare, hence the attack on the Lombards.

In 1306, he turned on the Jews of France and expelled them from the kingdom.[29] But expropriating their assets did not resolve the currency crisis. Historian, Ignacio de la Torre, believes that it was at this moment, 'the Temple's fate was sealed as the Templar treasury was probably the only remaining source of silver able to provision royal mints'.[30]

It's widely asserted that when Philip's officials broke into the Paris Temple, the cupboard was bare. But not everybody accepts this. There are records of the amounts obtained from the Templars in Cyprus and England that are eye-watering and one Templar's testimony in 1308 claimed that Jacques de Molay had returned to Paris from Cyprus with 600 kilogrammes of gold, and possibly an equivalent amount of silver. De la Torre believes that Philip got exactly what he wanted from the Temple and the knights' extensive bullion stores, which were melted down for use in the royal mints. Suddenly, Philip's financial woes were resolved. Crushing the Templars had made great economic sense.

There are two contradictory views of King Philip of France. One is that his reign saw French royal power reach its absolute height, which it would not experience again for many generations. Another view is that he was a 'shadowy, elusive figure' who lurked 'behind a screen of bureaucrats'.[31]

Either he was a very hands-on monarch involved in the minutiae of decision making, or he was laissez-faire in his approach, leaving the running of the kingdom to a succession of ruthless but competent ministers. The truth probably lies somewhere in between. However, one thing is certain, he was intimately involved when it came to the trial of the Templars and the other heresy-related proceedings. No other monarch of the Middle Ages could be said to have been one of the architects of the witch hunting mania that was about to explode across Europe.

At the Church council in Vienne in 1311–1312, where the Pope officially banned the Templars, the monarchs of Europe and many bishops were notable by their absence. There was widespread disgust and suspicion at the treatment of the knights by the king and Pope. But one figure loomed in the background, brooding, stroking his chin, nudging his ministers, following the debates intensely. Philip sat in the shadows, his stare fixed on Clement, determined that the Templar heretics and sodomites would face the flames.

Chapter Three

Pope Clement Versus the Templars

The trials of the Knights Templar created an unbearable tension between King Philip IV of France and Pope Clement V, two men who had known each other since their youth. A monarch who believed he had a divine right to rule versus a Pope who was painfully aware of the royal assault on papal power. The king's ministers hardly masked their contempt for the leader of the Roman Catholic Church while the Pope's cardinals urged their boss to push back against this overbearing monarch.

The first rumblings of the future witchcraft mania can be clearly detected in Philip's reign with its many heresy and sorcery trials. The king's belief in supernatural forces ranged against God exceeded that of the Pope. He saw covert demonic conspiracies everywhere. Clement, meanwhile, was a beleaguered pontiff ceaselessly bullied by the king and yet, when it came to the Templars, he managed to score some small victories against his determined rival. Though in the end, the order was doomed.

In late 1305, a Gascon, Bertrand de Got, was elected Pope after months of deliberations by the cardinals. Gascony was part of Aquitaine – a territory covering south-west France, dating back to the Roman provinces of Aquitania Prima and Secunda. In 1152, Eleanor of Aquitaine (1122–1204) married Duke Henry of Anjou (1133–1189) who, two years later, became King Henry II of England. From that moment, Aquitaine was governed from England until France took complete control of the territory in the 1450s. However, at the time of Bertrand's birth, the future Pope Clement V was an English subject who would have spoken Occitan, a lyrical language that the poet Dante Alighieri (*c.*1265–1321) believed was perfect for verse – a point proven by the medieval troubadours who sang in Occitan of chivalry and courtly love.

Bertrand was not present at the conclave's secret deliberations in 1305 as he was not a cardinal. Yet that proved no barrier to putting his name forward. His family pedigree was perfect for the job. The new pontiff's father was Bérard (or Beraud by another spelling) de Got, lord of Villandraut, Grayan, Livran, and Uzeste, descended from the noble houses of Mauléon, Farges, Savignac, and Prevssac. His uncle was Bishop of Agen while his deceased older brother, Bérard (*c*.1250–1297) had been Archbishop of Lyon and Cardinal-Bishop of Albano. Another brother was a papal chaplain while Bertrand's grandfather had been the brother of the Bishop of Bazas. So, this was a family with a plethora of ecclesiastical connections.[1] The sacred college of cardinals, locked in a very rancorous conclave, eventually compromised and picked Bertrand to be Pope.

At the time of his election to the papacy, Bertrand was Archbishop of Bordeaux, effectively the capital of the Duchy of Aquitaine, which was held by the Angevin monarchs of England, on condition they pledged fealty to the king of France. The young Bertrand lived in a thriving city that enjoyed a free trade status with England. It exported wine in return for English imports of cloth and wheat. But the prosperity of this medieval metropolis was menaced by dark clouds gathering on the political horizon.

The Capetian kings of France had never accepted the loss of Aquitaine to the Angevin dynasty that ruled England and Aquitaine. This was a centuries old sore that they picked at. Meanwhile, Edward I of England (1239–1307), a man not noted for his tact, chafed at having to bend the knee to Paris. But Philip IV was in expansionist mode, determined to extend his tentacles southwards. What he saw in southern France was galling for him. England was in control of the south-west while the south-east was governed by independently minded barons and the Holy Roman Empire. Displaying an almost incipient nationalism, Philip wanted to bring all these duchies, principalities, and archbishoprics firmly under the control of Paris, creating the France we know today.

It was only going to take the smallest of provocations for Philip to let his armies loose, but little could he or Edward have realised that their spats over fealty would erupt into the Hundred Years' War that would rumble on long after their deaths. This would be a momentous conflict in which England and France would draw the rest of Europe into a bloody series of battles stretching from 1337 to 1453.[2] The result would be the full realisation of Philip's ambitious vision and the final ejection of England from French soil.

In May 1294, Philip seized Aquitaine from England. This was a personal slap in the face to Edward who had spent much of his youth in the duchy and was in no mood to be denied its revenues and fine wines. This whole thing about being a vassal to the French king was a recent development having been negotiated by his father, Henry III (1207–1272), from a position of weakness. Edward wanted to restore absolute English control over the duchy, only now he had lost it completely.

Philip used an unseemly punch up at sea between English, Gascon, and French sailors as a pretext to invade. The resulting occupation by France was a dreadful experience for the local nobility which was subjected to imprisonment and interrogation. Bertrand's family became involved in the on-going fraught diplomacy that rumbled on between the English and French. Philip was determined to hold on to his new province, while Edward needed more time before striking back as his hands were full fighting in Wales and Scotland.

In 1295, Bertrand's brother Bérard was tasked by Pope Boniface VIII with trying to secure peace between England and France and in August that year, he met King Edward in London. England would eventually regain Aquitaine, but it was in this precarious environment that Bertrand developed his cautious diplomatic skills, often construed as weakness. He performed a constant, delicate balancing act, seeking to simultaneously appease Boniface, Edward, and Philip to further his career.

As early as 1289, in his mid-twenties, Bertrand wrote a stiff letter to Edward, as the ruler of Aquitaine, begging for a better paid job in the Church. At that stage he had received a top-class education at the universities of Orléans and Bologna, before becoming a canon at Bordeaux, Saint-Caprais in Agen, Tours, and Lyons. Barely out of his teens, Bertrand was acting as a lawyer for the English king at the French court.[3] But these positions, attained at a young age, were of insufficient status and revenue for an ambitious fellow like Bertrand de Got. The king responded to his gripes by granting the grasping young cleric a generous stipend until a better position could be found.

By 1297, he had secured the archbishopric of Bordeaux, at the height of the conflict between France and England over who would govern Aquitaine. English control was eventually restored but throughout this crisis, Bertrand maintained a placatory correspondence with both Edward and Philip. His instincts were to calm the situation, pouring oil on troubled waters, but he had the misfortune, throughout his career, to have to deal with some very combustible monarchs, with the worst of all being Philip IV of France.

Could Bertrand de Got have imagined that within eight years, he would be catapulted into the papacy without even being a cardinal? Bertrand's election as Pope Clement V in 1305 was the result of unseemly haggling between French and Italian cardinals during which he emerged as a compromise candidate acceptable to both camps and welcomed by the now reconciled kings of England and France.

For the faithful, he was a contentious figure. Italians dismissed him as a Frenchman. The French looked down their noses at the new Pope as a Gascon.

The cardinals around him had chosen a man outside their ranks and these princes of the Church would not allow him to forget that fact. At this time, the cardinals were becoming ever more powerful as advisors and framers of policy. With every step he took, Clement needed to secure the support of the sacred college that had elected him, especially the French faction that took its cues from Philip IV. In short, the Pope was not his own man, exercising absolute power. He needed to negotiate treacherous waters to survive.[4]

It must have been glaringly obvious to him from day one that his position as Pope had been primarily due to the machinations of the King of France. It was certainly clear to Philip who regarded Clement V, as Bertrand was now styled, as his puppet pontiff. But Pope Clement had a long history of diplomatic tightrope walking and despite the enormous pressure put on him from Paris, he kept on good terms with England and attempted to maintain the dignity of his office by pursuing his own path.

However, Clement had good reason to be nervous about the French king. The years leading up to his election saw Philip in a state of perpetual war with the papacy. Taxing the Church in France without papal permission, to fund his wars with England, resulted in Pope Boniface threatening him with excommunication. This led to astonishing scenes at the papal palace at Anagni in 1303 when France's chief minister, De Nogaret, and Sciarra Colonna, assaulted the Pope by slapping him in the face repeatedly with a gauntlet. Clement had not forgotten this incident. It illustrated only too well Philip's lack of respect for the papacy.

Clement was elected by the cardinals at Perugia, where the one-year reign of Pope Benedict XI had ended with his sudden death. During his brief pontificate, Benedict excommunicated De Nogaret over the assault on Boniface, which led to rumours that the French had the Holy Father poisoned. This exclusion of De Nogaret from the Church would become a contentious issue for Clement, who refused to lift it for several years.

Clement decided not to process to the Lateran Palace in Rome for his coronation. Instead, he travelled north to the city of Lyon, which was part of the Holy Roman Empire before France annexed it in 1312. It was there that the papal tiara was placed on his head, on 14 November 1305. Clement's own choice of Vienne, just south of Lyon, was vetoed by Philip, and the new Pope meekly acquiesced.

The decision to move the papacy out of Rome was not that difficult for a non-Italian pope with no connections to the gangster-like families that dominated the city's life. However, this was a highly controversial move. Papal power, after all, rested on the belief that the apostle Peter, in the aftermath of the crucifixion, had journeyed from the Holy Land to Rome and became the first pope, before being martyred. All successive popes claimed their legitimacy from this account. Yet here was a pope refusing to rule from the eternal city and instead, skulking in France.

On 14 November 1305, the papal coronation was held in Lyon with due pomp until disaster struck. John II, Duke of Brittany (1239–1305), was leading the Pope's horse through the crowds, many of whom were crammed on top of the city walls. As the Pope passed by, a section of the walls gave way and collapsed on top of his party. Clement was thrown from his horse but survived. The duke, however, took four days to die. In the resulting confusion, a precious garnet stone went missing from the papal tiara, never to be seen again. Hardly the most auspicious start to a pope's reign and surely a sign of divine disapproval.

Despite this, Clement established his headquarters in the city of Avignon, which was also, like Lyon, nominally part of the Holy Roman Empire. Today both cities are in modern France as Philip intended. This was dubbed The Avignon Exile and lasted from 1305 to 1378 under successive popes. Some have even called it a Babylonian Captivity of the popes on French soil. In 1378, the Church attempted to relocate to Rome and elected the first Italian in many years to be crowned on the papal throne. Only Avignon was not prepared to fade away. From 1378 to 1417, there were two rival popes – one in Rome and one in Avignon – demanding the loyalty of Catholics everywhere.

This caused a split across Europe with France, Aragon, Castile, Scotland and Wales recognising the Avignon pope while England, Portugal, Ireland, Poland and others backed the pope in Rome. In 1409, a third pope emerged in the Italian city of Pisa, though this 'antipope', proclaimed as John XXIII (*c.*1370–1419), organised a council where he resigned along with the Roman pope, and the Avignon pope was excommunicated. Then another cardinal, Oddone Colonna, was elevated as Pope Martin V (1369–1431), and the Church was reunified.

For those who argue that Clement was a ruinous leader of Roman Catholicism, this rivalry between papal claimants, dubbed The Western Schism, was proof of his poor strategic decision making that resulted in a permanent weakening of the pope's power.

In the months after his election, the new Pope holed up in Bordeaux as he experienced the first of many bouts of ill health that would eventually culminate in terminal stomach cancer, which physicians attempted to halt with oral infusions of crushed emeralds. This was a time when cancer was misunderstood as 'an imbalance of the humours' and characterised as 'an eating worm or wolf'.[5] The persistent challenges he faced during his reign cannot have helped his physical wellbeing, especially the perceived ever-present danger of heresy.

It was in response to the proliferation of heretics across Christendom that his predecessors had developed the Inquisition, a body of highly trained interrogators and sadistic torturers that would loom large in the centuries ahead. In the minds of the inquisitors, heresy had many faces, but its devilish tails were linked together.[6] It presented itself as a vast array of false theologies and charismatic movements, but the devil was pulling all the strings. Heresy, to the Church, was a many-headed hydra, the serpentine monster of mythology, and it was the Herculean task of the Inquisition to lop off one venomous head after another.

Dealing with individual heretics, once identified, was relatively straightforward: build a case against that person, bring them to trial, and either force the person to recant or face the consequences. But the Cathar heresy of the thirteenth century had been a mass movement, drawing in thousands of people, that swept across southern France and parts of Italy. It had convinced Rome that something far more robust and institutional was needed to tackle large-scale disobedience. It would need to be a round-the-clock effort by a specially trained corps of dedicated, legally minded clerics to root out the enemies of Catholicism.

One notable leader of the Church in the early thirteenth century grappled with this challenge. Pope Gregory IX (1145–1241) was elderly but energetic, possessing a fine legal mind. He reorganised the Church's haphazard heretic hunting activities into the Papal Inquisition, a notorious body that would strike terror into many communities across Christian Europe. It's been argued that Gregory's inquisition originally had benign motives – to stop random lynchings, by zealous mobs, of individuals suspected of heresy. However, it was also about centralising and controlling anti-heresy activity, ensuring that only the prelates of the Church could authorise a heresy hunt. Rome, a cynic might observe, felt it should have sole control over lynching heretics.

The new Papal Inquisition led to a boom in talented young men studying canonical jurisprudence at universities like Paris and Bologna. The whole process of judging heretics would be done with proper rigour. Gregory drafted in bright but steely-eyed souls from the Dominicans and Franciscans to fan out across Christendom in search of those undermining Church power. His Inquisition was going to be methodical and well organised.

Alarmingly, this new beefed-up Inquisition made growing use of torture, sanctioned by Rome, and an early target were Jewish people. In a document, the Decretals, issued in 1234, Gregory declared the doctrine of *perpetua servitus iudaeorum*: the perpetual servitude of the Jews. They would be regarded as inferior until Judgment Day.[7] While Gregory offered some protections to synagogues, he granted those crusaders who had fought the Cathars a moratorium on their debts to Jewish moneylenders. He took children from their Jewish mothers and entrusted them to the father, if he had converted to Catholicism, and forbade

Jews to have Christian servants. He also called for the burning of copies of the Talmud, the Jewish scripture, in public squares.[8]

Gregory's approach to rooting out heresy gave the accused a path to follow that could lead either to absolution or execution. They had a period in which to make themselves known, for witnesses to come forward, and a process for determining whether they could be brought back to the bosom of the Church. But by 1252, Pope Innocent IV (*c.*1195–1254) decided a tougher approach was required. He issued a papal bull with the ominous title *Ad extirpanda* (to eradicate), which authorised the use of torture by the Inquisition. Law 25 in the bull explained how torture should be carried out:

> *The Podesta or Rector has the authority to oblige all heretics that he may have in his power, without breaking limbs or endangering their lives, to confess their errors and to accuse other heretics whom they may know, as true assassins of souls and thieves of the Sacraments of God...*[9]

The forms of torture used by the Inquisition have been a source of unseemly curiosity for centuries: the strappado, rack, and the Judas Chair reducing accused heretics to blubbering wrecks. To be shown the instruments of torture was deemed in some instances to be sufficient to extract a confession. In each town where the Inquisition came to investigate, the inquisitor would work with the local bishop and the secular authorities, who were obliged as good Christians to help him in his work. That included providing accommodation and somewhere to conduct operations.[10]

Why did the Church embrace this institutionalised cruelty? The reason was that as papal power had increased during the Templar period, so had resistance and disgust. The sight of jewel encrusted abbots, bishops, and cardinals may have impressed some, but others felt it was a complete break with scripture. Where was the poverty in the Church, let alone the humility? The Cathar heresy spread like wildfire on the back of widespread resentment throughout society at the obscene wealth of the Church. Roman Catholicism began to appear like a scam that exploited the credulity of the faithful.

Rebellious heretics proliferated everywhere. From the 1260s, a sect called the Order of Apostles spread throughout northern Italy, believing that they were as legitimate a religious order as the Franciscans, who also advocated the sanctity of poverty. The apostles were founded in Parma by Gherardo Segarelli (*c.*1240–1300) after the Franciscans had rejected his request to become a friar. With a certain degree of theatricality, Gherardo grew his hair long and cultivated a straggly beard in imitation of Christ's apostles.

Initially, he attracted a ragtag band of misfits around him, but his cult became so popular, across several kingdoms, that it was banned by a Church council in the English city of Chichester in 1289. By 1300, his followers were popping up all over the place on the Iberian Peninsula, especially in Galicia. In that year, Segarelli was brought in for questioning by the Grand Inquisitor of Parma, who judged he was a relapsed heretic and ordered him to be burned at the stake.[11]

However, it was not enough to kill Segarelli, the Church propaganda machine needed to bury every heresy in an avalanche of counter-arguments and smears lest the faithful ever be tempted to stray from the correct path in future. To denigrate the Order of Apostles, the Franciscan chronicler, Salimbene of Parma (1221–*c.*1290) claimed that Segarelli's followers spent 'every day running throughout our cities seeking out women' and on their many travels 'they turn aside to prostitutes, or if, in the places they stay, lascivious women, and little is the apostles' resistance'.

Segarelli, like the Cathars, permitted women to be preachers and ministers on equal terms to male apostles. A surprising number of medieval people agreed with giving women access to the pulpit, to which the Church responded hysterically by casting them as whores. This can be seen with the previously mentioned Beguines, communities of women who took vows of chastity and poverty and lived in houses called Beguinages. They prayed, fasted, self-flagellated, and performed acts of charity in towns and villages. Normally from wealthy backgrounds, they had rejected the material world to serve God through goodly works. Many, including male Church chroniclers, felt inspired by the Beguines, cheering them on as brides of Christ and living saints. But they rose and fell in tandem with the Templars. As the knights were burned to death, so were the Beguines. Women who had gone from being models of piety to objects of fear.

Three years after Segarelli was executed, a member of his movement, Fra Dolcino (*c.*1250–1307), brought together some survivors and established the Dulcinians. They combined a belief in the virtue of poverty with the justification of violence, even murder, against those who betrayed them. Their egalitarian views, and strident tactics, made the Dulcinians heroic figures to Italian socialists in the nineteenth and early twentieth century.[12] For years, they hid in the Alps and often unable to source food, lived off tree bark and the roots of plants. One account asserts that they began eating their fellow Dulcinians who had died of wounds sustained in raids, the freezing cold, or hunger.

Fra Dolcino was eventually captured in 1307 alongside his partner and fellow preacher, Margaret of Trent. Bernard Gui, the inquisitor, described her disparagingly as Dolcino's 'amasia', which translates as concubine. Yet again, an example of denigrating an assertive and pious woman. However, Gui was eventually forced to admit that the two prisoners were not in a sexual relationship, and that she was simply 'his partner in crime and heresy'.

The year before, 1306, Clement had declared a crusade against the Dulcinians, so when the Bishop of Vercelli contacted the Pope asking what should be done, the response was unequivocal.

> *The news thus conveyed threw the pope into an ecstasy of delight… and on that very same evening or the ensuing night, he wrote with his own hand a long letter to his patron and very good master, Philip IV, the Fair of France, bidding him rejoice that the son of Belial, that incarnate fiend, the arch-heretic, Dolcino, had by God's own interference, after infinite trouble, peril, and sacrifice, at last been overcome by the Christian arms.* [13]

Gui wrote, with indecent relish, that Margaret was torn to pieces in front of Dolcino and he was then castrated and dismembered. The remains of their corpses were cremated in public view as an example to all. However, accounts of their executions do vary with this even more ghoulish description of Dolcino's ignominious end:

> *Next came the turn of Dolcino: he was seated high on a cart drawn by oxen; and thus, paraded from street to street all over Vercelli. His tormentors were all around him. Beside the cart, iron pots were carried, filled with burning charcoals: deep in the charcoals were iron pincers, glowing at white heat. These pincers were continually applied to the various parts of Dolcino's naked body, all along his progress, till all his flesh was torn piece-meal from his limbs; when every bone was bare and the whole town was perambulated, they drove the still living carcass back to the same arena, and threw it on the burning mass in which Margaret had been consumed.*

The Dulcinians were not the only violent heretics met with equal force by the Church. The thirteenth century witnessed several crusades, many now forgotten, against groups of heretics who fought back. The most famous such group were the Cathars who took the full brunt of the Albigensian Crusade (1209–1229), which involved the unleashing of crusader armies against cities and towns suspected of harbouring Cathars. This was going on while the Templars were running preceptories nearby and fighting on crusade in the Holy Land.

There was also the Stedinger Crusade (1233–1234) in Germany against serfs who had rebelled against their lord, the Prince-Archbishop of Bremen. What began as a tax revolt was characterised by the Church as an assault on God, with the peasants accused of killing priests and desecrating the Eucharist. Pope Gregory IX was soon on board and excommunicated all those involved in a stirring letter that described their orgies and worship of demons.

Dominican inquisitors then fanned out across the area warning the faithful of dire consequences for their souls if the Stedinger rebels were not turned over to the authorities. In the same year that this crusade was initiated, the Pope had begun another crusade against alleged devil worshippers in central Germany and in the year before, a crusade had just concluded against the Drenthers in the Netherlands who had killed the Bishop of Utrecht in a full-blown battle against his soldiers.[14]

So, by 1307, when the Templars were arrested, the papacy had endured a string of heresies, some of which had posed a direct threat to the lives of senior clergy as well as the destruction of Church property, the mocking of sacraments, and the stamping underfoot of crucifixes. An example of the latter was the twelfth-century Petrobrusians who smashed and burned crosses and rejected Roman Catholic communion because, in their view, Jesus only gave his flesh and blood once to his disciples and that miracle could not be repeated at every mass. It was in response to this kind of heresy that the papacy built a sophisticated inquisitorial apparatus staffed by Dominicans who had now, very literally, racked up decades of experience.

They were ready for the increased workload as knights were dragged into dungeons across France, initially, and then the rest of Catholic Europe. Despite misgivings in some quarters, the Templars were very quickly subjected to torture. Many were old men by the standards of the time yet had their ageing bodies broken to extract confessions. Methods trialled on Jews, Cathars, and Dulcinians were now unleashed on these holy warriors, previously the poster boys of the Crusades. There were few qualms about imprisoning, torturing, and executing fellow Christians.

At the many judicial hearings held between 1307 and the burning of the last Templar grand master, Jacques de Molay in 1314, there were several accounts of torture from the knights. The former preceptor of Gentioux, Peter of Conders, told the Pope to his face at a hearing in 1308 that he had been shown the instruments of torture and confessed immediately.[15] Braver Templars were subjected to the strappado, where the accused's hands were bound at the wrists, behind his back, and he was then hauled upwards. At some point, his shoulders would be dislocated. To maximise the pain, the torturer pulling the rope bounced the knight up and down or attached weights to his ankles, or a combination of both. One knight, Gerard du Passage, testified that he had weights attached to his genitals. Another favoured form of torture was to rub fat into a knight's feet and roast them at a fire. In one incident, this resulted in the accused's bones falling out of his foot.

Even when torture resulted in a confession, the inquisitor might return for more information. Ithier of Rochefort had been the preceptor of Douzens in the diocese of Carcassonne, which had been a nest of Cathars in the twelfth and thirteenth centuries. After one torture session, he had revealed all about spitting on crucifixes and obscene kisses at the base of the spine. On reflection, however, the inquisitor was sure Ithier was holding out on more salacious details. Further torture sessions ensued with the focus on alleged idol worship. However, Ithier stood firm, insisting that he had divulged everything.

The arrest of the Templars dominated the papacy of Clement V. The events of that fateful day, Friday, 13 October 1307, were detailed by the contemporary chronicler Jean de St Victor, who was clearly taken aback by what occurred. It began with the dawn arrest of Jaques de Molay at the Temple in Paris.

> *On the same day, all Templars in France were suddenly arrested and incarcerated in various prisons. Everybody was stunned by such action but assumed it was ordered by the Roman curia in consultation with the king.*

Thousands of knights, chaplains, sergeants, and farm hands were rounded up, with only a few escaping the long arm of the law. The operation, coordinated by De Nogaret, was impressive, even by modern standards, and left no time for dissenting voices to oppose the action. However, the king soon put out a statement declaring that Clement had been consulted. This was essential not only for opinion within France, but also to bring on board the monarchs of Europe. The papal stamp of approval universalised this action against the Templars. Now it was the Christian duty of every king and prince to follow the example of France.

Did Clement know what was about to happen? All indications are that he was taken completely by surprise. There had been correspondence between the Pope and king about reforming the Templars and the Hospitallers, but Clement was not expecting a wave of arrests. He immediately convened an emergency meeting of top clerics in Poitiers and then, by all indications, festered for a fortnight until his feelings exploded to the surface. For a Pope usually written off as weak and compliant, the letter he sent to Philip, in the form of a papal bull titled *Ad preclaram sapientiae* (to the eminent wisdom), was a brave missive:

> *You, our dear Son … have, in our absence, violated every rule and laid hands on the person and properties of the Templars. You have also imprisoned them and, what pains us more, you have not treated them with due leniency … and have added to the discomfort of imprisonment yet another affliction… You have laid hands on persons and property that are under the direct protection of the Roman church… Your hasty act is seen by all, and rightly so, as an act of contempt towards ourselves and the Roman church.*[16]

Earlier that year, Philip and Clement had met to discuss the logistics of a new crusade in the Holy Land, the ongoing diplomacy between England and France, and the rumours of criminal behaviour swirling around the Templars. The king may have dropped hints at this encounter about his future approach to the Templars and a contemporary chronicler, Tolomeo of Lucca (*c.*1236–*c.*1327), wrote that the cardinals around Clement were concerned about comments he was making. They believed the king was trying to assume papal powers. It's very likely that when the arrests came, it was these same cardinals who urged Clement to take a tough line with Philip, hence the harsh tone of his letter.

In August 1307, Clement told Philip that he was going to investigate the various allegations being made against the Templars. But as with previous popes, who had been drip fed poison about the order from the knights' enemies within the Church, the intention was to give the Templars a clean bill of health. Once the inquiry was completed, Clement would announce that everything had been examined, and there was no cause for concern. De Molay was on board with this and expected his order to be fully exonerated and life to resume as before.

However, Philip saw an opportunity to pounce. In fact, there was never going to be a better moment to destroy the order. A question mark now hovered over the knights and the king had to act while doubts were being raised about the order's conduct. In retrospect, it's hard to understand how the Pope failed to see what Philip would do next.

While the Templars did not anticipate their mass arrest, they must have sensed that Philip was circling them with malign intent. Maybe they feared a raid on the Paris Temple's cash – a royal bank robbery. This would not have been unprecedented. English and French kings had previously kicked the door down and helped themselves to Templar cash in times of need. De Molay had seen Philip extort money from France's Jews, Lombard merchants, and monasteries, so he would have been apprehensive about his order's very visible wealth.

However, by coming to France in 1307, the grand master must have hoped that he could defuse the situation. He would be in proximity to the Templars' protector, Pope Clement, and have access to the king. This was poorly judged optimism. Instead, the grand master was positioning himself at the very centre of the Capetian spider's web with Philip preparing to suck the order dry.

When the Templars were rounded up, the chattering classes were stunned. Chroniclers divided between those who were appalled and others who welcomed the action against the knights. In the Holy Roman Empire and Italy, the view was that this was all to do with furthering French interests, with one contemporary Italian voice describing the Templars as martyrs.[17]

Philip's financial motives were suspected very early on with John of Viktring (*c.*1270–1347) mentioning the plundering of Jewish wealth by the king across France in 1306, while Walter of Swinbroke (died 1360), an English chronicler also known as Geoffrey the Baker, believed the king had been turned down for a loan by the Templars and never got over the humiliation, resolving to revenge himself. The majority opinion among the elite outside France was that Philip was pursuing a crazed vendetta against the Templars and that the Pope was being bullied into rubber-stamping his moves.

Clement was undoubtedly upset at Philip's heavy-handed tactics, but the king got what he wanted. By January 1308, nearly all the 138 Templars arrested in Paris had given full confessions supporting the charges against them. Of course, the king denied that these had been obtained by torture in his dungeons, but their physical appearance at the court hearings said otherwise. The imprisoned knights, broken by the inquisitors, looked to their grand master, De Molay, but he too was confessing to everything. Disorientated and downcast, De Molay agreed he spat on the crucifix during this initiation many decades before, although he spurned the accusations of sodomy. But others would come forward with lurid tales about the grand master's sexual proclivities.

Faced with the crumbling resistance of the Templars, Clement issued a papal bull in November 1307, *Pastoralis praeeminentiae*, ordering the arrest of the knights throughout Christendom. There are two ways of looking at Clement's pronouncements following the arrests. On the one hand, he was striving to marginalise Philip and place himself at the centre of the investigation into the Templars. To dilute the king's role, he involved every Christian kingdom in Europe and pushed to put clerics in charge of the trial proceedings.

On the other hand, he was buckling by degrees to Philip. Clement imagined he could clamber back into the saddle and lead the process, but ultimately, the king outmanoeuvred him.

The trials of the Templars ground on for seven years between 1307 and 1314 when De Molay was fastened to a stake near Notre-Dame cathedral in Paris and burned alive for heresy. Why did the judicial process take so long?

One big reason was Clement's many vacillations, which undoubtedly emboldened some of the Templars to retract their confessions. Two months after admitting to spitting on the cross, De Molay took back his confession on Christmas Eve, 1307. Philip was furious and through gritted teeth pointed out that he had only arrested the Templars once papal approval had been given and the Inquisition was completely on side. Furthermore, any monies derived from the Templar estates would be used to fund future crusading in the Holy Land. Perish the thought that Templar gold would find its way into royal coffers.

The imprisoned knights were hoping that Clement would recover his nerve and even threaten Philip with excommunication, forcing him to back down and end these grotesque trials. In the previous century, popes excommunicated several crowned heads of Europe, forcing them to beg for forgiveness. King John of England was cast out of Catholicism in 1208; King Afonso II of

Portugal in 1212; James II of Aragon, 1286; Eric VI of Denmark in 1298; King Andrew II of Hungary in 1231; and the Holy Roman Emperor Frederick II was excommunicated on three separate occasions, and this is by no means an exhaustive list.

But the balance of power between popes and kings was shifting and Philip was very much alive to this trend. He was resolved to have the whip hand over the Pope and not the other way round, a point he had made in stark terms when Boniface VIII tried to excommunicate him. Clement, a man in delicate health, had no wish to be struck repeatedly by a henchman's gauntlet.

Then, the unexpected happened. In February 1308, Clement slammed on the brakes. The Inquisition was stood down and the Templar trials brought to a complete halt.[18] His Holiness had finally snapped. After months of being pushed around by the king, Clement recovered his nerve. An exasperated Philip turned to the University of Paris for an expert opinion to legitimise the arrests and trials. Instead, the learned scholars, while praising the religious zeal of the king, ruled that he had no right to act alone and only the Church could decide the fate of the Templars. This was maddening for Philip. One can visualise the scenes of volcanic rage that must have ensued in the royal palace.

Languishing behind bars, tens of Templars were dying from disease, torture, and poor living conditions. The sight of Templar corpses being stretchered out of French prisons was not winning the king any friends. Frantic to get the trials back on track again, Philip called an assembly of nobles, clergy, and commoners at the city of Tours to back his persecution of the order, just as he had convened the same body, in the same place, to condemn Pope Boniface VIII a few years earlier. When the assembly met, some bishops and nobles were absent, registering their disapproval. But that was a godsend for Philip, leaving him with a thumping majority in favour of prosecuting the Templars.

Philip then met Clement in May 1308 and read him the riot act. The message was clear. All of France was backing the king. Pope Clement V risked being placed on the same level as the late Boniface VIII, who Philip had condemned as a heretic, diabolist, and sodomite. Should Clement not come to his senses, and resume the trials, he would face similar consequences. How much clearer did the king have to be?

To put Clement in his place, the king turned to a very talented legal mind at his court, Guillaume de Plaisians, who was also gifted with a razor-sharp tongue. He consulted ancient Roman law, proving that Philip had every right to dominate the Pope. As a result of his extensive research, he coined the phrase: 'The King of France is Emperor in his Kingdom' (*Le Roi de France est empereur en son royaume*).

De Plaisians accompanied the king to meet the Pope on 29 May 1308 and told an astonished Clement that Philip had been chosen by God, as his representative on Earth, to defeat the heretical Templars and by winning this battle, he would save humanity. It's hard to imagine how affronted the Pope and his cardinals must have been to hear these almost blasphemous words delivered in Latin:

> *God's providence chose a minister for this business, namely, the King of France, who in his kingdom is God's temporal vicar, and certainly no one could have been found more suitable for this.*
>
> *(Dei providentia elegit ad hoc negocium ministrum scilicet regem Francie, qui in regno suo est Dei vicarious in temporalibus, et certo nullus ad hoc magic idoneus inveniri potuisset.)*

The Roman Catholic Church had insisted for centuries that the Pope was Christ's vicar on Earth, which was why all secular rulers must defer to their Holy Father in Rome. Now, Philip was saying that within the borders of his kingdom, the role of Christ's vicar on earth fell to him, and him alone. Not even the Pope could claim that role within Philip's realm.[19]

At this point, there was a risk that public sympathy might start to swing behind the jailed Templars. They cut a pathetic sight by now. Bedraggled figures, half-starved, limped before the hearings to croak their confessions or declarations of innocence. Hardly the image of rich and devious Satanists that the king wanted to project. What the situation demanded was a terrifying conspiracy theory. Astonishing proof that the knights were in league with Christ's enemies. A rumour suddenly began to circulate that fugitive Templars had fled to the Emir of Granada, the Muslim ruler of southern Spain, and together with an army of Moors and Jews, was plotting an invasion of the Christian kingdom of Aragon.

Worse, these Templars had converted to Islam to please their new Muslim masters. This smear spread so widely that the co-ruler of Andorra, Gaston I, Count of Foix (1287–1315), wrote to the King of Aragon asking if the story was true. Those with a keen sense of history would have recalled the treacherous Templar, Robert of St Albans (died 1187), who converted to Islam in 1185 and led Muslim soldiers against his former Templar colleagues at the Battle of Hattin in 1187. Whisperings of collusion with the world of Islam had burbled under the surface throughout the two centuries of Templar activity. Philip's ministers latched on to these longstanding slurs, gleefully feeding the rumour mill as part of their relentless propaganda campaign.

All this piled the pressure on Clement. Fighting to stay on top of the situation, he now demanded access to Templars held in royal prisons to hear their testimonies in person. At the end of June 1308, Philip grudgingly supplied seventy-two Templars for Clement to question. They trooped in front of the pontiff at a hearing held in Poitiers, within the kingdom of France, and murmured their confessions one after another, leaving Clement even more concerned about their condition. Despite having been vetted by the king, some had the courage to comment on their dreadful treatment. However, they all declared that their confessions were true and given voluntarily.

Absent from the hearing in Poitiers was the leadership of the Knights Templar. De Molay and other top figures had been diverted to Chinon. Clement tasked a very resourceful cardinal, with experience of delicate diplomacy and espionage, Bérenger Fredoli (1250–1323), with a risky mission: reach De Molay and obtain his side of the story. Pose the questions for which the Pope wanted answers. Was he a heretic? Was he a sodomite? Had he plotted to overthrow the king and Pope? Did his knights venerate an idol some claimed was the demon, Baphomet? Clement wanted to hear the truth from De Molay's lips. Fredoli got access to De Molay and what he heard convinced Clement that the grand master was no heretic.[20]

The evidence for the Pope's apparent willingness to save the Templars has only been rediscovered recently. Barbara Frale is a noted medievalist at the Vatican's Secret Archives who has written extensively about the Templars. In 2001, she chanced upon a 'misplaced' document in the archives, the Chinon Parchment, which cast the Pope in a whole new light. He absolved the Templars of the lurid charges: denying Christ, spitting on the crucifix, and worshipping idols. They had committed grave sins, he conceded, but the knights were not heretics as the king claimed.[21] The testimonies obtained by Fredoli stiffened Clement's backbone.

He issued two papal bulls on 12 August 1308 that riled the king. The first, *Regnans in Coelis* (Reigning in Heaven) convened a special council of the Church to pass final judgement on the Templars. Philip must have hit the roof when he saw the date: 1 October 1310. In fact, the council would not meet until a year after that. The Pope was now moving at his own stately pace. He also announced that the council would be held in Vienne, where Clement had wanted to be crowned before Philip vetoed that in favour of Lyon. The significance of Vienne is that while it's located in modern France today, it was part of the Holy Roman Empire in 1308, and so not under the king's direct jurisdiction.

The other bull, *Faciens misericordiam* (Granting forgiveness) brought the whole trial process firmly under papal control. Special commissions of bishops and other Church worthies were to be established to hear the testimonies of the Templars. The fate of the order, Clement decreed, rested with him and nobody else. So much for Philip being the vicar of Christ in France. One might be forgiven for thinking that there was a hint of sarcasm in the bull when it described Philip's motives for rounding up the Templars:

> *But then our dearest son in Christ, the illustrious King Philip of France, to whom the same crimes had been indicated, not out of avarice, because he did not intend to sell the Templars' possessions, nor appropriate them, but totally kept his hand from them...*[22]

What followed next panicked the king into the most drastic action. The Templars themselves, from their dungeon cells, attempted a fightback. What was there to lose?

From 1308 to 1310, the Templar trials moved at a snail's pace. Clement spent an inordinate amount of time travelling around France on papal business and establishing his new court at Avignon. Meanwhile, the king sent royal officials to asset strip Templar preceptories, impatient to get his pound of flesh out of these proceedings. Simultaneously, he kept up a steady flow of badgering correspondence with Clement, pointing out that if the Pope did not move faster, more knights would retract their confessions.

In their cells, the knights began to reconsider their position. Some threw in the towel and confessed, even winning their freedom from a grateful king. Others, however, hardened their position, even after suffering behind bars. One knight, Aymon of Barbonne, had endured the medieval equivalent of waterboarding with a 'cucufa' stuffed in his mouth and water applied. These knights endured unspeakable pain in the faintest hope that Clement would come to their aid.

One such knight was Ponsard de Gizy, the preceptor of Payns. In prison, he conferred with two legally trained Templars, Pierre de Bologna and Renaud de Provins. The former was about 44 years old and when arrested in November 1307, admitted to denying Christ, spitting on the crucifix, kissing on the buttocks, and other crimes, without having been tortured. He had subsequently retracted all of this. De Provins was younger, about 36 years old, and had considered becoming a Dominican friar before joining the Templars. If he had chosen the Dominicans, he might have ended up becoming an inquisitor, but fate led him to be an accused heretic instead.

Both men urged Ponsard to go for an aggressive defence. He needed little encouragement. After his arrest, before confessing, Ponsard had been placed in a dark pit with his hands tied so tightly that 'the blood ran to his nails'. He told the papal commission that he would defend the order with his dying breath, whether he was executed by fire, beheading, or being boiled, but what he could not suffer again was prolonged torture. Faced with the pit, he would say anything.

But for now, given a public platform, the jailed knight was going to make his feelings known. On 27 November 1309, Ponsard raged at the commission that the Templars had been framed by four ungodly individuals.

> *These are the traitors who have falsely and disloyally accused the Temple: Guillaume Robert the monk, who had them put to the torture; Esquin de Floyran of Beziers, Prior of Montfaucon; Bernard Pelet, Prior of Maso, Philip's envoy to England; and Gérard de Boyzol, knight of Gisors.*

As he was getting into his stride, the commission brought his testimony to an abrupt and humiliating halt. They wielded a previous confession from Ponsard that damned the order in his own words. Worse, it included accusations never heard before and not included in the arrest warrant drafted by De Nogaret back in 1307. For example, Ponsard had told an inquisitor that the Templars admitted women members on condition they observed the vows of poverty, chastity, and obedience, and then raped them. There is evidence of Templar 'nuns' and female donors living inside or near the preceptories, but only Ponsard alleges sexual abuse. He went on to allege that illegitimate children born from these rapes were then initiated into the order.

Looking rather compromised, Ponsard blustered that he had made the confession in a moment of anger directed at senior members of the order. The commission waved him away. He was led back to his cell, dejected. It seemed as if the spirit of rebellion, growing among the brothers in their dungeon cells, had been broken. But this was not the case.

Any Templars pinning their hopes on the grand master, Jacques de Molay, were going to be disappointed. His long-anticipated testimony between 26 and 28 November 1309 was the rambling of an old man still disorientated by the turn of events. Some suspected he was playing for time in the hope of being able to make a direct appeal to Clement, the order's protector. Ending his shambolic defence, De Molay murmured that Templar churches had always been well maintained, the knights had given alms to the poor, and that they had spilled their blood in the Holy Land in the name of Jesus Christ. What more did Christian Europe want of them?

At which point, De Nogaret appeared, as if in a puff of smoke. Nobody had invited him but beyond doubt, the king had sent him. Standing before the assembled bishops and the Templar grand master, he railed against the order. When Saladin had led the Saracens, De Nogaret thundered, the Templars had bowed down to him as their true leader. Yes, they had fought at the Battle of Hattin against Saladin and defended Jerusalem against Muslim scimitars, but they had lost because 'they were afflicted by the vice of sodomy and because they had violated their faith and law'. De Molay's jaw dropped in astonishment as the history of his order was rewritten. As intended, De Nogaret's hysterical stream of invective drowned out the grand master.

That winter's poor weather slowed everything down. But by February 1310, the Pope's officials agreed that any Templars wishing to defend the order could be heard in Paris. They were anticipating a handful of diehards – not the 532 that demanded their day in court. The majority were sergeants while knights accounted for 32 of that number plus 60 chaplains. It took a while for everybody to arrive but there was almost a holiday atmosphere as hundreds of Templars, many who were still imprisoned, turned up at a mass hearing in the grounds of the bishop's palace in Paris on 28 March 1310. Clement had given them permission to state their case, and they were not going to miss the opportunity.

Pierre de Bologna and Renaud de Provins led the defence of their brother Templars, who were now imprisoned at various sites around the city, for which they had to pay rent and the cost of food. These improvised prisons included churches, the private residences of abbots, and the Paris Temple, transformed from the order's headquarters into a jailhouse. Many were in chains and required to pay their jailer to remove their shackles and manacles when they were taken to the commission and then make a further payment to be chained up again in the evening as if this was a service.

A complex defence of the Knights Templar was mounted, tying up the Pope's lawyers who darted around interviewing the accused at multiple locations. Successive French kings, it was pointed out, had employed the Templars as treasurers and political advisers. Would they have done this if the knights were evil? Everybody knew how the Templars operated, and the commission was reminded of their service to past great monarchs like the saint-king Louis IX. They possessed many holy relics such as the heart of Saint Euphemia, which worked miracles for those pilgrims who prayed before it. Did this suggest divine disapproval of the Knights Templar?

Pierre de Bologna pleaded the order's case very eloquently. The Templars were 'untainted by all defect and all uncleanliness of any vices'. Initiates received the kiss of peace and not the indecent kisses described by De Nogaret. With pride, the knights wore their white mantles, emblazoned with a red cross that reminded them of the sacrifice of Christ at Calvary. Those making scandalous allegations against them were 'shameful, horrifying, and detestable'. They were the real heretics and 'seducers of the Holy Church', motivated by greed and shoring up their lies with the testimonies of those expelled from the order like 'sickly cattle were thrown from the fold'.[23]

It really felt as if the Templars might force Clement's hand to end the trials and free his loyal and faithful knights to resume their crusading for Christ. But as ever, Philip was watching in the wings. De Nogaret had failed to derail this Templar fightback, so the king turned increasingly to his finance minister, Enguerrand de Marigny (*c.*1260–1315) for advice. He begged the king to let his brother Philip (*c.*1260–1316), the Bishop of Cambrai, fill the vacant position of Archbishop of Sens. The king twisted Clement's arm who then put the newly minted archbishop in charge of the Templar trials. Brimming with ambition, the De Marigny brothers realised that their political future depended on the complete destruction of the Templars.

The Templar defence team recognised the threat posed by the archbishop and begged the commission not to recognise his authority. But then, on 12 May 1310, the unthinkable happened. The archbishop, who had only been enthroned days before, ruled that retracted confessions were proof of heresy. He ordered guards to round up 54 Templars and transport them in wagons to the Porte Saint-Antoine – one of the medieval gateways into Paris. Beyond the city walls were fields and just in front of the priory of Val des Écoliers, a large pyre had been constructed with multiple wooden stakes. Greeted by that sight, one might have expected the Templars concerned to beg for their lives. But the inquisitor Bernard Gui was astonished as every man present retracted the confessions made after they were arrested. All of them, according to the contemporary chronicler Guillaume de Nangis, went to their deaths loudly proclaiming their innocence.

Minutes later, the flames engulfed the prisoners. De Nangis noted that many in the crowd struggled to watch the grisly spectacle. Days after that, further burnings of Templars were conducted. The effect on De Molay and the knights was devastating. Their will to defend themselves crumbled overnight. Pierre de Bologna disappeared into the ether with rumours that he had escaped, though more likely he was murdered in his prison cell. De Provins tried to continue with the Templar defence but all around him, knights were sheepishly caving in to the inevitable.

De Provins seems to have avoided being burned to death himself but vanishes from the public record, presumably dying in prison. Once more, the accused lined up to admit they had spat on crosses, kissed each other on the naked flesh, and worshipped a demonic head. Though some struggled with the details. William of Arreblay, Preceptor of Soisy, thought the head in question might be one of the 11,000 virgins who had suffered mass martyrdom alongside Saint Ursula at the hands of the Huns in the fourth century CE. By this stage, the Inquisition was not too fussed with the finer points. The aim now was to bring this whole sorry affair to a conclusion and finally shut down the Knights Templar.

The Council of Vienne, which Clement had called for in 1308, finally convened in 1311. Three years before, Clement had indicated to the Templars that while he was suspending their order, he would permit the knights to defend themselves at the papal commissions. The deluge of retracted confessions that followed had taken the Pope by surprise and horrified the king, leading to the burning of 54 Templars at a gateway into Paris. Now, at Vienne, Clement assumed that the knights were reconciled to their fate and all signs of revolt were extinguished. So, it came as something of a shock when seven Templars burst into the first session of the council demanding to make their case for the order, claiming there were up to 2000 brothers at large in the region who could descend on Vienne at a moment's notice.

Panicking, Clement wrote to Philip to say he had 'taken measures to reinforce our security' and that the king should do likewise. The Pope was also alarmed by reports that in England, Aragon, and other countries, those Templars taken into custody were being treated like princes, able to bring their own furniture and servants to their prison quarters. William de la More, grand master of England, was arrested at Temple Bruer in 1308 and by all accounts was in quite plush settings, or so the Pope was told. This was not good enough. His orders were not being taken seriously. Clement began cajoling these Christian kingdoms to make conditions harsher and torture the knights for confessions.

Finally, in March 1312, as the Council of Vienne dragged on, Clement issued the bull *Vox in Excelso* (a voice on high) that dissolved the order. Seated on one side of the Pope was King Philip and on the other side was his son, the future Louis X of France (1289–1316), then king of Navarre. While Clement towered above them on a raised dais, he was painfully aware of being flanked by the French monarchy. His pronouncement ending the existence of the Knights Templar was stuffed with ominous biblical references:

> *They have built the high places of Baal to consecrate their sons to idols and demons… Not slight is the fornication of this house, immolating its sons, giving them up and consecrating them to demons and not to God, to gods whom they did not know… About the time of our election as supreme pontiff before we came to Lyons for our coronation, and afterwards, both there and elsewhere, we received secret intimations against the master, preceptors and other brothers of the order of Knights Templar of Jerusalem and also against the order itself.*

The Church had honoured these knights, showered them with privileges, recognised the order as 'special warriors of the Catholic faith and outstanding defenders of the Holy Land'. But they had fallen into the sin of 'impious apostasy', 'the abominable vice of idolatry', 'the deadly crime of the Sodomites', and heresy. Yet, Clement conceded, the papacy had refused to believe the reports because they had fought so bravely in battle against Christ's enemies.

He detailed their crimes and the investigations conducted by the papal commissions. Now, four fifths of the cardinals and council members demanded the destruction of the Templars. Clement was duty bound to act:

> *Therefore, with a sad heart, not by definitive sentence, but by apostolic provision or ordinance, we suppress, with the approval of the sacred council, the order of Templars, and its rule, habit and name, by an inviolable and perpetual decree, and we entirely forbid that anyone from now on enter the order, or receive or wear its habit, or presume to behave as a Templar.*[24]

This set in motion the chain of events that led, on 18 March 1314, to the burning to death of the last Templar grand master, Jacques de Molay. As the flames lapped around his 70-year-old body, the old man was said to have croaked a final curse at his tormentors calling on both Philip and Clement to be dragged before the judgement seat of God. Barely a month later, the Pope was dead while Philip would meet his maker in November that year.

De Nogaret died a year before De Molay, replaced in the king's affections by his new chief minister, Enguerrand de Marigny, whose brother the Archbishop of Sens had burned so many Templars. The De Marigny brothers were instrumental in applying the final required pressure on Clement in the run up to Vienne to secure the winding up of the order. However, in an ironic twist, Enguerrand would fall victim to the growing trend for sorcery trials. When the king died, his brother, Charles of Valois (1270–1325), accused Enguerrand of using diabolic magic to kill the new king, Louis X, Charles himself, and other nobles using wax dolls. These were baptised in the devil's name and the intended victims 'would have gradually pined away and died'. Enguerrand was hanged like a common criminal alongside a young male sorcerer, called Paviot, while a female witch, also involved, was burned at the stake.[25]

Was Clement a complete failure in his dealings with the king and the jailed Templars? In truth, he probably went as far as he could in resisting Philip's demands. For example, his predecessor, Boniface VIII, was not declared a heretic, sodomite, diabolist, and every other crime the king had itemised. Clement refused to lift the excommunication on the king's minister, De Nogaret, until the very last minute and only then on condition he serve five years in the Holy Land on crusade, which he avoided by dying shortly afterwards. Templar assets became the responsibility of the Church and not a piggy bank for a king. However, a cynic might counter that any concessions Clement won, only gave him the illusion of control over the trials as the verdicts were a foregone conclusion.[26]

On 20 April 1314, Clement V died on a trip to his native Gascony. His body was reportedly left unburied for at least a day while his fellow countrymen looted his palaces. When it was transferred to the designated burial place, contemporary chroniclers gleefully reported that an accidental fire consumed half the corpse before the funeral. Was this a further manifestation of Jacques de Molay's dying curse?

In 2007, the Knights Templar received a heavily qualified pardon from the Vatican. Seven hundred years after their torture, trials and execution, the order, accused of heresy and sodomy in the year 1307, was partially absolved. The Holy See made the astonishing decision to release a mass of trial documents it had held under lock and key for centuries. They were published in a weighty tome, the *Processus Contra Templarios*, (Papal Inquiry into the Trial of the Templars), retailing at an eye-watering US$8,333.[27]

For Templar enthusiasts, this was an opportunity to own reproductions of original legal texts, written in Latin, as well as replicas of the wax seals used by the fourteenth century inquisitors who interrogated the Templar knights. For reasons best known to the Vatican, only 799 numbered copies of the *Processus* were to be put on sale. Pope Benedict XVI (1927–2022) received his own personal copy. One of the parchments was an impressively sized half a metre wide by two metres long. with the original staining replicated.

A posthumous pardon for the Knights Templar was to be welcomed – but little comfort to those who were thrown into dungeons, tortured, brutalised, and burned at the stake.

Chapter Four

Quest for Templar Treasure

The Knights Templar were crushed but one question endures: did they escape with their fabled treasure? If so, what was that treasure? Aside from gold and silver, many have wondered whether they discovered sacred artefacts under the Temple Mount in Jerusalem. These might have included the 'passion relics' from the crucifixion of Jesus, such as his burial shroud and the Roman spear that pierced his side. Or the Templars may have been directed by a secret map to the long-lost treasures of Solomon's first temple, destroyed by the Babylonians in the sixth century BC, particularly the Ark of the Covenant that was housed in the temple's Holy of Holies and contained the Ten Commandments.

However, the holy relic that has provoked the most interest among Templar enthusiasts is the Holy Grail: the cup that contained some of the blood of Christ. Its association with the Templars is fixed in the popular imagination, even if there is not a shred of evidence confirming they ever possessed it. The knights are the grail keepers sworn to protect it, keeping its true meaning a jealously guarded secret. Seekers of sacred treasures have sought this one item above all others, scouring Templar sites in the hope of finding it concealed or buried. The most notorious group of grail hunters worked for the Third Reich.

In 1941, a group of Nazi commandos, under cover of night, made their way to the ruins of Glastonbury Abbey in south-west England. Their objective was to locate, excavate, and bring back the Holy Grail to their Nazi paymasters.

> *Although brilliantly executed, the Nazi raiders – who landed from a submarine in the Bristol Channel, achieved complete surprise, and were able to carry out their mission – found nothing remotely resembling the object of their search.*[1]

This was at the height of the Second World War, fought between the Allies (United States, United Kingdom, France, Soviet Union, etc.) and the Axis Powers (Germany, Italy, and Japan). In Berlin, the Third Reich's Führer (leader), Adolf

Hitler (1889–1945), suspected the British may have sent the grail, along with the crown jewels of the monarchy, to America's banking fortress, Fort Knox, for the duration of the war. This military base in Kentucky houses the gold reserves of the United States under the most secure conditions and during the war, the American Declaration of Independence and the constitution written by the Founding Fathers were also put there for safekeeping.

A superstitious man, steeped in the occult, Hitler was convinced that his enemy's continued possession of this holiest of artefacts ensured that the British could not be annihilated, no matter how many German bombs were dropped on British cities such as London, Coventry, Glasgow, and Liverpool. Its protective power would shield the enemies of the Third Reich until it was taken from them. However, the grail remained beyond the grasp of the Nazis who went on to lose the war, with Hitler committing suicide in his bunker as Soviet forces advanced towards him.

Since the war, the grail has turned up in some curious places including an attic in Rugby, a town in the British Midlands, and under a manor house near Burton-upon-Trent. The least spectacular contender for the grail is the Nanteos Cup in Wales – a broken medieval drinking bowl. However, it has a small army of fervent advocates. In 2014, the cup was stolen from the house of a seriously ill woman to whom it had been loaned, in the hope its magical power would cure her. That July, a West Mercia police spokeswoman told journalists: 'I don't want to say we are hunting the Holy Grail, but police are investigating the burglary'.[2] At one point in their quest for the grail, the police allegedly locked the doors of a fifteenth-century pub, keeping the staff inside, while they searched the premises, only finding a modern bowl, 'used to serve mixed salad to customers'.[3] Frankly, that was probably the original use of the Nanteos cup, which was eventually recovered.

Across Europe, there have been some 200 chalices all laying claim to be the Holy Grail since the Middle Ages.[4] Three of the most notable examples are the Santo Caliz in Valencia, the Sacro Catino in Genoa, and the Caliz de Doña Urraca in León. Arguably the most eye catching is the chalice of Abbot Suger of St-Denis (*c*.1081–1151) who purchased a superbly crafted onyx cup dating to Egypt in the first century before Christ, which he then mounted in a gilded silver stand, encrusted with jewels. It's now displayed at the National Gallery of Art in Washington DC.

The grail is usually described as a cup from which Jesus Christ drank at the Last Supper and in which his uncle (or great uncle), Joseph of Arimathea, caught some drops of his divine nephew's blood as he hung, dying on the cross. This ghoulish incident does not feature in the four gospels of the New Testament but was part of an embroidering of Joseph's life that got underway from the second century onwards in the 'apocryphal' (not accepted) gospels and medieval legends.

To summarise the various stories about Joseph of Arimathea, from biblical and non-biblical sources, he was a wealthy man, trading in precious metals, who obtained permission from the Roman governor, Pontius Pilate, to remove the body of Jesus from the cross, and then paid for his burial in a rock tomb. Joseph was a member of the Sanhedrin, the council of Jewish elders in Jerusalem. They turned on him for burying the blasphemer Jesus, a heretic who had impudently claimed to be the son of God. In their opinion, his naked body should have been left exposed to be pecked at by the crows. Joseph's punishment was to be entombed alive and starved to death. But luckily, Joseph had the grail on his person, and it miraculously nourished him, producing food and water every morning. The account of his incarceration appears in the apocryphal Gospel of Nicodemus, which is not included in the Christian Bible.

Having survived his imprisonment, Joseph travelled to England, which he had visited years before with the young Jesus. Uncle and nephew based themselves in the village of Priddy, trading in lead and tin, which was plentiful in this area. Returning to England as an old man, Joseph chose to live at a raised spot surrounded by low lying farmland and marshes. This foggy, mystical place was known as Ynys Witrin, meaning the Island of Glass in the pre-Roman Brittonic language. It was also referred to as Avalon, but today it's better known as the town of Glastonbury, most famous for its annual music festival.

Full of grief and realising that death was near, Joseph hid the grail in the form of two vials, one containing the blood of Jesus and the other his sweat, at a place called the Chalice Well. He then founded the first Christian Church that endured as a thriving monastic community until it was smashed up in the Protestant Reformation of the sixteenth century, leaving only the very characterful ruins that can still be visited today.

The first monks lived in timbered buildings, replaced by stone after 712 CE. Among them were Irish monks who played a leading role in re-converting England to the Christian faith after the Romans quit the province of Britannia in the fifth century. The Romans were followed by the Saxons and their kings enriched Glastonbury, with two monarchs being buried within its walls. The Benedictine rule was introduced, regulating the monks' everyday existence, and when the Normans invaded in 1066 CE, Glastonbury boomed, becoming the wealthiest monastery in the country. Pilgrims were drawn to the abbey by its sacred well and the direct connection to Jesus, through Joseph of Arimathea. In the fourteenth century, the monks evidenced this with a large book proudly displayed to visitors, the *Magna Tabula Glastoniensis*, telling the story of Glastonbury from 63 to 1382.[5]

Holy relics were big business in the Middle Ages and Glastonbury was dripping with sacred artefacts. There was an icon of the Virgin Mary lovingly crafted by the very hands of Joseph of Arimathea. The monks informed pilgrims that local people had been hostile to Joseph when he first arrived. So, to convert these heathens, he struck his walking stick into the ground, and it miraculously took root and blossomed, creating the Glastonbury Holy Thorn. Pious Catholics venerated this tree until it was cut down by puritans during the English Civil War. A 1950s replacement was removed in 2019 by the landowner. In addition to the Marian icon and sacred tree, the relics of some 300 saints were held at the abbey including Patrick, Bridget, and Aidan of Lindisfarne. Plus, Joseph had buried the Holy Grail at Glastonbury near the Chalice Well. Its waters still run red today on account of the rich iron content, though medieval pilgrims believed it was Christ's blood bubbling to the surface.

There was an undeniable whiff of corruption around Glastonbury. God's displeasure with the venal monks was made manifest when the entire monastery, bar the bell tower, burned to the ground on 25 May 1184. However, the Benedictines did not allow this calamity to dampen their spirits, and entrepreneurial flair, for very long.[6] In the year 1191, the monks announced an incredible find. Between two stone pyramids, they unearthed the bodies of the legendary King Arthur and his queen, Guinevere. Their remains had been 'buried deep in the earth' and only came to light because the monastery was being comprehensively, and expensively, rebuilt after the disastrous fire. On the underside of a large stone was affixed a lead cross and an inscription:

> *Here lies buried the glorious king Arthur and Guinevere his second wife in the Isle of Avalon.*[7]

The skeleton of Arthur revealed a giant of alarming proportions:

> *His skull, too, was large and capacious like a prodigy or wonder, to such a degree that the space between the eyebrows and between the eyes was more than a palm's width.*

The canny monks were latching on to the growing fascination with the figure of King Arthur, lionised in a history of the kings of Britain penned by Geoffrey of Monmouth (*c.*1095–1155), as well as subsequent chroniclers who linked Arthur to the Holy Grail and the Knights Templar.

King Arthur, Glastonbury, and the Templars are intertwined. Too much ink has been spilled trying to prove Arthur was a late Roman general or a Dark Ages warlord, when in truth, this legendary king was a literary creation, conjured into being by storytelling troubadours. A thoroughly medieval character intended to personify the bold and pious crusader monarch, who should be emulated by the crowned heads of Christian Europe. Authors like Chrétien de Troyes (*c.*1160–1191), Robert de Boron (active in the thirteenth century), and Wolfram von Eschenbach (*c.*1160/80–*c.*1220) were striving to transform crusading into a sacred mission. They wanted to flatter their patrons who were nobles actively engaged in the crusades, fighting alongside the Knights Templar.

These writers were depicting their patrons and vassals as King Arthur and his Knights of the Round Table. As for the Templars, they were the grail knights devoted to protecting the holiest relic in Christendom. This was not literally true. It was a propaganda fantasy that elevated the sordid business of war and slaughter into something more agreeably spiritual.

Bit by bit the grail story was constructed. Chrétien had a knight called Percival being taken to the grail castle, but the nature of the grail is never fully explained in his incomplete story. De Boron established that the grail was used to collect the blood of Christ at the crucifixion and that it was guarded by grail keepers. Eschenbach's hero, Parzival, placed the grail at a place called Castle Munsalvasche (later referred to as Montsalvat) where the 'Templeise' barred entry to unwelcome visitors. This included Parzival who, in a very stirring scene, is confronted by a Templar knight and forced to fight for his life. Before they charge at each other, the Templar gives Parzival one last chance to turn around:

Sir, said he, it displeases me
That you beat a track thus, wantonly,
Through forest owned by my good lord
I shall you this warning afford
Such a one as you will regret
Munsalvasche must never let
Any man close, nary a knight
Without demanding that he fight
In fierce encounter, or doth proffer
Such amends as death doth offer.[8]

Parzival survives his fight with the Templar, but only just.

At Munsalvasche, he gains an understanding of the grail, but its definition is annoyingly vague, best summed up as a magic crystal reminiscent of the Philosopher's Stone: an alchemical object, recorded in ancient times, with the power to turn base metals into gold and grant eternal life. Parzival relates how the phoenix sits on the grail stone and is then consumed by flames before being reborn.

This is the 'Lapis Exilis', the stone of exile, around which angels cowered during the titanic battle between Lucifer and God for control of the heavens, as described in the Book of Revelation. It was after his defeat that Lucifer, the rebel son of God, transformed into Satan, Lord of Darkness. In another legend, not mentioned by Eschenbach, the Lapis Exilis was an emerald that popped out of Lucifer's crown as he was flung downwards, out of the celestial realm, by his heavenly father.

Eschenbach never states that explicitly, even though subsequent nineteenth-century commentators tried to suggest he had. What Eschenbach describes is a mysterious and powerful stone that has originated in the heavens, is placed in a grail castle, and is then guarded by the Templars, the grail knights, over whom the stone seems to exercise some kind of mind control.

Eschenbach claimed he had learned of the adventures of Parzival from a troubadour poet, Kyot of Provence, who had found the secret of the grail in a manuscript lodged at the Moorish libraries of Toledo, a city taken by crusaders in 1085. Some have speculated that Kyot was a Cathar heretic who transmitted Gnostic ideas from the east into the heart of Europe and that Eschenbach's Parzival is a kind of Gnostic manifesto.[9]

During the Templar period, there was an explosion of pilgrim activity across Europe and the Middle East as the religious travelled enormous distances to venerate bits of bone, splinters of wood, and pieces of cloth associated with saints, biblical figures, and the son of God. These were often housed in bejewelled reliquaries displayed in chapels, churches, and cathedrals, and it was big business. Monks and priests were incredibly inventive in using scripture to conjure up relics. So, for example, one church in the northern English city of York claimed to have the silver tray on which the severed head of John the Baptist was given to Salome. Many Catholic places of worship today claim to have either John's entire skull or fragments, which if added together would culminate in an enormous head.

Yet of all the relics, the most enigmatic must be the Holy Grail. However, the medieval texts, contemporary with the Templars, cannot agree on what it is. Option one is a cup or chalice that contained the blood of Jesus. Option two is a stone that fell to earth like a meteorite, the Lapis Exilis, which might have popped out of the crown of Lucifer as he was thrown into hell. Option three focuses on the etymology of the word 'grail', resembling the Latin word 'gradale', meaning a platter. But the idea of the grail as a dining plate has not had many takers. Or finally, the favoured option of Templar conspiracy theorists in recent decades, that the grail is the bloodline of Jesus Christ.

This latter option assumes that the San-graal, the medieval French word for Holy Grail, is a corruption of *sang real,* meaning 'royal blood': the bloodline of Jesus from the womb of his consort, Mary Magdalene. To most people, however, the grail is that cup-like object featured in the Hollywood movie *Indiana Jones and the Last Crusade*, guarded by an ancient Templar, with the power to heal and bestow eternal youth. This is the supernatural cup that the Nazis were desperate to find.

On 13 March 1939, the body of a 35-year-old man was discovered by some children on the snowy slopes of the Tyrolean mountains. He had taken an overdose of sleeping pills. But when his death was made public, it was attributed to a 'mountaineering accident', with his corpse found frozen solid. The deceased was a former Nazi SS officer, Otto Wilhelm Rahn (1904–1939), who had devoted his life to seeking the Holy Grail without success.

His fruitless quest had been funded by Reichsführer Heinrich Himmler (1900–1945), leader of the SS (Schutzstaffel), the black-shirted elite force tasked with protecting the Führer, Adolf Hitler, and implementing the more brutal policies of the Third Reich, such as the extermination of millions of people in concentration camps. Rahn had been forced to enrol in the SS as a condition of obtaining funding for his expeditions, but he was less than comfortable in his new role, being quite open about his homosexuality and, worse, in Nazi eyes, being of Jewish descent.[10] However, as he admitted to friends, he needed the money badly.

Rahn's writings on the more esoteric and mystical side of the Middle Ages chimed with the obsessions of certain leading Nazis, especially those who had been members of the secretive Thule society (or *Thulegesellschaft* in German). The society was named after a mythical northern land, mentioned in Greek mythology, which early twentieth-century Völkisch racists came to believe was the original source of the Aryan race. Thule was led by Baron Rudolf von Sebottendorf (1875–1945), real name Adam Glauer, whose associates included several future, leading Nazis: Rudolf Hess, Dietrich Eckart, and Alfred Rosenberg.

Many of Himmler's racist infatuations, such as proving that Jesus was an Aryan, finding the Holy Grail, and casting the Nazis as medieval holy warriors, were rooted in Thule-generated theories. In 1935, Himmler set up a new SS division, the Ahnenerbe (Ancestral Heritage), made up of academics and scientists instructed to build the case for Aryan racial superiority. The team included archaeologists, anthropologists, ethnologists, and linguists who, under Himmler's watchful gaze, manipulated data from historic sites and excavations to build his Aryan narrative.

The Ahnenerbe generated some off-the-wall theories. For example, that the witchcraft trials from the fifteenth century onwards had been an organised attack on German womanhood by a coalition of Jews and the Roman Catholic Church. Thousands of documents were harvested from around Germany to try and back up this assertion – though nothing by way of hard evidence was forthcoming. Nevertheless, speaking to the Imperial Farmers Assembly at Goslar in 1935, Himmler thundered that those witches burned at the stake had been Aryan women who had fallen victim to this dastardly conspiracy.[11]

Neighbouring fascist states were drawn into the Ahnenerbe's ahistorical fixations. In 1939, Spain, then under the dictatorship of General Francisco Franco (1892–1975), collaborated with the Ahnenerbe on the excavation of a Visigoth necropolis near Segovia. The Visigoths were a Germanic people who had been settled by the Romans in southern France but had then crossed the Pyrenees, overwhelming the empire's provinces in modern Spain and Portugal during the fifth century. Their control of the Iberian Peninsula lasted until the Muslim invasion of 711 CE. Spanish fascists gifted Visigoth gold and bronze cups, necklaces, and even human bones to Himmler to affirm the common Aryan heritage of Spain and Germany. In 2016, the Spanish government demanded that Germany hand those items back.[12]

In October 1940, Himmler paid an official visit to Spain and in a meeting with the Commissioner-General for Archaeological Investigations, Julio Martínez Santa Olalla (1905–1972), the Spanish announced they would establish their own version of the Ahnenerbe.[13] During his visit in 1940, Himmler was driven in a convoy to the striking, pink-coloured jagged hills known as Montserrat. Nestled in the shadow of this rock formation is the sprawling abbey of Santa Maria de Montserrat. Himmler had come to this place with a single objective: to find the Holy Grail.[14]

But why would Himmler care about an ancient chalice linked to the Jewish messiah? Firstly, he did not regard Jesus as Jewish, but Aryan. Nazi theorists in the 1920s and 1930s set out to prove that Jesus was an Aryan preacher whose ideas had been distorted by Jewish gospel writers. They portrayed Galilee as a Hellenised, Aryan part of the Middle East up against Jewish-controlled Judaea and the city of Jerusalem.[15]

This was a distortion of the Bible that was of little interest to Jewish people, who had far bigger concerns about the Third Reich, but it did rile the Roman Catholic Church that resented the Nazis usurping their role in interpreting scripture. When Himmler arrived at Montserrat, the abbot was in no mood to meet a Nazi promoting heretical views of Jesus. He sent a German speaking monk, Andreu Ripol Noble, to give the unwanted visitor a tour.[16]

Himmler pestered the young monk for information on the Holy Grail and whether Montserrat was the true location of Eschenbach's Munsalvasche, which had been re-imagined as Montsalvat in the opera *Parsifal*, composed by Richard

Wagner (1813–1883). Wagner had been dead for six years when Hitler was born but his influence on the Nazi leadership was immense. In *Parsifal*, they saw not just a quest for the grail but a hymn to Aryan racial supremacy.

Wagner transformed German history into a mystical fairytale peopled by Teutonic superheroes whose lives and struggles were played out against stirring musical scores. Fans of Wagner have long been irked by claims the composer was a proto-Nazi and even deny that Hitler adored this opera. Yet facts are a stubborn thing. Hitler's medievalism was evidenced in a 1936 portrait, *Der Bannerträger* (The Standard Bearer), where the Führer is depicted as a Teutonic Knight wearing shimmering steel armour, seated on a black horse, with a swastika on the banner he holds in his right hand. It could easily have been a very kitsch theatre poster for *Parsifal*. As for Himmler, his passion for the grail, and all things Wagnerian, led him to a Benedictine monastery in 1940 where he believed the sacred cup might be hidden.

Not only was the blood shed into the grail cup from an Aryan Jesus, but Himmler cast the Knights Templar as racially pure guardians of true Christianity against an impure Catholic Church.[17] This linkage between the Templars and German racist ultra-nationalism originated with an ex-Catholic occultist who influenced early Nazi thought.

Jörg Lanz von Liebenfels (1874–1954) was a former Cistercian monk, bookish and bespectacled, who developed the pseudo-science of 'theozoology' and in 1900, founded the Ordo Novi Templi (New Templar Order), which used the swastika as an emblem, many years ahead of the Nazis. The order had seven levels of membership with the most junior being 'servers' who were either suspected of racial impurity or had not yet undergone a rigorous racial test. Lanz publicised the order, and his racist ideas, in a disturbingly popular publication: *Ostara, Briefbücherei der Blonden und Mannesrechtler* (Ostara, Journal of the Blondes and Men's Rights Activists). The ex-monk turned Aryan supremacist later complained to Hitler in the 1930s that he had not been given enough credit for his influence on the ideology of National Socialism. Not long after his plea, the Ordo Novi Templi was suppressed by the Third Reich.[18]

By the time Himmler was touring Montserrat, his former employee Otto Rahn was dead – possibly murdered by the SS. Rahn came to Himmler's attention with a book titled *Crusade Against the Grail* in which he linked the Templars, Cathars, and Catholic Church with the true secret and location of the grail. Rahn believed that Eschenbach's *Parzival* was not a mere work of fiction but a guide to finding this most sacred of artefacts. What directed him to that point of view was his hero worship of the German archaeologist Heinrich Schliemann (1822–1890), whose excavations at Troy transformed the literary works of the eighth century BCE Greek writer Homer from myth to historical fact. If Schliemann had made Troy a reality, then Rahn could do the same with *Parzival.*

Consequently, he became convinced that the Cathars and Templars truly were the guardians of the grail against the medieval Catholic Church and its false version of Christianity. They espoused a Gnostic theology that rejected the Jewish god, Yahweh, and heroized Lucifer, the bringer of light, who was not the devil depicted in the New Testament but a divine instructor who seeks to lift our sights beyond the material world in which we are trapped by the evil god. As for the grail, it somehow embodies this truth and poses an existential threat to the Catholic Church. The Cathars and the Templars were the carriers of an Aryan religion linked to the grail that originated in Tibet, northern India, and Persia. It was then transmitted through the Celts to the Gothic tribes of Europe who were implacable foes of the Roman Empire.

The papacy was the continuation of that empire with the popes performing the role of emperor. These anti-Aryan, anti-Gnostic, and anti-grail despots, ruling in the name of an evil god, hunted the Cathars and the Templars to extinction. Both groups of grail keepers were heavily intertwined. Rahn described the Cathars and Templars using the same caves in the Pyrenees to escape the forces of the Pope as they bore down on them. They knew their way around these treacherous, dark passageways that took them deep into mountains and underground with occasional precipitous drops down which their pursuers fell to their deaths.

> *Serious clues remain that the white cape of the Templars, on which glittered the eight-pointed red cross, lies together with the black garments and yellow crosses of the Cathars someplace in the shadowy caves of the Sabarthès.*[19]

There would be no happy ending for either the Templars or the Cathars, pursued relentlessly by the Papal Inquisition. In the shadow of the Pyrenees, and close to the border with Spain, is the French village of Luz-Saint-Sauveur. It has a church attributed to the Templars, though it may have been built by the rival Hospitallers. Rahn described an inscription on a stone slab within this holy place:

> *In the crypt, nine Templar skulls can be found; every night on 13 October, a voice can be heard in the church that asks, whispering like the wind, 'Has the day for the liberation of the Holy Sepulchre arrived?' The nine skulls mumble, 'Still not…'*

So, where was the grail hidden?

According to a Pyrenean legend, the Grail moves farther away from this world, and upward toward the sky, when humanity is no longer worthy of it. Perhaps the Pure Ones of Occitania keep the Grail on one of those stars that circle Montségur like a halo, that Golgotha of Occitania.

Himmler was not about to bankroll Rahn if the grail had disappeared into the heavens. The slightly built academic, who was always short of cash, accepted the Nazi offer of money, promising his SS overlord that he would find the grail. Montségur, a former Cathar stronghold, was one of his first ports of call. So began a journey that indulged all Rahn's academic interests. Yet at the same time, he must have felt as if an hourglass was draining away. Himmler was not paying for a travelogue, published for the amusement of German history fans. He fully expected to be in possession of the Holy Grail at the conclusion of this odyssey. No other outcome was permissible.

Let's follow Rahn's grail quest. It begins in Germany, then on to France, Italy, Switzerland, Germany, and finally, north to Iceland. Everything is detailed in a log that would inform the resulting book: *Lucifer's Court: A Heretic's Journey in Search of the Light Bringers*. Compared to *Crusade Against the Grail*, *Lucifer's Court* is a far poorer piece of writing. It's a series of disjointed observations on each port of call with very little to report. One can almost sense Rahn looking over his shoulder, to his Nazi paymasters, wondering how this is all going to land. When it was eventually published, the Nazi censors spiced it up with additional anti-Semitic material before sending the manuscript to print and distributing thousands of leatherbound copies to party members.

In the first chapter he mocks the Catholic Church's denigration of the Cathars as heretics who rode to nightly orgies on the 'backs of large crabs', kissed the rear end of black cats, and reduced 'murdered children to a powdery form in order to cannibalise them more easily'. Then he heads for Montségur, his favoured location for the grail. He strolls past the Camp des Cremats (Field of Fires) where Dominican monks, working for the Papal Inquisition, burned over 200 heretics to death. 'Not far from the well, jutting out of a stone block, is a wrought-iron cross with two swords, positioned across it'.

Hanging from the upright beam of the cross is a whip, a cane, and a crown of thorns – as well as the keys of Saint Peter. The papacy had stamped its mark on this one-time Cathar stronghold. Rahn meets an engineer from Bordeaux who is digging for treasure at the nearby castle and hopes to find the 'authentic Book of Revelation' as well as the Apocalypse According to John, a forbidden text that the Cathars jealously guarded, believing it contained the true message of Jesus. Long after the Cathars had been exterminated, the engineer explains, Catholic inquisitors were burrowing into the mountains looking for those dangerous texts but to no avail.

Rahn investigates the castle where the last Cathars held out until local shepherds, bribed by Dominican monks, told the Pope's crusaders how to breach its walls. Before the castle fell, one of the Cathar leaders, a woman named Esclarmonde, threw the grail into the mountain gorge which miraculously opened wide like a gigantic mouth then closed again, swallowing the holy relic. Once the Cathar defenders were rounded up, the mass burnings got underway, on Palm Sunday, 1244. 'All who refused to recognise the supremacy of Yahweh, the authority of Peter's keys, and Rome's dogma were burned alive.' Hundreds more were cast into dungeons where most perished. As for Esclarmonde, she was transformed into a dove and 'flew off to the mountains of Asia'.

All of this makes for a fun fireside chat, but Rahn needs results for the SS leader. Questioning the locals further, he is informed that the grail was last seen in a cave in the forest, blocked by a massive stone. Within were hundreds of vipers guarding the grail. Only on Palm Sunday, while the priest was saying mass, did the vipers fall asleep, affording a window of opportunity to steal the grail. 'But God help the person who has not left the cave before the priest has sung *Ite Missa Est!* At the end of the Mass the slab closes again, and the intruder suffers a terrible end as he is bitten to death by the newly awakened vipers.' One of the locals tells Rahn that his grandfather found the spot, deep in the forest, but had been unable to move the stone, despite it having an iron ring attached. He returned to the village for assistance but then was unable to find the cave again. Rahn begins to despair.

The weather was cold and when Rahn attempts to climb the northern slope and reach the castle, he is met with 'an unassailable wall of ice'. Disheartened, he retreats to a farmer's warm kitchen and re-reads *Parzival*. 'Wolfram's poetry fills me with unbridled joy. Isn't every man who seeks justice just like Parzival?' The grail, Rahn opines, is eternal, known to Hercules and Alexander the Great. It fell to earth and ever since has been kept in a grail castle guarded by grail knights. Parzival gained entrance and became the grail king. His son, Lohengrin, was made the grail herald 'travelling in a boat pulled by a swan to all people suffering injustice'. Surely, Rahn reasons, Montségur must be the grail castle in Eschenbach's story? The place he calls Munsalvasche while Wagner refers to it as Montsalvat. That translates as 'mountain of light' but can also mean 'secure mountain'.

Leaving Montségur, Rahn travels to Toulouse where he stays with a Gnostic aristocrat, the Comtesse Miryanne Pujol-Murat, who claims to be descended from Esclarmonde, as well as other Cathars who defended the castle against the Pope's crusaders. While she sits, knitting, Rahn reads one of the books from her large library that describes a macabre Cathar grave where twelves bodies are arranged so that their skulls form the hub of a wheel, and their bodies radiate out like spokes. What can this mean?

Rahn's next stop is the visually stunning medieval, hilltop citadel of Carcassonne. Even though this glory of the Middle Ages was heavily (and controversially) restored by Eugène Viollet-le-Duc (1814–1879), who also embellished Notre-Dame in Paris, it remains a breathtaking example of a fortified urban centre from the Templar and Cathar period. Or as Rahn puts it: 'Beautiful and solemn Carcassonne! Nowhere in the Western world is there anything comparable. The massive walls of your towers and parapets rise up defiantly, and they speak'. But tragically, the story those walls relate is one of bloodshed and betrayal.

On 15 August 1209, the Cathar-held city surrendered to the Pope's crusaders though, unlike neighbouring Béziers, they were not slaughtered in the streets, men, women, and children. Instead, the Cathars of Carcassonne were ordered to strip to their undergarments and leave by the gates, never to return. They departed 'carrying nothing but their sins', as a Cistercian chronicler, and witness to this spectacle, spitefully noted.[20]

Rahn stands before the Tour de l'Inquisition that, as its name suggests, once housed the Papal Inquisition. Within that forbidding place, a knight who was being interrogated by the inquisitors, declared that he would never swear on the crucifix. Rahn finds this very telling: 'Which holy symbol would he have preferred to the cross? The Grail?'

Then he gazes at the Visigoth towers and the Treasure Tower wondering if the Holy Grail has ever been concealed there. The Visigoths overran France in the closing decades of the western Roman Empire and Rahn believes they brought the grail from Rome to Carcassonne after their leader, Alaric, had sacked the eternal city in 410 CE. All this information is cunningly concealed in the text of *Parzival*, 'a literary work that was certainly dictated by Cathars'. Rahn is sure that Kyot of Provence was a Cathar troubadour who had related the truth about the grail to Eschenbach. That made *Parzival* a road map which, if interpreted correctly, would lead Rahn to the grail.

Despite Himmler's later visit to Montserrat, Rahn pours scorn on the idea that the grail made its way to Catalonia: 'The Grail was never kept on Montserrat. Never'. He skips past Montserrat and heads towards Lourdes, the great French pilgrimage site, which he finds impressive. But time is marching on, and he crosses the border into northern Italy, noting that it was a centre of Cathar activity as much as southern France.

In Genoa, he remarks on the lack of belief among local people that the relic known as the Sacro Catino is the grail. This is a bright green glass vessel, believed to have been carved from a single emerald, and brought to the city in the early twelfth century after the sack of Caesarea in 1101 during the First Crusade. It was once revered by the faithful and placed in the cathedral of San Lorenzo, but the adoration suddenly stopped at the end of the eighteenth century.

In 1798, Genoa was under French occupation and the Emperor Napoleon had the Sacro Catino taken to Paris for examination by a group of academics. Their damning assessment was that the cup was made of coloured glass, and not an emerald. Furthermore, it dated to anywhere between first-century Roman to tenth-century Fatimid Egypt and was unlikely to have existed when Jesus was crucified. They then returned it to Genoa broken into about ten pieces.[21]

Heading north for Geneva, Rahn receives news that his friend, the comtesse, has died. She would often regale him with implausible tales about her ancestry. Suffice it to say her family tree would have passed a Nazi racial purity test with flying colours. Her bloodline begins with the Nordic peoples, then the Celts and on to the Hellenic and after that, the Goths who had resisted the might of the Roman Empire. Then in the Middle Ages, her Cathar forebears were annihilated in the Albigensian crusade unleashed by the Pope. How terrible that in her own lifetime, France has abased itself as the faithful daughter of Rome: 'My ancestors cry aloud. Listen to them'. Mourning his friend, Rahn promises himself that he will. But time is running out for his Nazi grail quest.

Rahn journeys through Germany to the capital, Berlin. From there, he moves on to Scotland and after a short stay in Edinburgh, Rahn boards a ship for Iceland. He is heading towards the mythical land of Thule in one last throw of the dice to discover the secret of the grail. Irish monks had sailed this way in the ninth century following the route taken by the ancient Greek explorer Pytheas (born *c.*350 BC) who had written of Thule, far to the north. Rahn hopes to find evidence of an Aryan homeland but instead his ship docks at the 'ugly city' of Reykjavik.

> *I was almost at my wit's end. And why? I dreamed of a fairy-tale land and suddenly found myself in a country that isn't at all like a fairy tale.*

Instead of majestic forests, he is faced with the 'gruesome reality' of 'tasteless houses jumbled together between shop counters, clothes shops, newspaper offices, and movie houses'. It resembles the frontier towns of the Klondike gold rush. There is no grail to be found in Iceland. His expeditions, archaeological digs, and avid reading have come to nothing.

If the Templars and Cathars had known the location of the grail, they had taken that secret to their graves. While Himmler printed thousands of copies of his travelogue, *Lucifer's Court*, he cannot have been impressed with the return on his investment.

Although Rahn remained in the SS, he was sent to perform guard duty at the Dachau concentration camp where German political prisoners were held in appalling conditions. It's been speculated that Rahn's sexuality, alleged alcoholism, or possible Jewish ancestry resulted in his final downfall. All that can be said with certainty is that on 13 March 1939, a slightly built man, dressed head to toe in black, was seen wandering into the snowy woods of the Tyrolean mountains from which he never emerged alive.

The association between the Third Reich and the Holy Grail required a gross distortion of medieval history that has lingered to the present day. Neo-Nazi groups, and other extreme Far Right elements, continue to appropriate Templar symbology with the words '*Deus Vult*' (God wills it) appearing on T-shirts, along with the Templar cross, to promote a narrative casting the Templars as defenders of western civilisation against Islam. This racialises the crusades in a way that would have been unrecognisable to anybody in the twelfth or thirteenth centuries. It also ignores accusations levelled against the Templars at the time that they had enjoyed too close a relation with their Muslim neighbours in the Holy Land, even learning Arabic to communicate with them.[22]

The fondness of some neo-Nazis for the Templars has nothing to do with the reality of the Middle Ages and everything to do with the outpourings of occult groups like the Ordo Novi Temple, and the Thule Society, which exercised a significant influence on Nazi ideology. These occultists were concerned with creating a pseudo-history of the world, putting the Aryan race at the top, even if this meant replacing Darwin's theory of evolution to have the master race evolving in an entirely different way to the rest of humanity. By twisting Greek and Norse mythologies and absorbing a slew of esoteric theories, particularly the theosophy of 'Madame' Helena Blavatsky (1831–1891), the Knights Templar, and even Jesus Christ, were transformed into Aryan superheroes.

While most neo-Nazis today would never have read the incomprehensible gobbledygook of the early-twentieth-century race theorists, they have absorbed some elements, hence the unquestioning assumption that they have something in common with the Knights Templar. The simple fact is they do not.

The Holy Grail eluded Otto Rahn. Its whereabouts remain a mystery. However, this was not the only sacred treasure associated with the Templars. Could the knights have got their hands on the passion relics: items directly involved in the crucifixion and resurrection of Jesus Christ?

These include the pillar to which Christ was bound and scourged, the veil used by Veronica to wipe his face as he carried the cross, splinters from the cross itself and the Crown of Thorns placed on his head, as well as the shroud in which he was buried. Conspiracy theorists have long argued that the knights resolved to find these sacred relics by digging underground on the Temple Mount in Jerusalem. Then, after the city fell to the Saracens, the Templars spirited these items westwards to their preceptories in Europe. If this is true – where are these relics now?

An obvious starting place to investigate is the centre of Roman Catholic power: Rome. A city brimming with holy relics, adorning the altars and side chapels of a thousand churches. At the Basilica of Santa Maria Maggiore, a below ground altar contains the crib of the baby Jesus, before which a gigantic statue of the nineteenth-century Pope Pius IX kneels in prayer. The preserved footprints of the Messiah can be viewed at San Sebastiano fuori le mura. And at the Basilica of Saint John Lateran, part of the table from the Last Supper is on display for the faithful.

The River Tiber in Rome is crossed at one point by an ancient bridge dating back to the Emperor Hadrian. The Ponte Sant'Angelo was completed in 134 CE and takes visitors today across the river to the entrance of the Castel Sant'Angelo, a circular fortress used in the past as a bolthole for the popes as invading armies approached. The core of the building, its impressive drum-shaped edifice, was once the tomb of Hadrian but later re-versioned as a papal castle after being sacked by the Goths in the fifth century.

On each side of the Ponte Sant'Angelo are seventeenth century statues of angels holding the passion relics. One angel clasps the marble column to which Jesus was tied and whipped before his crucifixion while another has the whips involved. One winged figure brandishes the Crown of Thorns. Another statue displays the Veil of Veronica used to wipe the face of Jesus as he carried the cross to Calvary. The other angels hold the cross itself, the nails, the inscription fastened to the crucifix, and the 'holy sponge', used to quench Christ's thirst as he gasped his last breaths.

The flow of relics from the Holy Land to Rome began in the fourth century CE when the Emperor Constantine (*c*.272–337) converted to Christianity. His mother Helena (*c*.246–330), the Augusta Imperatrix, became an enthusiastic patron of the newly legalised religion. On a visit to Jerusalem between 326 and 328 CE, Helena uncovered one passion relic after another in what were undoubtedly stage-managed discoveries.

She just happened to unearth the crucifix of Jesus along with the two crosses on which the two thieves were executed on either side of him. Then the nails driven into Christ's hands and feet turned up as well as the tunic stripped from his body before being fastened to the cross with a length of rope that the lucky empress also chanced upon. Helena, who would be declared a saint soon after death, tore down the temple to Venus that the pagan emperor, Hadrian, had erected over the site of Christ's death and resurrection. In its place, she commissioned the Church of the Holy Sepulchre, which would become the holiest site in Christendom and a destination for Christian pilgrims whom the Templars were sworn to protect.

Back in Rome, Helena commissioned the transformation of a large secular meeting hall into a Christian church to house some of her haul of relics. The Basilica di Santa Croce in Gerusalemme is still one of the seven most important Catholic sites in Rome today. In a side chapel, the faithful venerate an impressive array of relics including two thorns from the Crown of Thorns, a crucifixion nail, parts of the true cross, and the Titulus Crucis. The latter is the wooden nameplate nailed to the crucifix above the head of Jesus that mockingly declared: *Here is the King of the Jews*. Radiocarbon tests in 2002 confirmed it's an early medieval forgery. Also in pride of place is the finger of doubting Thomas that was placed into the very wounds of Christ.

If the Templars possessed any of the passion relics, then the shroud that covered the dead body of Jesus comes closest to having supporting evidence. Accounts of a cloth bearing the imprint of Jesus date back to at least the sixth century but there is a fundamental difference of opinion. The object in question is either Veronica's Veil, used to wipe Christ's face as he carried the cross to Calvary, and therefore bearing only a facial image, or it is a full-body shroud. Linking this passion relic to the Templars means proving it is the latter.

Turning to the canonical gospels offers no help. The story of Veronica originates in the apocryphal Gospel of Nicodemus and, as with so many medieval accretions to scripture, acquired more details with every telling. By the Middle Ages, a woman called Veronica obtained an imprint of Jesus on a piece of cloth that she then used to cure the Roman Emperor Tiberius of a serious illness.

Her name, according to the medieval chronicler Gerald of Wales (*c*.1146–*c*.1223), derived from the Latin 'vera' (true) and 'icon' (image). Even though her story did not originate in the four accepted gospels of the New Testament, she became very popular with the faithful. Pilgrims during the Templar period loved to collect badges from shrines they had visited, emblems to commemorate their long journeys. Gerald relates that those returning from Rome proudly sported badges of the Veil of Veronica. That might be pinned alongside a cockle shell motif from Santiago de Compostela or an ampule of water mixed with the blood of the martyred Thomas Becket from a visit to Canterbury. The Veronica badge was the must-have souvenir, and some lucky pilgrims would have got to see the actual Veil, owned by the Pope, being given a public airing.[23]

This revered face cloth, or 'sudarium', was something entirely different to the full-body shroud of Jesus. That was held by the Byzantine Emperor in Constantinople as part of his vast collection of relics. There it remained until the year 1204 when a crusader army breached the once impregnable walls of Constantinople, looting and burning on an epic scale. A horrific act of violence by Christians against other Christians.

This was a moral low point for the entire crusading venture when the Fourth Crusade was diverted by the Venetians, who were bankrolling the crusaders, to attack their maritime rivals the Byzantines, instead of prosecuting the war against the forces of Islam. Not a single church or monastery was spared as the knights from the west stripped the glories of eastern Christendom, even digging up the tombs of the emperors back to Constantine the Great. Saint Mark's Basilica in Venice still displays four bronze horses stolen from the old Roman hippodrome, though many of the treasures were melted down for their scrap value.

During this orgy of criminality, the shroud disappeared. It then re-emerged in April 1389 when it was put on permanent public display by Geoffroi de Charney. That should have a ring of familiarity as a man of the same name, the Templar preceptor of Normandy, was burned at the stake alongside Jacques de Molay in the year 1314. Suggestions that there was a familial link between these two De Charneys has not been definitively proven, even if it seems very compelling. Nevertheless, it's the name De Charney that suggests the Templars may have owned the shroud up until their destruction.

There is a fog of uncertainty around the shroud's whereabouts between 1204 and its reappearance in 1389, a gap of 185 years. In 1978, author and historian Ian Wilson (born 1941), published a bestseller, *The Turin Shroud*, that set out to resolve that conundrum.[24] He believed that the shroud stolen from Constantinople originated in Edessa where it was known as the Holy Mandylion. But was this Veronica's Veil or, as Wilson argued, the full-body Shroud of Jesus folded into four with only the face visible?

Over the centuries, it went on a very long journey, passing through Byzantine and then Templar hands, during which time it may have been housed in Cyprus, the knights' headquarters, after losing their last strongholds in the Holy Land, then eventually ending up in Turin cathedral in the sixteenth century, where it has remained ever since.

How did the Byzantines come to own the shroud before they lost it in 1204? And crucially, can it be dated back to Jesus himself? Possible answers can be found in apocryphal gospels and early Christian writings.[25] The story begins with an Arab king who ruled Edessa during Christ's ministry, Abgar V Ukkama (died *c.*50 CE).

The fourth century Church historian and propagandist Eusebius of Caesarea (*c.*260–339) claimed that Jesus and Abgar had been in correspondence, with the king pleading to be cured of his chronic leprosy and gout. Jesus responded that he was rather busy carrying out his ministry in Judaea, but after his resurrection, a disciple would be in touch.[26] Judas Thaddeus was the disciple assigned to the task whose name was later shortened by translators of the New Testament to Jude to avoid confusion with Judas Iscariot, the betrayer of Jesus. Armed with the sacred relic of the now dead Jesus, Judas Thaddeus went to Edessa and healed the king.

In a Syrian version of the story, the shroud was presented to Abgar, and its mere presence banished the disease. Given its proven miraculous power, the image was venerated in the city, paraded around in times of strife, until it was transferred to the Byzantine capital, Constantinople, in 944 CE.

Historians then divide on the question of whether it was an image of the face of Christ or his entire body. For Wilson's hypothesis to stack up, the image must be a head-to-toe representation of Jesus. This would ensure the Turin Shroud's provenance tracing it back through the Byzantines, to the kings of Edessa, and on to Jesus. However, the image held by the kings of Edessa is often described as just Christ's face. One explanation given for this is that the shroud was routinely folded to only show the face and the resulting creases can still be seen on the Turin Shroud.

The arrival of this passion relic at the centre of Byzantine power was celebrated by the Emperor Constantine VII Porphyrogenitus (905–959 CE), who was a prolific historian and bibliophile. It was also mentioned by the archdeacon of the Hagia Sophia, Gregory Referendarius, who noted not only Christ's face, but evidence of blood from the Roman spear plunged into the torso.[27] That clearly suggests a full-body image. Gregory's sermon was only rediscovered in the Vatican archive in 1986, with the most accurate English translation made in 2004, and it seems to validate Wilson's hypothesis.

In addition, there is the begging letter sent by the Byzantine Emperor Alexios I Komnenos (*c.*1057–1118), at the end of the eleventh century, calling for western help against the invasion by the Muslim Seljuk Turks. This was the missive that sparked the crusades, offering European knights all the sacred treasures of Constantinople, including 'the linen cloths found in the sepulchre' after the resurrection of Christ. That certainly infers a whole-body shroud was held by the emperors. There are also several accounts by pilgrims in the twelfth century and first years of the thirteenth century that support a full-body image on a long cloth.

In April 1979, the BBC broadcast a documentary, *The Silent Witness* (part of its Everyman strand), that examined these new theories about the shroud's authenticity. Wilson presented his research, backing up his claim that it dated back to the time of Jesus. He believed that after it was stolen from Constantinople during the Fourth Crusade in 1204, it was held by the Templars and formed the basis of the head-worshipping rites mentioned in their trials. Evidence to back up this argument was uncovered in 1945, beneath the crumbling ceiling plaster of an outhouse to a medieval cottage off the high street in the English village of Templecombe. What emerged was a haunting image of the head of Jesus, painted onto an oak panel, later carbon dated to between 1280 and 1340.

Templecombe was once home to a Templar preceptory, located in the county of Somerset, where Jesus and Joseph of Arimathea were reputed to have spent some time trading in tin and lead, according to medieval legends. The oak panel had been hidden face down for centuries. Wilson argued that this image was linked to the shroud owned by the knights and that they secreted this religious icon away in 1312, when the preceptory was shut down.

By this time, the actual shroud was in France with the De Charney family, but images of it were secretly circulated among Templars across Europe. 'Satellites such as the important preceptory at Templecombe would have had painted representations for religious purposes', according to Wilson.[28] The outside world was not told that the Templars had the shroud because it formed a vital part of their clandestine rites of initiation.

But Professor Malcolm Barber, an authority on the Templar trials, wonders why the knights would not have capitalised on their ownership of such an incredible relic from Christ's Passion. It would have been unprecedented to keep the ownership of such an amazing holy artefact under wraps. The Templars were not usually shy about being associated with venerated objects linked to the life and death of Christ. In the Holy Land, they rode into battle with the True Cross carried before them. And like every religious order, they leveraged their relics for publicity and fundraising.

The remarks from one man who worked closely with the knights, and gave evidence at their trials, seems to back this up. Antonio Sicci di Vercelli was an Italian notary who worked for the Templars over a forty-year period. In March 1311, he was called before the papal commission investigating the order and gave testimony. What he said may have been extracted under torture but nevertheless, he revealed how the Templars made money from relics that were otherwise of inconsequential worth:

I saw many times a certain cross, which at first sight seemed to be of no monetary value, and was said to be from the tub or trough in which Christ bathed, which the brothers kept in their treasury; and several times I saw that, when excessive heat or drought occurred, the people of Acre asked the brothers of the Temple that that cross should be carried in a procession of the clergy of Acre... When these processions were carried out in this way, by the cooperation of divine clemency, water came from the sky and moistened the land and tempered the heat of the air.[29]

Not only was this a rain-making cross, but it could also banish a 'malign spirit' out of a possessed sinner, foaming at the mouth, and in dire need of an exorcism. If Sicci was right, and the Templars brandished this relic very publicly, then why not the shroud? Possibly because it was reserved for the clandestine, nocturnal rituals of the Templars, which were not for public consumption.

So where was it kept? The most likely venue would have been the heavily fortified Paris Temple, where it would have disappeared behind the impregnable walls. If the shroud was then spirited away before the mass arrests of the Templars, the knights would have needed advance notice of their fate. Wilson argues that the knights were tipped off in time to flee with their treasure, though Barber disagrees. He is convinced King Philip sprung his trap before the Templars could react. Outside of France, Templars might have escaped the Inquisition. But not within France.

Did that mean the shroud was seized by the authorities? If it was in Paris, then it would have been within reach of the king's commissioners. The only way it could have eluded them would have been if the shroud was kept in Cyprus, the order's global headquarters. But Wilson maintains it was seen at chapter meetings in Paris and ended up with Geoffroi de Charney, preceptor of Normandy. Therefore, the shroud was in France and nowhere else.

During the trials, the Templars were accused of worshipping an idol of some description that had various magical powers and gave them instructions. The idol was usually identified with a head, possibly of a demon. But according to Wilson, despite its fierce countenance, this head was of Jesus Christ as it appeared on the shroud. It was therefore two-dimensional and not three dimensional. However, Templar testimonies at their trials in France do not support this.

One Templar who gave evidence in the French hearings, Rainier de Larchant, said the head was of a bearded man 'which they adored, kissed, and called their saviour'. Raoul de Gizy told the hearings the head was a frightening, devilish thing 'that he could scarcely look at it, except with the greatest fear and trembling'. According to him, the head was brought to their meetings in a bag and was possibly human – which hardly concurs with an image on cloth.

Etienne de Troyes saw a bearded head placed on an altar and believed it was the mouldering remains of Hugh de Payens, first grand master of the order.

Again, this does not lead one to believe that the head mentioned in the trials was a flat image. It sounds more like a grisly statue or a decaying skull. The only feasible explanation is that the Templars manufactured three dimensional images of the body on the shroud for veneration at secret rituals in their preceptories around Europe. The knights would have understood that the solid head before them was based on the true image of Christ on the shroud.

In 1389, De Charney publicly displayed the Shroud of Jesus. He had inherited it from his father, yet another Geoffroi de Charney (*c*.1306–1356), who had been a celebrity knight of the fourteenth century, achieving glory in the Hundred Years' War against England until he was killed at the Battle of Poitiers, bravely clutching the sacred banner of the kings of France. He wrote books on chivalry and was a leading member of the Order of the Star, which was intended to overshadow England's rival Order of the Garter.[30] Wilson argues that the Order of the Star was a de facto revival of the Templars under a different brand name. This order was established at a time when interest in the Arthurian romances across Europe was booming. De Charney most likely dreamed of evoking the Knights of the Round Table but whether he was seeking to resurrect the Templars is far less clear. If he was, the venture fell apart in the years after his death at Poitiers.

With the valiant and chivalrous De Charney dead, his son resolved to share this curious family heirloom with the faithful. But the Church had already expressed its reservations about the shroud and took a dim view. Two bishops of Troyes, a city with strong historic connections to the first Templars, complained to the Pope about the shroud being promoted by the De Charney family. They argued that it was a cunning forgery – a painting of Christ's body. Bishop Pierre d'Arcis was particularly vexed when he fired off a letter to Pope Clement VII (1342–1394) in Avignon.[31] However, the letter was not well received.

The 'Babylonian captivity' of popes in Avignon was supposed to have ended with Pope Gregory XI (1329–1378) when he returned the papal court to Rome after a seventy-year absence. But his successor, Urban VI (1318–1389) was such a polarising figure that the Church split with the kingdoms of France, Castile, Aragon, and Scotland backing a rival 'antipope', Clement VII, who continued to rule from Avignon. He needed powerful friends, and so instead of backing his bishop, gave De Charney permission to display the shroud, removed any threat of excommunication, and injuncted the bishop to perpetual silence. The only proviso was that religious ceremonies around the shroud were heavily restricted, and the shroud was not to be presented as authentic, but a likeness.

From that time to the present day, it has continued to provoke controversy and heated debate with no amount of carbon dating bringing a resolution.

Whether or not the Templars were the guardians of the Turin Shroud during its missing years remains a mystery.

The Templars are reputed to have held other passion relics, for example the Spear of Destiny, the Roman lance that pierced the side of Jesus on the cross, hastening his death. Also known as the Holy Lance, there are three main contenders today in the Vatican, Vienna, and Armenia. Only in the Gospel of John do we get an account of the Roman centurion thrusting his lance into Christ's body 'and immediately blood and water flowed out'. In later accounts, this soldier acquired the name Gaius Cassius Longinus and was described as shortsighted. But when the blood of the saviour splattered on his eyes, his vision became perfect. As Jesus gave up his last gasp and died, a terrible earthquake shook Jerusalem. Longinus, fearful and awestruck, immediately became a Christian. Returning to his native Cappadocia, he was martyred for his new faith after smashing the idols of his persecutors and conversing with the demons within them.

In various traditions and pseudo-histories, the spear has been given both a prequel and a sequel. There are claims that it was already over a thousand years old at the crucifixion and originally fashioned by Phinehas who was the grandson of Aaron, the brother of Moses, and high priest of the first temple in Jerusalem. Phinehas used the spear to kill an Israelite prince and a pagan Midianite with a single thrust as they were in the act of making love, within sight of Moses.

Centuries later, King Herod was said to have owned the spear and then, somehow, it ended up in the hands of Longinus. After news of this Roman soldier's conversion to Christianity reached Pontius Pilate, the governor of Judaea, he wrote to the Emperor Tiberius asking for advice. The response came back – cut the centurion's head off. Not only did Longinus become the patron saint of the shortsighted but an impressive statue was erected in the Vatican and his martyrdom is celebrated today in the Philippines and Brazil.

After Longinus, the spear was owned by Maurice, an African Roman soldier who, according to early Christian writings, commanded a garrison in Thebes. In 287 CE, he was ordered to put down a revolt in Gaul (modern France). This was done successfully, and the troops were then expected to make the obligatory sacrifice of thanks to the cult of the divine emperor. But Maurice had converted his entire garrison to Christianity, and they refused. Their stubbornness led to all of them being executed. In one account, the number martyred is given as 6666.

The spear then falls into the hands of the first Christian Roman Emperor, Constantine, but is then stolen by Alaric, the Gothic leader who sacked Rome in 410 CE. After his death, it is briefly held by Atilla the Hun but then returned to the Romans and is a prized possession of the Emperor Justinian. He sends it to Jerusalem but after that city is invaded by the Persians in the seventh century, an old tradition has it ending up with the English king, Athelstan, who used its sacred power to repel a Viking onslaught. After that, in the eighth and ninth centuries, the spear becomes part of the royal treasury of the Emperor Charlemagne and takes pride of place in the imperial regalia of the Holy Roman Empire. This empire, founded by Charlemagne, endures for nearly a thousand years with the spear housed in Prague, then Nuremberg, and finally Vienna. Not everybody agreed this was the genuine article, hence the rival spears in Rome and Armenia.

In fact, during the First Crusade, at the Siege of Antioch in June 1098, a soldier from Provence, Peter Bartholomew, claimed Saint Andrew told him in a dream that the spear was buried within that city. Sure enough, it was then dug up by Peter in front of an amazed group of fellow crusaders, though sceptics poured scorn on his discovery. Enduring a year of malicious gossip, Peter demanded an ordeal by fire where he carried the alleged Holy Lance through a narrow gap between two blazing piles of wood. He suffered horrific burns, dying shortly afterwards. But the Spear of Destiny endured, finding its way to the Byzantine capital, Constantinople. Then it either fell into crusader (or Templar) hands after the destruction of the city in 1204 or other sources say that an Ottoman sultan gave it to the Pope as a diplomatic gift, who then placed it under one of the pillars supporting the dome of Saint Peter's Basilica.

In 1912, a young Adolf Hitler saw the Spear of Destiny on display in the Hofburg Palace in Vienna, by then the capital of the Austro-Hungarian Empire, and resolved to own it one day.[32] In 1938, when Austria was annexed to Germany, his dream came true, and the spear was brought back to Nuremberg. It was given a position of honour in Saint Katherine's Church until 1944 when it was moved to a secretly constructed vault to protect it from the constant barrage of Allied bombing. Otto Rahn failed miserably to find the Holy Grail and paid the ultimate price, but the Third Reich managed to rob one passion relic that had pierced the very body of Jesus. To Hitler, and the occult-obsessed Himmler, this was a talisman of breathtaking power.[33] However, when the Nazis were defeated in 1945, at the end of the Second World War, American troops recovered the spear and returned it to Vienna.[34]

Trying to prove that the Knights Templar owned a vast treasure, including the passion relics of Christ, which they then hid away in one or more locations after 1307 is an unenviable task. The knights themselves left no written records. Their enemies were certainly none the wiser.

The main evidence for the Templars absconding in the dead of night, after the arrest warrants had been issued, with items of immense value rests on the testimony of just one knight: Jean de Châlons. In 1308, at a hearing in Poitiers during the Templar trials, he had quite a tale to tell, though torture may have loosened his tongue. According to this jailed Templar, the order's leadership clearly knew they were about to be imprisoned by order of the king. So, they made for the coast in a convoy of carts and horses where they were met by eighteen ships to ferry them and their precious cargo onwards.

There was nothing unusual about the Templars having access to ships, which doubled for both merchant and military use. They may have been owned outright or rented by the order. A thirteenth-century Templar church in San Bevignate, in the Italian region of Umbria, includes a fresco depicting the stern and mast of a Templar caravel. There is even a suggestion that some Templars engaged in piracy on the high seas.

One brother knight, Roger de Flor (1267–1305), had grown up among the Templars as a child before joining the order. He became the captain of *The Falcon*, helping to rescue Christians from the siege of Acre in 1291, though for a price. This vessel was regarded as a jewel in the Templar fleet and proves that many of the knights had considerable maritime prowess. However, De Flor was a controversial figure who came to occupy a grey area between policing piracy and becoming a pirate himself.[35] Indeed it's been suggested that quite a few Templars sank into piracy after the order was suppressed as a way of using their skills profitably. Eventually the Pope signalled his displeasure at De Flor's activities, and he quit the Templars to become an overt and unashamed pirate until he was assassinated.[36]

La Rochelle is often cited as the port from which the Templars fled with their treasure, a bustling hub for all types of trade, but especially wine. The knights used it extensively for mainly commercial purposes. It was not a useful point of embarkation for the Holy Land but gave access to Scotland and Portugal – two possible destinations for the treasure of the Templars.

Chapter Five

Fleeing to Scotland

Jacques de Molay, the last grand master of the Knights Templar, had just been burned at the stake near Notre-Dame cathedral in Paris, the grimmest form of medieval execution. In the dark of night, a group of Templars disguised as stone masons approached the still flickering embers and thrust their swords into the glowing pyre, coating the blades with ashes. They uttered a single, top-secret word under their breath, still used today in Masonic rituals. Then, turning their backs on the grisly scene, the group departed for Scotland.[1] Their leader was the provincial grand master of Auvergne, Peter d'Aumont, and he was accompanied by two commanders and five knights on the arduous journey by sea.

The Masonic tradition has the Templars dividing into four groups after the death of De Molay. One group re-emerged in Portugal as the Order of Christ. A second group recognised D'Aumont as the new grand master, electing him to the position after arriving on the Scottish island of Mull. A third group claimed that a knight from Outremer, Jean Marc Larmenius, was the only true grand master and they will be examined in a later chapter. While a fourth group refused to accept either D'Aumont or Larmenius with some of them fighting alongside Robert the Bruce (1274–1329), king of Scotland, in his wars against the English, while others were absorbed into the Knights Hospitaller. One Masonic version of events goes on to assert that Robert the Bruce created the Order of the Thistle as a new home for the Templars, from which modern Freemasonry emerged centuries later.

Does any of the above possess a shred of truth? These tales only emerged over the last 300 years. Dates and names in the eighteenth- and nineteenth-century source material are sometimes incorrect or confused. Yet the legend of Templars fleeing to Scotland from France, laden with treasure of incalculable value, has endured. As is so often the case with the Templars, fact and fiction have become intertwined and disentangling them is an unenviable task.

Christianity first arrived in Scotland when the Romans still governed Britannia, the province south of Hadrian's Wall that covers modern England and Wales.

Contact with Roman soldiers who had converted to Christianity and the brave efforts of missionaries saw the first Scots embrace the gospels. But most people continued to worship the gods of their ancestors. It took the diligent work of Irish monks, who sailed over from the fifth century CE onwards, to win over Scotland to the Christian faith. And even then, it was a Celtic version of Catholicism, often at odds with the official version mandated by Rome.

There is a legend that a certain Saint Regulus, also known as Saint Rule, sailed to Scotland from Constantinople, capital of the eastern Roman Empire, around 345 CE, with the bones of Andrew the apostle. Andrew was a fisherman who became an itinerant preacher after the death of Jesus but was then martyred at the Greek speaking city of Patras in 60 CE by being bound, not nailed, to an X-shaped cross, or 'saltire'. The Saint Andrew Saltire flag, with a white cross on a blue background, is still the Scottish flag today. He was accompanied by a very pious woman, Saint Triduana, whose beauty attracted unwanted attention from the local Pictish king, which she resolved by gouging her own eyes out and handing them to the offending suitor. This echoes a similar story in the life of Saint Lucy who, like Triduana, removed her own eyes and subsequently became associated with curing eye disorders. A lavish cathedral was built in the twelfth century to house Saint Andrew's relics but was then destroyed in 1559 during the Protestant Reformation.

These sixteenth-century Protestant zealots, who believed Christians should avoid embellishing scripture, sought to root out apocryphal tales and legends that infested the Bible like weeds. Take for example a widely believed story that Pontius Pilate was born in the tiny Scottish village of Fortingall, Perthshire. Reportedly, both he and Jesus Christ spent time in Scotland and were initiated into the Druidic rites on the isle of Iona. Pilate was the illegitimate son of a Roman soldier, and a local woman related to the local Scottish king, Metallanus, who enjoyed a productive relationship with the Romans as his kingdom sat on large deposits of iron, lead, and copper.[2] Pilate somehow worked his way up the imperial career ladder, becoming the governor of Judaea. Clearly there was no honour among Druids as Pilate, in his new elevated role, allowed fellow Druid Jesus Christ to be nailed to a cross. One small niggling factual point about this tale is that the Romans were not in Scotland during the reigns of Augustus and Tiberius when Pilate and Jesus were both reputed to be there.

In England, there were similar stories of the teenage Jesus living in the Somerset village of Priddy with his uncle, Joseph of Arimathea, during the missing years between his childhood and ministry at the end of his life. Joseph was apparently a tin and lead merchant, and the duo may even have got their hands dirty doing some mining for the valued metals. But Scottish medieval storytellers persisted with their rival claim to being the home of the teen messiah.

In 1933, a British Museum curator, Henry Jenner, visiting the Hebrides, noted 'a whole set of legends of the wanderings of the Holy Mother and Son in those Islands'.[3] Whether or not Jesus spent time in Scotland, the kingdom was thoroughly Christianised by the medieval period thanks to the missionary work of Irish monks and the introduction of the great monastic orders: Augustinians, Benedictines, Cistercians, and Premonstratensians.

In 1128, the first Templar grand master, Hugh de Payens, arrived in Scotland as part of a European tour to drum up interest in his new order of holy warriors. He got a warm welcome from the king, David I (*c.*1084–1153), who had spent his formative years in Normandy and at the Anglo-Norman court of England's Henry I (*c.*1068–1135). This meant that far from being isolated from the royal courts of Europe, David was plugged into a Norman network stretching from England, down through Normandy, and on to southern Italy. He was very receptive to De Payens, and his new order of monastic knights. So much so that he green lit a Templar headquarters to be established at Balantrodoch, not far from Edinburgh. The name 'Balantrodoch' roughly translates as 'town of the warriors' in Gaelic but today is known simply as Temple. This Templar preceptory would be followed by a second one at Maryculter in Aberdeenshire.

During his stay, De Payens became associated with a Viking-Scottish noble family that plays a prominent role in the various narratives about what happened to the Templars after their downfall: the Sinclairs. Also spelt St Clair, this aristocratic dynasty was responsible for building Rosslyn chapel and, according to some commentators, helped the Templars escape their persecutors, possibly making their way to the New World.

There was a growing tension in the thirteenth century between European monarchs and the Templars on their soil. The kings of Portugal, Castile, Aragon, France, and England increasingly wanted to know – on whose side were these armed bodies of men? There was a nascent nationalistic spirit leading kings to question whether the loyalty of the Templars should be to them or the Pope. For the English king, Edward I (1239–1307), this became a pressing issue as he pursued an aggressive policy on several fronts towards his enemies in France, Wales, Ireland, and Scotland. He expected the total loyalty of the Knights Templar and Hospitaller within his expanding empire. Astonishingly, both orders complied with the king's demands even though it was in clear breach of their rules. When the Templars had first been established, they swore to never take sides in wars between rival Christian princes. Their swords would only be raised against the Saracen or the Moor. But that principle was now completely undermined through pressure from Edward as he set out to earn the well-deserved soubriquet – Hammer of the Scots.

The Templars sought for as long as possible to maintain good relations with the Scottish kings, even while the English massed at their borders. After all, King Alexander II (1198–1249) and his successor, Alexander III (1241–1286), had granted lands to the Templars. But the knights finally caved in entirely to the English when Alexander III died with no heir. A series of events led to King Edward installing a compliant monarch, John Balliol (*c.*1249–1314), on the Scottish throne, but when he was overthrown by his own nobles, Edward launched a full-scale invasion that sparked the Wars of Scottish Independence. The Scottish Templars were directed by their line manager, the grand master in London, to support Edward.

This inevitably led to the Templars in Scotland being viewed as nothing more than an arm of the English state, especially as their leadership hailed from south of the border. Disgusted patriotic Scots needed a Templar villain to exemplify the perfidy of these treacherous knights. An evil figure that would loom large in fireside storytelling. Step forward Brian de Jay (died 1298), preceptor of Balantrodoch and grand master of both England and Scotland. His family estates were in what was then the English county of Shropshire but is now part of Herefordshire. De Jay pledged himself and the order to Edward's cause becoming an instant bête noire to the Scots. Clearly this was a man of low moral character, and a good yarn was needed to illustrate the point.

The ensuing tale was a classic piece of anti-Templar propaganda. It involved De Jay, plus, a grieving widow and an estate at Esperston in Midlothian. A man called William, son of Geoffrey of Halkerston, bequeathed his wife Christiana's estate to the Templars for the remainder of his life. He then became a Templar, living at Balantrodoch. A modern analogy would be an elderly person going into sheltered accommodation, remortgaging his property to pay the bills. His wife and children were permitted to occupy a small house in a corner of the estate from which the Templars now creamed off the profits. At his death, William intended the estate to revert to his wife, but De Jay decided otherwise. When the old man passed away, he evicted the widow and children. In fact, De Jay turned up in person with some armed heavies to perform the task. Christiana turned out to be quite a spirited individual and put up a fight, clinging with both hands to the front door, until one of her fingers was cut clean off with a dagger.

Later, when the English king, Edward, was lodging at nearby Newbattle Abbey, run by the Cistercians, Christiana paid him a personal visit, falling at the monarch's feet and demanding justice. In an uncharacteristic display of mercy, the king ruled in the widow's favour. A furious De Jay bided his time and at an opportune moment, threw the widow out again.

By the year 1298, De Jay was grand master of the Templars throughout Britain. He was back at Balantrodoch with a large group of Welsh mercenaries, preparing to fight alongside Edward against the charismatic William Wallace (*c.*1270–1305), better known to moviegoers as 'Braveheart', at the battle of Falkirk. In desperation, the widow's oldest son, Richard Cook, went to De Jay and pleaded his mother's case. The Templar feigned compassion and promised that if Cook safely chaperoned his mercenaries to Falkirk, then the family estate would be returned to his mother. An overjoyed Cook agreed without realising that De Jay had instructed the mercenaries to murder their guide the moment they arrived at their destination, which they duly did.[4]

Still, De Jay then got his comeuppance from Braveheart's soldiers at Falkirk. He was cut down fighting alongside Edward's forces, which was maybe divine retribution for his breach of the Templar code as set down by Saint Bernard of Clairvaux. The order retained control of the widow's estate up until 1312 when the family finally managed to get their property back, as Templar assets were being broken up across the country. At a judicial hearing in Holyrood Abbey to investigate the Templars, it was alleged that De Jay had always extended hospitality to the rich but had shown nothing but contempt for the poor. One witness even claimed that De Jay once threw a farthing in the freezing mud to enjoy watching beggars competing to pick up the coin with their mouths.

The Templars in Scotland made many enemies in their last decades of existence. This was not helped by English domination of the order, north of the border. But it's worth bearing in mind that by 1307, we are talking about a very small group of people. Templar numbers, never very high in Scotland, had dwindled significantly. At the Holyrood hearing, only two rather forlorn knights appeared: Walter de Clifton and William de Middleton. Both were English. Queuing up to testify for the prosecution were local Scottish monks who had been neighbours of the Templars and had racked up a mass of grievances which they vented against the duo. De Clifton and De Middleton were forced to sit through a litany of petty slights and baseless rumours, defending themselves as best they could.

This was in marked contrast to the way the Templars were treated in the Iberian Peninsula where the relationship between monasteries and Templar preceptories was very different. In Portugal, the monks directly benefited from the Templars grabbing more territory from the Islamic caliphate. As the knights expanded the Christian realm, the Cistercians moved in to set up their medieval agri-businesses behind the frontlines. Everybody benefited financially.

But there was no such dynamic in Scotland. Quite the contrary. If the Templars were given land, the monks thought it was at their expense.[5] At Maryculter, the second largest Templar preceptory in Scotland, the monks at nearby Kelso Abbey believed the knights owed them tithes. The Templars disagreed. They had brought unpromising land into cultivation that would have remained unused and so had performed a public service from which they should alone benefit. It was this kind of dispute that brought monks and friars to Holyrood to unleash years of frustration against the Templars.

Central to the belief that the Knights Templar fled from France to Scotland after King Philip and Guillaume de Nogaret served their arrest warrants, is the idea that the Scottish king, Robert the Bruce (1274–1329), was a natural ally. That he alone, among Europe's crowned heads, would offer the Templars sanctuary from the forces of the Papal Inquisition. Why? Because Robert had been excommunicated by the Church and was therefore an enemy of Pope Clement – and any foe of the pontiff, logic dictates, must be a friend to the knights.

Robert was a direct descendant of David I, the Scottish king who had welcomed the first Templar grand master, Hugh de Payens, into his kingdom and showered benefits on his new order of knights. Most accounts have him born at Turnberry Castle in Ayrshire, which was the seat of the Earls of Carrick. But the fourteenth-century English chronicler, Walter of Swinbroke claimed he was born at Writtle in the southern English county of Essex.[6] This is not totally far-fetched as Robert's family was a mix of Scottish and Anglo-Norman nobles with estates in England and Scotland. That included Essex where the Bruce (or Brus) clan held lands in Writtle, Hatfield Broad Oak, Terling, Hatfield Peverel, Lamarsh, and Southchurch.[7] Therefore Robert the Bruce, Scotland's greatest hero, may have been an Essex lad.

Robert's grandfather, Robert V de Brus (*c.*1215–1295), fifth lord of Annandale, was one of two claimants to the Scottish throne in 1290 after a 7-year-old princess, Margaret (1283–1290), Maid of Norway, who was due to be crowned queen of Scotland, dropped dead. Eleven years later a German woman claiming to be Margaret, alive and well, was burned to death as an imposter dubbed 'False Margaret'.[8]

For two years, the Scottish throne lay vacant with the country ruled by the so-called Guardians of Scotland – a committee made up of two bishops, the high steward, the Earl of Fife, and two members of the powerful Anglo-Norman Comyn family who would figure prominently in Robert's life. There were about thirteen nobles insisting they should be ruling Scotland but two figured prominently: Robert V and John Balliol (*c.*1249–1314).

These were two formidable and ruthless figures and the Guardians, displaying a distinct lack of backbone, asked Edward I of England to arbitrate. He recognised a golden opportunity to insert himself permanently into Scottish politics and chose John Balliol in 1292. The Balliols originated in Picardy, France, and the new king's parents founded the prestigious Balliol College at Oxford University. John Balliol grew up on the family's English estates in Northumberland and Durham but now, with the support of the Comyns, he readied himself to be crowned as ruler of the Scottish. One condition of Edward choosing Balliol over Robert was that the new monarch pledge himself as a vassal to the English king, which he duly did. However, two years into his reign, John flatly refused to forcibly enlist his Scottish subjects to help Edward with his wars in France. Worse, he reached out to Philip IV to forge a Franco-Scottish alliance against Edward.

The English king was noted for his volcanic temper and made his feelings plain by sacking the city of Berwick-upon-Tweed in March 1296, killing thousands of its inhabitants. Arguably, this barbaric act was one of the worst war crimes of the Middle Ages.[9] The Scottish army was then routed at the Battle of Dunbar on 27 April. John was captured and forced to abdicate. He was stripped of his titles and imprisoned in the Tower of London until 1299 when he was allowed to retire to the family estates in Picardy. Having got rid of John, Edward established direct rule over Scotland. In his view, the fiction of an independent Scottish monarchy was over. To ram home the point, Edward removed the Stone of Destiny, over which all Scottish monarchs were crowned, from Scone Abbey, taking it to Westminster Abbey in London. It remained there until 1996 when it was returned to its homeland. Quite what the stone is or signifies remains a mystery. Legend has it that it was the pillow on which Jacob rested his head, as described in the Bible, while some researchers believe it is a Bronze Age measuring weight that somehow acquired mystical meaning.[10]

These traumatic events ignited the Wars of Scottish Independence leading to the famous campaigns of William Wallace (aka Braveheart) and his stunning victory over the English at Stirling Bridge on 11 September 1297. Wallace was made Guardian of Scotland in March 1298, leading to an all-out invasion by Edward in July that year with Braveheart defeated at the Battle of Falkirk. He then handed over the guardianship to Robert the Bruce and John Comyn (*c.*1274–1306), nephew of John Balliol. By now, Robert had succeeded his father and grandfather to be the head of the family. The two new Guardians despised each other and the Bishop of St Andrews, William de Lamberton (died 1328), tried in vain to keep the peace between them.[11]

The story of Robert the Bruce versus John Comyn is replete with accusations of treachery and double dealing, leaving neither party covered in much glory.[12] Both men had a strong claim to the Scottish throne but only one was going to occupy it. The other man would have to step aside. Or, as Robert determined, he would have to be removed permanently from the equation. Robert's grandfather had failed in his attempt to be king, losing out to John Balliol. The grandson was resolved to win his fight, even if it meant risking civil war at a time when the English were in a powerful position.

What happened on 10 February 1306 before the high altar of Greyfriars Church in Dumfries is still disputed today. The two rivals agreed to meet in a place where a Christian could expect to be safe, even if the murder of the Archbishop of Canterbury, Thomas Becket, in Canterbury Cathedral in December 1170 should have cast doubt on that notion.

From the scant details available it seems that a heated argument broke out between Robert the Bruce and John Comyn, leading to the former stabbing the latter to death on the altar steps. John's uncle was also slain in the fracas. Was the murder premeditated? Supporters of Robert the Bruce argued that it was an attempt at reconciliation that went badly wrong. Those in Comyn's camp believed this was nothing more than the brutal and calculated removal of a political obstacle. This view was supported in an account by the fourteenth-century chronicler John of Fordun, who claimed that Comyn survived the initial attack. A monk, leaning over the injured noble, asked if he thought he might live, and Comyn replied yes. At which point, Bruce or an associate walked over to coolly finish the job.

In the years that followed, Robert expressed no remorse for this assassination in a holy place. There was no public act of penance or pilgrimage to cleanse his soul. Leaving the altar of Greyfriars splattered with Comyn's blood was a necessary act over which he had no regret. However, the Pope took a different view and shortly afterwards, Robert was excommunicated from the Church. Members of the Scottish clergy who stood by their hero faced a similar fate. Clement V effectively cast Scotland out of the Christian fold and urged Edward in England to bring the Scottish to heel. But on Palm Sunday 1306, in open defiance of the Pope, four bishops crowned Robert as the new king of Scotland at Scone. One of those bishops was Lamberton. Later captured and interrogated by the English, Lamberton tried to claim that he was not present at the coronation, but few had forgotten him being there, giving his episcopal blessing. This meant that, in effect, the people, Church, and king of Scotland had all parted company with the papacy.

This situation has led many to speculate that Templar knights fleeing France in 1307 most likely made a beeline for Scotland because the king there was pitted against the same Pope who had just ordered their destruction. Ergo, they would get a friendly reception from Robert the Bruce who had also been so badly treated by the papacy. He might also value their military muscle. In 1307, this did not look entirely implausible. Though later when the Scottish bishops tried to repair the relationship with Avignon, blatant support for the heretical Templars would not have helped matters. However, those overtures were unsuccessful for a long period and King Robert remained cast out of the Roman Catholic Church until his death in 1329.[13]

Just over a year after the excommunicated Robert the Bruce was crowned king by his equally excommunicated bishops, the orders went out from Avignon to arrest, imprison, and interrogate the Knights Templar. Robert had been hounded out of his kingdom by the English and was holed up on an island off the Irish coast. For now, the English were in control of Scotland. Obedient to the Pope, they set about confiscating all Templar assets north of the border and handing them over to two commissioners appointed by the Hospitaller grand master.

Edward I was dead and a new English king, his son Edward II (1284–1327), had severe misgivings about the papal orders to arrest the Knights Templar and shared his thoughts with other European monarchs, though not the French king obviously. However, medieval realpolitik meant he gave in to the Pope's demands, and so sheriffs were soon appearing at Templar commanderies to arrest everybody present and make an inventory of the goods on site. The prisoners were escorted to the nearest castle or wherever they could be kept under lock and key. The grand master of England, who also oversaw Scotland, was William de la More, who ran one of the wealthiest preceptories in England at Temple Bruer in Lincolnshire. He was apprehended there along with the grand commander of the Auvergne and other top Templars who were then bundled away to Canterbury Castle. Breaking their own rules to fight with the previous English king in his wars counted for nothing as they were clapped in irons.

Many Templars decided not to sit patiently waiting to be arrested and fled. Some cast off their sacred white mantles, hoping to blend into the population. The authorities were hampered in their attempts to track them down by their own lack of records on the Templar order. There was no comprehensive list of names to tick off, so they needed Templars to either voluntarily turn themselves in or be betrayed. The only way to be sure that an individual was missing from a preceptory was to rely on hostile non-Templars to snitch on them. Fortunately for the sheriffs, local priests and bishops rushed forward eagerly with the names of absconding Templars.

The man put in charge of suppressing the Knights Templar on both sides of the border was a bishop who was happier wielding a sword and mace than a crozier and censer. Antony Bek (*c.*1245–1311) commanded military campaigns in Wales and Scotland while simultaneously being a priest who experienced a meteoric rise through the Church ranks, becoming Bishop of Durham and Patriarch of Jerusalem. Taking time out from saying mass in church, he led an English army division at the Battle of Falkirk in 1298, which saw the defeat of 'braveheart', William Wallace (*c.*1270–1305). The Benedictine chronicler, Robert de Graystanes (died 1336), fulminated against this militaristic prelate:

> *This Antony was of a lofty disposition, second to none in the kingdom in splendour, dress and military power, concerned rather with the business of the Kingdom than the affairs of his Bishopric.*[14]

Pope Clement, though, had a high regard for his abilities and he was tasked with rooting out Templars in the British Isles. On 23 September 1309, Bek wrote a letter, co-signed by other leading English clerics, insisting that the Scottish Templars be rounded up. They addressed the letter to senior Church figures in Scotland that were less vocal in their support for Robert the Bruce, or even sympathetic to Edward.[15] The result was a trial of the Templars led by none other than Bishop Lamberton, and a papal representative, John de Solerio.[16] The fact that Lamberton had crowned Robert the Bruce king and was then imprisoned by the English proved to be no obstacle. Following his release, the bishop rapidly developed a strong survival instinct, maintaining friendly relations with both the Scottish and English monarchs. The venue for the trial was Holyrood Abbey in Edinburgh, a city still under English rule in 1309.

Unlike in France, Castile, and Portugal, there were not a considerable number of Templar knights to interrogate, and the leaders were English. Walter de Clifton and William de Middleton gave testimonies. De Clifton, the commander of Balantrodoch, candidly admitted that the initiation rites of the Templars did indeed excite interest because they were conducted in secret. But the rumours of demonic idols and cat-like creatures being worshipped were nonsense. He then went on to discuss the command structure and how Scotland was subordinate to England which in turn received its orders from the grand master in Cyprus.

This was followed by a predictable procession of monks, friars, and abbots who finally had an unmissable opportunity to air their gripes against the knights in public. Adam of Wedale, a Cistercian monk, complained that the Templars were selfish and bad neighbours. Robert, chaplain of Kirkliston, made the remarkable

Roman Catholic monk burns in hell in a Portuguese altarpiece.

Christ embraces Templar champion, Bernard of Clairvaux, in this unusual depiction from a convent in Funchal, Madeira.

King Louis IX, grandfather of Philip IV, was canonised as a saint.

Éliphas Lévi created the image of the demon Baphomet that is known today.

Philip IV of France wanted Templar assets but also sincerely believed in heresy and sorcery.

Edward I of England pledges fealty to Philip IV of France but resented this demeaning act.

The Templars were accused of a kiss not dissimilar to the 'Osculum Infame' delivered by witches to the backside of the devil.

The Beguines — a movement of holy women crushed at the same time as the Templars.

Pope Boniface VIII is captured by Guillaume de Nogaret and Sciarra Colonna before being assaulted.

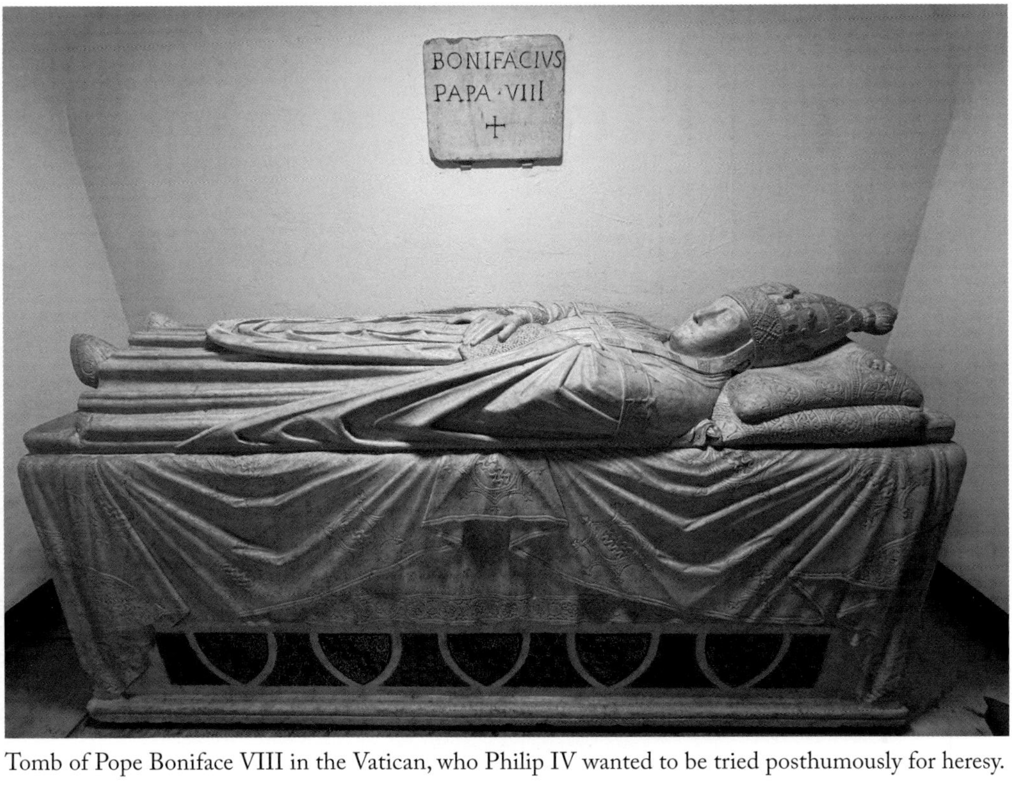

Tomb of Pope Boniface VIII in the Vatican, who Philip IV wanted to be tried posthumously for heresy.

Pope Clement V who presided over the trials of the Knights Templar.

Inside the papal palace at Avignon.

The chapter house of Lincoln Cathedral where local Templars were put on trial.

Temple Bruer — the ruins of a preceptory where the English grand master was arrested.

Templar grand master, Jacques de Molay, is burned at the stake in 1314.

Fra Dolcino led a movement of heretics brutally suppressed by Clement V.

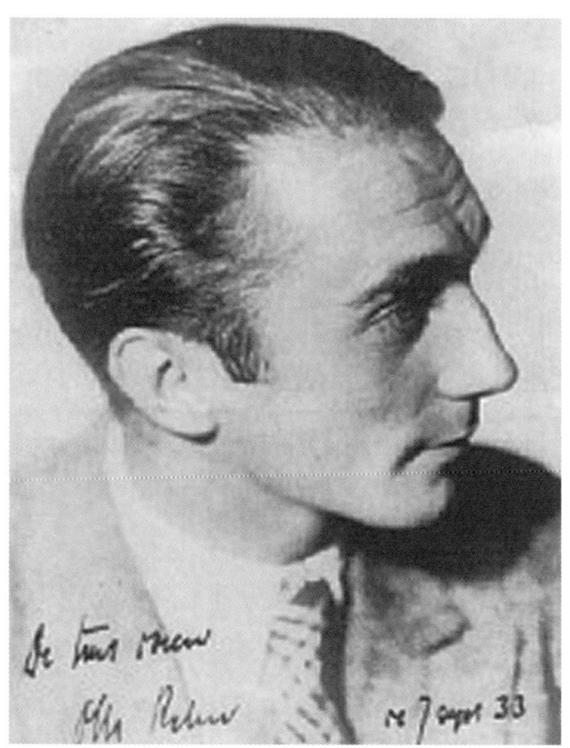

Otto Rahn hunted for the Holy Grail across Europe in an expedition funded by the Nazis, but failed in his mission.

Leading Nazi Heinrich Himmler was obsessed with finding the Holy Grail.

Christ collects his own blood in this curious fifteenth-century statue at the Victoria & Albert Museum, London.

The ruins of Glastonbury Abbey, long claimed to be the home of the Holy Grail.

The Mandylion, some believe to be the Shroud of Jesus, arrives in Constantinople.

Rosslyn Chapel in Scotland, built by the Sinclair family and linked to the Knights Templar.

Afonso Henriques, first king of Portugal, gave huge privileges to the Church and Templars.

The headquarters of the Order of Christ at Tomar that formerly belonged to the Templars.

Christopher Columbus — there are claims of a connection to the Knights Templar.

Pierre Plantard, holding his son, who promoted the idea that the shadowy Priory of Sion had founded the Knights Templar.

French presidential candidate François Mitterrand visits Rennes-le-Château in 1981 with his old friend Roger-Patrice Pelat, wrongly named as a grand master of the Priory of Sion.

Ivanhoe — the nineteenth-century novel by Walter Scott cast the Templars as the villains.

The Knights Templar as zombie demons in this 1970s Spanish horror movie.

Templar knight on Castle Street in Liverpool in 2024 — as popular today as ever.

claim that 'he had never known when any Templar was buried or heard of one dying a natural death, and that the whole order was generally against the holy church'. Abbot Hugh of Dunfermline remarked that the Templars were 'ungracious to the poor, practicing hospitality alone to the great and wealthy, and then only under the impulse of fear'. He added for good measure that if they had been 'good Christians, they would never have lost the Holy Land'. A Franciscan friar, Adam Hercton, told the hearing that as a child, boys at his school would yell: 'Beware of the Templar kiss'. It was now all too clear what that meant — the touch of the sodomite on the lips and base of the spine.

Secular witnesses perjured themselves describing lurid goings-on inside the order. It was highly unlikely they had seen anything because firstly they would have been barred from the order's internal ceremonies and secondly, new initiations had been quite rare in Scotland for some time. Quite what motivated these people to come forward and denigrate the knights is something of a mystery. Though there are some clues.

The renowned Templar historian Helen Nicholson gives a good example of the kind of cynical calculation that was in play during this hearing. Fergus Marshal, a noble, claimed his grandfather had joined the Templars in good health but then died suddenly three days later because he had refused to submit to their sordid demands. But Marshal's grandfather was typical of elderly men of the nobility who entered the order as their life was ending. To ensure a place in heaven, they willed their property to the knights as a final good deed. Only their families might have been hoping to inherit those assets. So, when the Templars were put on trial, individuals like Fergus Marshal seized the moment to try and grab back estates legally gifted to the knights.

In the aftermath of the trials, the assets of the Knights Templar were in the hands of the Hospitallers but in Scotland were managed separately from the rest of the order's estates. As late as 1488, the register of the great seal of Scotland contains a document confirming land grants to an entity referred to by the Latin: *Sancto Hospitali de Jerusalem, et fratribus ejusdem milita Templi Salomonis*. This implies a continued legal recognition of the Templars, distinct from the Hospitallers, although the knights had now vanished. In 1563, the Hospitallers handed over their Templar assets to the Scottish Crown although as late as 1748, it was recorded that owners of former Templar properties were still exempt from taxes, jury service, and compulsory membership of trade guilds. These were privileges dating back to the glory days of the Templars from the twelfth to fourteenth centuries.

The arrest warrants for the Templars were issued to law officers around France a month before they were served and the arrests commenced in late 1307. Central to the hypothesis that Templar knights were able to flee with treasure from France to Scotland is the claim that the issuing of the warrants was leaked. Templar leaders knew in advance what was coming in their direction and acted. The preceptor of France, Gerard de Villiers, fled with fifty horses and set sail with eighteen ships of the Templar fleet. Another Templar, Hugh of Châlons, took the order's treasure to a destination where it would be safe.[17]

There is an oft-repeated theory that the Templars made their way, under cover of night, to the port of La Rochelle and set sail for Scotland. Other theories have the Templars departing from Italy or Aragon, bound for Scottish shores with incalculable wealth. The route taken might have avoided the English Channel and North Sea where English forces could have spotted this maritime convoy. Instead, it's been conjectured that the Templars were forced to travel up the western coast of Ireland, around the Jura, to Argyll. Whichever route they took, evidence for this odyssey is thin on the ground. Undeterred, some have pointed to gravestones in churchyards at Kilmory, Currie, and Culross that are deemed to have Templar characteristics proving the knights were present in these places.

All of which brings us to the Battle of Bannockburn, fought on 23 and 24 June 1314, that pitted the forces of Robert the Bruce against the English army of King Edward II, who needed a victory to stabilise his rule in England. He marched over the border with a vast force of English, Welsh, Irish, and Gascon soldiers believing that he would be unstoppable on the battlefield. His first task would be to relieve the Scottish siege of Stirling Castle and then deal with the resurgent Robert the Bruce. But as the eighteenth-century poet Robert Burns (1759–1796) noted in his famous poem, 'To A Mouse': '*The best laid schemes o' Mice an' Men; Gang aft agley*' (the best laid plans of mice and men often go astray). Edward's plan was about to unravel horribly.

Despite heavily outnumbering the Scots, the English underestimated Robert's strategic brilliance and the high morale of his troops. The Scottish king deployed his soldiers carefully, manoeuvring them on to the most advantageous terrain. Robert had learned from William 'Braveheart' Wallace about the effective use of the 'schiltron', a compact phalanx of pike-wielding infantry, likened to large hedgehogs. During the battle, these advanced then charged at alarming speed, sewing confusion in English ranks. King Edward fought bravely but there was a degree of complacency in his leadership and at a key moment, his forces fled at the sight of the Scottish baggage train yelling and screaming into the fray. Robert had ordered male and female auxiliaries to join battle with whatever they had to hand, giving the impression his army was bigger than perceived. What followed was a bloody rout with the English slaughtered as they sped towards the border. This defeat ended the Wars of Scottish Independence, leaving Robert secure on his throne. Eventually, even the Pope acknowledged his kingship, but without removing the excommunication.

Yet not everybody is convinced that Robert's quick wits won the day against superior numbers. There is an alternative view, promoted by the Victorian historian Reverend Alfred Coutts, that what provoked the English into a panicked retreat was the sight of a Knight Templar cavalry charge heading towards them. Far from overwhelming the English, Robert the Bruce was in trouble until 'a small detachment of armoured knights appeared'. Their white mantles emblazoned with red crosses were unmistakable, as well as the beausant which fluttered over their heads. Grateful for being sheltered by Robert, they now bore down on Edward's troops who dispersed in terror.[18] It was not the baggage train that won the day but the greatest fighting force in Christendom, making their swansong at Bannockburn. Suffice it to say that Scottish nationalists have reacted negatively down the years to the view that foreign Templars drove the English away, as opposed to valiant Scots.

In 1329, Robert the Bruce lay on his deathbed. He begged his close confidante James Douglas (*c.*1286–1330), Lord of Douglas, to take his embalmed heart to the Holy Land and place it in the Holy Sepulchre. He had promised God to go on crusade but fighting the English had always taken precedence. Now he was slipping away in an excommunicated state with his soul unlikely to enter heavenly glory. Here was a gesture that might free him a little sooner from purgatory, that waiting room in the afterlife for those whose sins prevented automatic entry to paradise.

When the king died, Douglas took the royal organ in a small casket, apparently worn around his neck, on a long journey that led him and his band of knights deep into the Iberian Peninsula. There he met King Alfonso XI of Castile (1311–1350) who was fighting the teenage Islamic sultan of Granada, Muhammad IV (1315–1333). Douglas and his Scottish compatriots offered their services. At a place called Teba, the Scots were attacked by a Muslim force and Douglas was run through with a Moorish scimitar. His mutilated body was retrieved by his comrades, the flesh then boiled off, and the bones returned, with Robert the Bruce's heart, to his native Scotland.[19] The dying king's last wish was never to be fulfilled.

When James Douglas was killed at Teba, two other Scots died alongside him. They were Sir William Sinclair and his brother John. The surname is also spelt St Clair, Saint-Clair, and Sanct-Claro, but for simplicity's sake, the name Sinclair will be used for all generations of the family. The Sinclairs occupy centre stage in the story of a Templar flight from France to Scotland. To fringe historians and enthusiasts, they were the protectors of the knights who gave them sanctuary at their lowest ebb and then helped them escape far beyond the boundaries of the known world. It's a fantastic tale resting on the flimsiest of evidential foundations but nevertheless is widely believed.

What are the facts about the Sinclairs? The first in the line was William Sinclair (*c.*1028–c.1078), son of Waldonius, count of Saint-Clair in Normandy, and first cousin of William the Conqueror (*c.*1028–1087). He fought at the Battle of Hastings in 1066, participating in the victory over the Saxons and consequent Norman invasion of England.[20] In a rather hazy sequence of events, Sinclair went to Hungary to rendezvous with a Saxon princess, Margaret (*c.*1045–1093), whose father had been forced into exile. He accompanied Margaret back to Scotland where she married King Malcolm III (*c.*1031–1093). This monarch would feature 500 years later as a lead character in Shakespeare's play *Macbeth* while his wife was canonised as a saint in the year 1250. William became the queen's cupbearer and was granted the Barony of Rosslyn in 1070 by a grateful Malcolm. Rosslyn is also spelt Roslin or Roscelyn, but Rosslyn will be used here.

The second baron of Rosslyn, Henry, accompanied the brother of Queen Margaret, Edgar Ætheling (*c.*1052–1125), on the First Crusade, taking part in the Siege of Antioch in 1098. In 1129, the first Templar grand master, Hugh de Payens, was in Scotland drumming up support for his new order. It's been asserted that the land granted at Balantrodoch to build what was effectively the Templar headquarters in Scotland came from the Sinclairs who were based nearby at Rosslyn. It's also stated that De Payens, before setting up the Templars, was married to a certain 'Margaret St Clair'.[21] This infers Sinclair involvement in the founding of the order through a close relationship with De Payens prior to taking his vow of chastity. However, the genealogical evidence points to De Payens having a wife called Elizabeth de Chappes, therefore no marital link with the Sinclair dynasty.[22]

At the end of the thirteenth century, the Sinclairs were swept up in the Wars of Scottish Independence and the sixth baron ended up imprisoned and dying in the Tower of London for his role in fighting the English. His son Henry (died *c.*1335), the seventh baron, was also held prisoner by the English at St Briavels Castle in Gloucestershire. Together with his two sons, John and William, Henry was alongside Robert the Bruce at Bannockburn. In the aftermath of that victory, he was a co-signatory of the Declaration of Arbroath in 1320, a plea sent by Scotland's nobles to Pope John XXII asking for their country to be recognised as an independent kingdom rooted in ancient history.[23] Sadly for Henry, both the sons that had fought and survived at Bannockburn were killed in Spain with Sir James Douglas, fighting the Moors.

It's with the ninth baron of Rosslyn, another Henry (*c.*1345–*c.*1400), that the Templar escape story to Scotland stretches credulity to breaking point. What is known for certain about this baron is that through his mother's ancestral line, he became a claimant for the earldom of Orkney, which was under Norwegian control. On 2 August 1379, Haakon VI (*c.*1340–1380), king of Norway, invested Henry as the new 'jarl' of Orkney and on paper, his loyalties were divided between the monarchs of Scotland and Norway. When appointed by Haakon, Henry swore an oath of fealty to the king, agreeing to supply soldiers when required to Norway. He also paid an enormous fee up front and promised not to build any castles without prior permission. Maybe thanks to his Norse familial connection, this Sinclair had access to Viking navigational maps that enabled him to take a group of Knights Templar all the way to the New World, a century before Christopher Columbus. That is the theory we now need to examine.

This is a bizarre story that has been built up in layers over the last 500 years linking the Knights Templar, the Sinclair family, and pre-Columbian North America. It all begins with a sixteenth-century Venetian politician and writer, Nicolò Zen the Younger (1515–1565), who in 1558 published the bestseller *Dello scoprimento dell'Isole Frislanda, Eslanda, Engroneland, Estotiland et Icaria fatto sotto il Polo Artico da due Fratelli Zeni* (On the Discovery of the Islands of Frislanda, Eslanda, Engroneland, Estotiland and Icaria made by two Zen brothers under the Arctic Pole). The book revealed, through a series of maps and letters, an expedition by the author's ancestors to America a century before Christopher Columbus.[24] Some spurned it as a desperate attempt by the Venetians, a long-time maritime power, to claim they had reached the Americas first, before Spain or England, but many others regarded the book as entirely credible and still do.[25]

Nicolò wrote about two ancestors, another Nicolò (*c.*1326–*c.*1402) and Antonio (died *c.*1403), who are often referred to as the 'Zeno' brothers. He discovered the story of their voyage into the northern Atlantic in the family archive, quite by chance, and felt obliged to share it with the world. It included a map dating from 1380 showing the unmistakable coastlines of Norway, Iceland, Greenland, and what could be taken for the eastern seaboard of America. Not completely accurate but enough to give the impression that the Zeno brothers knew America was there.

In one voyage into the north Atlantic, Nicolò was shipwrecked on the island of Frislanda but then rescued by the mysterious prince of a neighbouring kingdom, Prince Zichmni. Nicolò joined his navy then wrote to his brother, Antonio, to make haste and join him. Zichmni conquered Frislanda (for which read the Faroes) followed by Eslanda (the Shetlands). After that, the prince's fleet sailed for Engroneland (Greenland), where they met fishermen who spoke of lands further west: Estotiland and Drogeo. They had been stranded in these strange places for twenty-five years where they had seen creatures that defied the imagination and encountered fearsome cannibals who they taught how to fish, which prevented them ending up in the pot themselves. Zichmni and the Zeno brothers set sail for the New World, where they arrived in 1398.

Cartographers, scientists, museum curators, and historians have rushed forward down the centuries to validate the story. Johann Reinhold Forster (1729–1798), a natural historian who accompanied the legendary Captain James Cook on his expeditions, believed the book was entirely truthful. But not everybody agreed. An 1898 report in *The Pall Mall Gazette* dismissed the voyage as 'a great and mischievous imposture'.[26]

There was one detail that has perplexed many and that was the identity of Prince Zichmni. Who was this intrepid warrior, conquering and exploring in the late fourteenth century? In the post-war years, author and historian Frederick Julius Pohl (1889–1991) was keen to prove pre-Columbian contact between the Old and New Worlds with particular emphasis on the Vinland Map, believed in the 1950s to be a genuine fifteenth-century map proving Norse exploration of North America.[27] It has now been comprehensively discredited. Pohl argued that the name Zichmni was a medieval Italian rendition of Sinclair's name, or title, and that after investigating the Stellarton area in the Pictou region of Nova Scotia, he claimed to have found clear evidence of Sinclair's presence there, as well as contact with the local indigenous people, the Mi'kmaq.[28]

Indeed, Pohl argued, it appeared that the native Americans venerated Sinclair as a god-like figure – Glooscap. The only problem with this hypothesis is that Glooscap, as described in Mi'kmaq mythology, is a giant so huge that Nova Scotia is his bed and Prince Edward Island, his pillow. One assumes that in the year 1398 the deity, for reasons best known to itself, shapeshifted into the body of a much smaller medieval Scottish noble. To the Mi'kmaq, Sinclair was the creator of the universe accompanied by other god-like figures – his Templar travelling companions. Together they founded some kind of colony of which no trace remains. But if this is true, they had beaten Christopher Columbus to the Americas. Imagine the sight of those white-mantled medieval knights greeting the local native Americans in what would have been one of the oddest civilisational encounters in history.

Many might scoff but others argue there is evidence for this incredible meeting in Nova Scotia in 1398. They point to the curious red cross on a white background that adorns the Mi'kmaq flag right up to the present day. It's an unmistakable crucifix flanked by a red crescent and red star that the native warriors allegedly copied from Templar iconography. However, sceptics counter that this emblem originated in the eighteenth century when the Mi'kmaq fought alongside the French speaking 'Acadian' population in what would become Canada, against the British. The French Jesuit priest Jean-Louis Le Loutre (1709–1772) helped form joint Acadian and Mi'kmaq militias during King George's War in the 1740s and was most likely responsible for the emblem being added to the tribal banner. It was not a symbol of peace as Le Loutre motivated his Mi'kmaq allies by offering a bounty for English scalps.[29] Alternatively, it could have been the work of another Catholic priest in the previous century. Chrestien Le Clerq was a Franciscan friar who conducted missionary work among the Mi'kmaq in the mid-1600s. In his 1691 account of his travels, *Nouvelle Relation de la Gaspesie,* Le Clerq claimed to have been rescued from starvation when lost in Quebec by the Mi'kmaq who already regarded the cross as sacred and told him this veneration went back deep into their history. This gives hope to those who believe the cross was copied from the emblem emblazoned on the white mantles of the Templars.

Then there is the puzzling engraving of the so-called Westford Knight. Having explored Nova Scotia, Sinclair and his party of Templars reportedly struck south, eventually arriving in New England. On a roadside in Westford, Massachusetts, there is an exposed rock that appears to depict a knight holding a sword, pointing downwards, and a shield. A faintly discernible coat of arms identifies this medieval soldier as Sir James Gunn who, it's argued, was a Templar. What transpired was that Sinclair's group arrived at Prospect Hill, near Westford, and at this point, from unknown causes, Gunn died. A 1983 article in *Atlantic Insight* described the other knights carving a life-sized memorial to their fallen comrade, which can still be viewed today – though it is very worn. In 2003, the *Massachusetts Archaeology Society Bulletin* took a wholly sceptical line declaring the markings were due to glacial erosion and 'not a depiction of a late fourteenth century knight…nor a knight's great sword, a shield, and a crest'.[30]

At the seaside town of Newport, Rhode Island, 100 miles south of Westford, there are the remains of a seventeenth-century windmill known as the Old Stone Mill. Its structure resembles windmills of that period back in England. Yet it's generated several intriguing theories, including the view that this was a small fortress thrown up by Sinclair and his band of knights after they trekked to this spot. From Nova Scotia, this is over 600 miles, which poses the question: why were they travelling such a huge distance? The tower has been the subject of considerable speculation over the years, being attributed to shipwrecked Portuguese sailors, ancient Phoenicians, Druids, or that it was even a fifteenth-century Chinese observatory. Back in 1832, the Danish historian Carl Christian Rafn (1795–1864) was convinced the Vikings were responsible for its construction.

Maybe though the most intriguing proof for a Templar flight to the New World is back in Nova Scotia on a tree-covered island off its south shore that has been attracting treasure hunters for over 200 years. In 1965, the mass-circulation monthly *Reader's Digest* introduced its readers to the fable of Oak Island and its mysterious 'money pit'. The story began in 1795 with a teenager, Daniel McInnes, paddling across to Oak Island to do some bird hunting. 'On a knoll at one end of the island he noticed an odd depression, twelve feet in diameter' and above this, hanging from a sawed-off tree limb, was an old ship's tackle block. He returned with two friends, Tony Vaughan and Jack Smith, and they began digging, convinced they had chanced upon a hidden treasure trove left by pirates.

At both ten feet and then twenty feet down, they hit what appeared to be platforms made of oak logs. All around on the walls, the boys glimpsed the pickaxe marks made by those who had dug the pit. Nearly a decade later, they got the backing of a local businessman, Simeon Lynds, who financed a much deeper dig down to ninety feet in 1804. At this depth, they found a large stone slab impeding their progress, carved with curious symbols. Later a cryptologist deciphered the scratching: *Ten feet below, two million pounds are buried.* Sadly, the slab has since gone missing. On digging further down, the pit flooded with water.

By 1849, McInnes was dead, but Vaughan and Smith persisted and were convinced their drill hit two wooden treasure chests piled one on top of the other but were unable to raise them because of further flooding. In 1850, they found evidence of what they took to be a conduit channelling sea water from the nearby beach into the pit, essentially a booby trap. A later excavation led by Nova Scotia businessman Frederick Blair drove through layers of wood, metal, and cement bringing up flecks of gold and a tiny scrap of parchment with the letters 'vi'. Blair would spend sixty years, and a lot of money, seeking treasure in the pit and was joined in his endeavours by a steady stream of adventurers including a young Franklin Delano Roosevelt (1882–1945), who would go on to become the thirty-second president of the United States.

Theories about what could be on Oak Island, and more specifically in the money pit, have included the Crown jewels of France, spirited away by a maid of the last queen, Marie Antoinette (1755–1793); an original folio of William Shakespeare's plays proving they were written by Sir Francis Bacon (*c.*1561–1626); and the pirate loot of the Scottish privateer, Captain William

Kidd (*c.*1654–1701). But among Templar enthusiasts, the question is whether the knights buried their priceless artefacts brought from Jerusalem, Cyprus, and Paris at this site. And would that have included the Holy Grail and the Ark of the Covenant?

This quest has formed the basis of a multi-season documentary series on History: *The Curse of Oak Island.* The series follows two brothers, Martin "Marty" Lagina (born 1955) and Rick Lagina (born 1952), in their bid to find evidence that treasure was buried in the money pit. Arguably the most notable Templar-related discovery has been the so-called 'Nolan's Cross', a crucifix-shape formed by six large boulders spaced out over a large area, originally identified by Oak Island landowner, Fred Nolan (1927–2016) back in the early 1990s.[31]

The idea that the Holy Grail could have been brought by Henry Sinclair, believed by some to have been a Templar himself, to the New World and buried at a location where it still lies has proven to be very appealing to American TV audiences. But there is another theory about the Sinclairs and the Grail that keeps this sacred chalice, and other holy relics found by the knights in Jerusalem, on the other side of the Atlantic. What if the fleeing Templars hid their treasure in Scotland?

Wind back for a moment to the first years of the Knights Templar. They are founded around 1118 and base themselves on the Temple Mount in Jerusalem, after which they are named. An order of holy warriors combining monastic prayerfulness with a fierce martial spirit. An order of celibate men (and some women) dedicated to fighting for the cross against the crescent. Their mission, as stated publicly, is to defend pilgrim routes to the Christian holy sites but some wonder if they have a clandestine agenda. The knights become very wealthy and establish themselves as bankers to the most powerful people in society. The popes shower them with privileges. Then everything goes into reverse. The Templars are condemned, their assets seized, and the leadership is executed. Stories that they may have found the greatest of biblical treasures cascade down the centuries with the most popular being their supposed ownership of the Holy Grail. Yet all these artefacts disappear into the ether.

When the arrest warrants are issued in France, the order is tipped off and a fleet embarks from La Rochelle, bound for Scotland. The Templars on board are warmly greeted by Sir Henry Sinclair who is not only a Templar himself but descended from two of the grand masters of the Priory of Sion, a secret society that founded the Templars as its military wing to protect the bloodline of Jesus

Christ. He is of Viking and Scottish ancestry and had access to ancient Viking navigational maps which he used to spirit the knights across the north Atlantic to the New World, a whole continent not yet known to medieval Europe. His family had been intimately associated with the Knights Templar since their founding and felt honour bound to accompany them to the ends of the earth if necessary. Sir Henry does eventually return to Scotland. But has he left a colony of Templars back in Nova Scotia?[32]

Fast forward, skipping a generation, and the grandson of Sir Henry is Sir William Sinclair (1410–1480), eleventh baron of Rosslyn and third earl of Orkney. It is this Sinclair who built Rosslyn Chapel, a medieval structure made world famous by the 2003 novel, *The Da Vinci Code* (discussed in more depth in a following chapter).

On a summer afternoon in August 2024, there was standing room only in the nave at Rosslyn as the official guide explained not only the mainstream history of this Gothic church but the many conspiracy theories that have become attached to it. Not least that within Rosslyn are Templar treasures including the Holy Grail and even the embalmed head of Jesus Christ.[33] This macabre item is variously claimed to be under the floor of the nave or within the so-called Apprentice's Pillar.

It is beyond doubt that this enigmatic place of worship is a feast for the senses. The vaulted ceiling is encrusted with curious designs while the walls include ghoulish depictions of the seven deadly sins, the dance of death, and an angel clutching the heart of the Scottish king, Robert the Bruce. The very heart that two Sinclairs died trying to convey to the Holy Sepulchre in Jerusalem. The actual heart was conveyed to the Cistercian abbey at Melrose, which is now a magnificent ruin having been shut down during the Scottish Reformation.[34]

The purpose of the secular, collegiate chapel at Rosslyn was primarily to pray for the soul of its founder, Sir William, and to promote spiritual knowledge. The stunted appearance of the chapel suggests it was intended to be part of a much bigger religious complex, but money problems and the Protestant Reformation from the sixteenth century onwards put paid to that. It's been argued that the striking internal and external imagery at Rosslyn points to Templar involvement in its construction and that it incorporates Gnostic and early Masonic symbols.[35] It's even been suggested that a rudimentary depiction of the crucifixion on the nave wall is in fact the burning of Jacques de Molay in 1307.

Down below in the subterranean sacristy, the walls are covered in mason's marks that have been construed as coded messages, even a Templar map evidencing a journey to the New World. While all over the church, images of vegetation have struck some observers as resembling crops like maize that were only introduced to Europe after the Spanish and Portuguese colonisation of

Latin America. Given that these were sculpted in the early fifteenth century, it therefore provides proof of Sir Henry's journey across the Atlantic a century before Columbus.

The theory of a Templar flight to Scotland has become embedded in neo-Templar and Masonic lore. In the latter version of history, the knights and medieval stone masons, who provided them with shelter and sanctuary, melded into each other forming what became Freemasonry. As will be seen, this has not only been rubbished by mainstream historians but bitterly opposed by non-Masonic neo-Templars over the last 200 years who argue that they alone represent an unbroken line back to the original knights. This will be explained and investigated further in the pages ahead.

It's not impossible that the Knights Templar, persecuted and broken across Europe, looked for a place of refuge. Many may have hoped that if they could lie low for a period, the storm might somehow pass, and the order could re-emerge vindicated.

Did these Templars, who refused to surrender to the authorities, look north to a kingdom ruled by an excommunicated monarch where they hoped to be shielded from the Papal Inquisition? Was the Sinclair clan recognised as faithful friends who would stick by them in their hour of need? And was Scotland a gateway for the knights to strange lands in the west where they could continue their mission? Assuming some knights did escape the clutches of the authorities, they may have headed for Scotland but there is another body of opinion that believes they went south to another kingdom which embraced them warmly.

Chapter Six

Fleeing to Portugal

The Templars were annihilated across Europe, their memory damned and existence wiped from the records, but something very different happened in Portugal. A new military organisation was created, the Ordem do Cristo (Order of Christ), into which Templar assets and knights were funnelled five years after the death of De Molay in 1314. Why was Portugal allowed to pursue a different strategy to the rest of Europe?

The answer lies in a bitter multi-generational feud between the papacy and the kings of Portugal. The thirteenth century saw multiple excommunications, interdicts, accusations of witchcraft, and violence between Church and State. Yet while successive Portuguese kings and popes engaged in a vicious war of words, the Knights Templar diligently continued to fight the kingdom's Muslim enemies, extending the frontiers of the realm.

They were key to consolidating the king's hold on the southern regions of the Alentejo and the Algarve, conquered from the Moors. So, when the rest of Christendom turned on the Templars, imprisoning, torturing, and executing them, Portugal resolved to take a unique approach.

The king who stopped the Portuguese Templars being jailed and butchered was Diniz (1261–1325), the sixth monarch of Portugal. His reign was long at forty-six years and in that time, he centralised royal power, curbed the privileges of the nobility and the Church, established two universities, reinforced the country's defence, and entrenched Portuguese as the national language. He was passionate about poetry as evidenced by the one hundred and thirty-seven poems, seventy-five love songs, and other literary output that he penned. Diniz aspired to be as much a troubadour as a monarch, earning the soubriquet the Poet King (*Rei Poeta*).[1] He was also known to his subjects as the Farmer King (*Rei Lavrador*) for repopulating the south and enacting much needed agrarian reform.

Diniz wed his wife, Elizabeth of Aragon (1271–1336), when she was just 11 years of age. The marriage was consummated in her late teens. As queen, she was noted for her devotion to the poor and would leave the palace in disguise to distribute food on the streets. The legend goes that the king became angry at this irregular conduct and forbade these free handouts. But she persisted. Until one day, Diniz intercepted his wife smuggling bread from the kitchens and asked what was hidden beneath her dress. 'Roses, my lord', she replied. He demanded to see these roses about her person. Obediently, she let her dress fall and miraculously, the bread had transformed into roses. As a result of this and other miracles, Elizabeth was canonised by the Vatican as a saint in 1625. This story recurs in the lives of several holy women including Saint Elizabeth of Hungary (1207–1231) who not only shared the same name as the queen of Portugal but was her great aunt. The two women were declared saints at different times, and both joined the Third Order of Saint Francis – a division of the Franciscans that permitted married people.[2]

Despite his wife's saintly ways, Diniz had a tense relationship with the Church. The problem ran in the family. Generations of Portuguese kings had been excommunicated, denied the sacraments of the Church, and sometimes the entire country was put under an interdict. That meant no church services could be conducted anywhere. The relationship with Rome had started out more promisingly with Portugal's first king, Afonso Henriques.

He had carved his new kingdom out of the neighbouring kingdom of León in 1139, besieging the Moorish city of Al-Usbunna, conquering it and renaming it Lisbon. He was a champion of the military orders, such as the Templars, and the monastic orders, especially the Cistercians. Yet it took until 1179 for the Pope to officially recognise him as a king of a legitimate and independent country.

Afonso was forced to endure decades of uncertainty with the King of León insisting he was a mere vassal. The Leonese monarch regarded Portugal as a region of León over which Afonso was a count, and certainly not a king. Rome eventually obliged Afonso as he had been such a faithful and obedient son. This was at a time of peak papal power in the twelfth century when a king, according to a pope in the previous century, should be 'as obedient and as humbly devoted and serviceable to the holy church'. Afonso displayed the qualities Rome demanded from secular rulers of 'usefulness' (*utilitas*) and 'suitability' (*idoneitas*).[3]

Or put another way, Afonso grovelled to Rome. He pledged himself and his kingdom to the Pope and pleaded to be put under papal protection. The Popes dragged their crimson-slippered feet when it came to obliging him. But in 1179, when the king was already an old man, Pope Alexander III (*c.*1100–1181) issued a bull declaring Afonso to be a bona fide king and Portugal was confirmed as a real kingdom. The deal was sealed on the proviso that the Portuguese agreed to hand over a one-off fee to Rome in the region of 1000 gold pieces. In addition, the papal bull, *Manifestis Probatum*, made it clear that further payments would be expected. After some glowing introductory remarks about Afonso being a 'devoted and glorious son', the Pope got down to business:

As tangible representation that said kingdom belongs to Saint Peter, you have determined as a testimony of great reverence to surrender annually two marks of gold to Us and Our successors. You and your successors will endeavour, therefore, to consign to the Archbishop of Braga pro tempore this census that belongs to Us and Our successors.[4]

This money grabbing document was the poison injected into the relationship between Portugal and Rome. The key clause was a demand that every year, the king send one of his retainers over to the primate of the Church in Portugal with a bag of cash, in return for which His Holiness would continue to shower the kingdom with his blessings. But if payment was not forthcoming, the bull concluded with a very direct threat that should 'anyone, in future, whether an ecclesiastic or secular person' decide not to abide by its terms, they would be 'held accountable for their iniquity before the Divine Judgement and be excluded from the Communion of the Most Holy Body and Blood of Jesus Christ, our divine Lord and Redeemer'.

Pope Alexander was desperate for money to fund his campaign against a rival pope who had been elevated by Rome's nobility, excluding him from entry to the city in 1179. He needed a war chest to topple the latest out of four antipopes who forced him into exile.[5] Aside from his financial woes, Alexander may have also delayed recognising Portugal as a new kingdom because he secretly hoped that once the Muslim emirs were driven out of the Iberian peninsula, then Castile, León, Aragon, and Navarre would reunite as a single Christian empire, as it had been under the Visigoths, before Muslim forces invaded in 711 CE. So, he reasoned, it was best to avoid creating yet another Christian kingdom that would delay that happy outcome. But by 1179, it was obvious that Christian Iberia was going to remain fragmented.[6]

Portugal, under its first king, acquiesced to the Pope's financial demands and allowed the Church significant powers within its borders. There is no doubt that Afonso bristled in private, cursing those puffed-up prelates in Braga, Coimbra, and Porto who exercised far too much temporal power for his liking. Yet while he fumed at the bishops, Afonso had nothing but praise for the Knights Templar, even if they were a military wing of the papacy. The king regarded himself as a 'co-frater', a brother of sorts, within the order. Through his family in Burgundy (his father was a Burgundian noble), Afonso knew many of the early leading lights of the Templar movement including their spiritual guide, Bernard of Clairvaux, with whom he corresponded.

Afonso's son and successor, Sancho I (1154–1211), had much need of Templar muscle after a fresh wave of Muslim forces, the revivalist Almohads, swept into southern Portugal, pushing the country's frontier back up to the River Tagus. It was during Sancho's reign that the Templars, at their fortress in Tomar, central Portugal, led by the ageing grand master Gualdim Pais (1118–1195), repelled a vast Almohad army, a victory that would become the stuff of legend. At one entry point to their fortress, the fighting was so fierce that the blood of the slain reputedly ran down the hillside, which is why today it retains the name: Porta do Sangue (gate of blood). With triumphs like this, Sancho had no hesitation increasing the grants of land and rights to the Templars, Hospitallers, and the Knights of the Sepulchre.

No Christian ruler in Iberia thought the era of Islamic rule was about to end. Therefore, Sancho still sought papal protection, paid the annual tribute due to Rome, and made further endowments to abbeys and monasteries. But points of conflict began to arise. These would lead to decades of tension between the papacy and Portugal in the run up to the destruction of the Templars. The kingdom would go from faithful son of the Church to truculent and rebellious teenager, punished repeatedly by the Holy Father. There were several signposts towards the total breakdown of the relationship between the popes and the kings of Portugal. When Sancho's daughter, Teresa (1176–1250) married Alfonso IX (1171–1230), king of León, the Portuguese king thought he had a good dynastic match that would guarantee peace on his northern border. But Teresa was Alfonso's cousin. The Pope threatened to excommunicate Alfonso if Teresa was not sent home immediately. To Sancho's horror, she reappeared on his doorstep, before shutting herself away in a convent.

Regarding the annual payments to Rome, arrears had been mounting up. The bags of cash never found their way to the Archbishop of Braga. But the matter was not pressed by Rome, so Sancho ignored it. But then Innocent III (1161–1216) was crowned Pope in 1198, a formidable character who was arguably the most powerful Pope of all time. He immediately demanded two of the outstanding amounts.[7] While not explicitly saying that Sancho was his vassal, the Pope made it very clear that he expected Portugal to show ongoing gratitude for all the assistance that had come from Rome.

But Sancho's position towards the Church hardened as his reign progressed. At his side was a wily figure, every bit as formidable as King Philip of France's notorious but brilliant adviser, Guillaume de Nogaret. This Portuguese political mastermind was a physician-cum-politician, Julião Pais Rebolo (died 1215), who was determined to defend the interests of the nation over that of the papacy. Together with the king, he explored ways to push back the power of the Roman Catholic Church in Portugal. They began floating uncomfortable questions. Why was so much land and property in Church hands? How were priests exempting themselves from military service? When could the country be truly independent and in charge of its own destiny?[8]

The average monk, friar, and even bishop kept silent. But Portugal's most senior clerics moved into action, desperate to defend their privileges and power. Astonishingly, an accusation of sorcery was levelled at the king. The Bishop of Coimbra, Pedro Soares, claimed that Sancho was harbouring a known witch inside his palace. Apparently a 'wise woman' who was consulted regarding affairs of state when no answers were forthcoming from his courtiers. The war of words between Sancho and Bishop Soares became so heated that the king had the prelate imprisoned in his palace, along with all his aides. One of them, however, managed to escape and fled to Rome where he briefed Pope Innocent who flew into a blistering rage, firing off a series of reprimands at Sancho. But the king remained defiant. He wrote back to the pontiff with veiled threats about confiscating all Church property in Portugal. His father, Afonso Henriques, had been far too generous, lavishing gifts on a parasitic clergy when he should have invested in those on the frontline in the war against the Islamic caliphate. Pope Innocent was taken aback by Sancho's lack of respect for Christ's vicar on earth:

> *No great prince, however powerful, unless perchance a heretic or tyrant, has ever attempted to write so irreverently or arrogantly to us or to our predecessors.*

However, Sancho was expressing the contempt that a growing number of Portuguese felt towards clerical power. In the kingdom's second city, Porto, the populace revolted against their own bishop, Martinho Rodrigues. This insurrection originated among the newer classes of merchants and traders, as well as waged workers, who were breaking away from the deference of the old feudal system. They felt the impact of episcopal corruption and graft every day of the week, resenting the taxes and levies that funded the bishop's ostentatious lifestyle.

The anger boiled over, leading to a popular invasion of the bishop's palace, a great hulk of a landmark in the city that could hardly be missed. The terrified prelate found himself barricaded inside with a mob baying for his blood. Martinho was besieged for five months until making his escape and dashing to Rome. There, he regaled the Pope with tales of mass sinfulness, convincing His Holiness to place the entire kingdom under an interdict. That meant churches were effectively closed, and the people could not receive any of the holy sacraments. Sancho ignored this inconvenience, encouraging his subjects to continue their lives as usual. But as he neared death, the king made his peace with the Church and handed over 100 golden marks to help bury the hatchet.

Sancho's son, Afonso II (1185–1223), was young but unhealthy, known rather unflatteringly as *O Gordo* (the fat) and *O Gafo* (the leper). Shortly after becoming king, Portuguese Templars joined forces with their Castilian counterparts, and crusaders from all over Iberia, to inflict a stunning defeat on a numerically superior Muslim army led by the Almohad caliph, Muhammad al-Nasir (died 1213). The Battle of Las Navas de Tolosa in 1212 is regarded as a key event in the 'Reconquista', after which Islamic rule on the Iberian Peninsula was steadily restricted to the southernmost tip. Though its impact should not be overestimated.

Las Navas de Tolosa is often presented as the last great military confrontation between Christian and Muslim forces on the Iberian Peninsula and that after that, the Islamic realm was reduced to a small, vulnerable foothold. That is not actually the case. The Islamic world was not prepared to abandon the Iberian Peninsula so easily and fought hard to regain control of what it had lost. As late as the 1330s, the Moroccan-centred Marinid Empire set out to revive the glories of Al-Andalus.

The Marinid sultan, Abu Al-Hasan 'Ali ibn 'Othman (*c.*1297–1351), received a cry for help from the Emir of Granada, Muhammad IV (1315–1333), whose domain covered the southern coast of what is now Spain, including cities like Málaga, Marbella, Ronda, and Almería. The kings of Castile and Aragon were invading, bent on driving him into the sea. Sultan Othman sent 5000 troops and seized Gibraltar from Castile in 1333. Six years later, Castile was back and its king, Alfonso XI (1311–1350), was determined to get Gibraltar back. Not for nothing was he dubbed The Avenger (*El Justiciero*) by his subjects. At the Battle of Río Salado on 30 October 1340, Alfonso of Castile and Afonso IV of Portugal defeated the combined forces of the Marinids and the Muslim army of Granada. Yet Gibraltar did not surrender, only falling to Christian forces in 1462. This shows very clearly that the Battle of Las Navas de Tolosa was by no means the end of Muslim rule on the Iberian Peninsula.

Yet victory at Las Navas de Tolosa provided a huge morale boost to the Knights Templar. They had endured the humiliation of seeing the Almohads reconquer everything south of the River Tagus during the reign of King Sancho. All that hard work, sacrifice, and training went to waste as the forces of Islam surged right back up to the gates of Lisbon. Now the Templars sought vengeance. They helped retake the town of Palmela, but in their sights was their previous stronghold of Alcácer do Sal – the northernmost outpost of Moorish control in Iberia.[9]

Fortune smiled in 1217 when a huge fleet that had set sail from the Dutch port of Vlaardingen, packed with crusaders on their way to the Holy Land, docked in Lisbon. There were an estimated 200 vessels with mainly German crusaders but also Flemish and English troops, all bound for the Fifth Crusade. Back in 1147, a similar force heading for the Second Crusade had been intercepted and convinced by the Bishop of Porto, Pedro Pitões (1108–1152), to help the new kingdom of Portugal take Lisbon from Muslim rule. Now it was the turn of the Bishop of Lisbon, Soeiro Viegas (died 1233), flanked by the Templars and Hospitallers, to convince the new arrivals to stay. Some preferred to continue to Outremer but others, including many English crusaders, saw a quicker opportunity for glory in Portugal. In no time at all, they were camped outside the walls of Alcácer do Sal constructing siege engines and sending sappers deep underground to undermine the city's fortifications.

The weeks dragged on without a breakthrough, and in September, an alarming number of Muslim reinforcements, possibly around 50,000 troops, arrived. They had been sent by the emirs of Seville, Badajoz, and other Moorish cities, keen to stem the Christian advance across the peninsula. Some disheartened crusaders peeled off and resumed their journey to the Holy Land. But the Templars boosted their own numbers with additional support from brothers who came to join them from León. They would provide the vanguard during the final assault on the city. On 12 September 1217, the resolve of the Templars ensured victory, and the Muslims were routed, with the knights pursuing the remnants of their army for three days. Here was proof that the Templars remained the most courageous and disciplined military force at the country's disposal.[10]

However, King Afonso was not present. Surrounded by a team of top jurists, he was figuring out how to boost his revenues at the expense of the country's bishops. His war was as much against the institutional wealth of the Roman Catholic Church as the Muslim Moors in the south and his troops were lawyers and accountants, not knights and squires. The Portuguese historian, Alexandre Herculano, once noted that 'never did so unwarlike a king fight so much' – he may rarely have lifted a sword, but he fought valiantly against bishops and priors with his pen and wax seal.

Afonso set about seizing Church property in earnest and enacting his father's proposals to make priests serve on the battlefield and appear before secular courts. At this stage, the Knights Templar were not viewed as any kind of threat, despite their loyalty to Rome. Afonso's ire was directed at the exceedingly wealthy bishops of Lisbon, Coimbra and especially Braga – the seat of the primate. The Archbishop of Braga, Estêvão Soares da Silva (died 1228), was so rich and powerful in the north of the country that the king barely felt he was in control of that region. The obvious solution was to take over his estates. But the archbishop was not going down without a fight.

The violence that ensued led to royal officials destroying part of the archbishop's palatial complex, forcing him to flee to Rome. Once more, a high-ranking

Catholic prelate was in the eternal city sobbing on the Pope's shoulder. Pope Honorius III (*c*.1150–1227) not only slapped another interdict on Portugal in 1221 but excommunicated the king in person. That meant any other Christian monarch could now invade Portugal with effective papal blessing. A fact not lost on Honorius who exhorted the neighbouring king of León to do exactly that.

Far from climbing down, Afonso got embroiled in an unpleasant row between the dean of the cathedral of Lisbon, Vicente Hispano, and Bishop Soeiro, who had been spending a great deal of time crusading alongside the Templars. Straight after the victory at Alcácer do Sal, Soeiro and the Templar leadership begged the Pope to let Portugal retain the foreign crusaders who had joined their forces. They wanted to create an unstoppable momentum that would destroy the rule of Muslim Al-Andalus once and for all. But they were slapped down by Rome as the Holy Land needed every soldier it could get. Portugal could retain its own native crusaders for the Reconquista but not purloin soldiers from other countries.

Soeiro's prolonged absence from Lisbon had not gone unnoticed in his diocese. Vicente, an ambitious dean, took full advantage of the bishop's extended leave on crusade to do things his way. When Soeiro returned, he was determined to reassert his authority over the dean. However, Afonso admired Vicente's administrative skills and spotted an opportunity to needle the Church, so supported the dean in his growing feud against the bishop. Vicente was no mild-mannered cleric but a ruthless character who attempted to murder his critics and even his own successor as dean. None of which had an adverse impact on his career as he went on to become the next king's first minister.

Afonso, meanwhile, was running out of time. His leprosy was killing him, and in a weakened state he extended the smallest of olive branches to Rome. But it was too late, and he died excommunicated. In one last act of ecclesiastical vindictiveness, the Archbishop of Braga refused to give the dead king a church burial. His hurt feelings, he declared, could only be assuaged by payment to himself of 6000 gold coins (called 'morabitinos'), the immediate repair of his property, another 50,000 gold coins to be deposited at the monastery of Santa Cruz in Coimbra, and the punishment of royal officials who had insulted his high office by their conduct. From the grave, the late king made his views known. His last will and testament pointedly left bequests to the Templars and Hospitallers but nothing to the bishops he so hated.

It was now very clear that Portugal had moved from beloved and obedient child of the Church, ever faithful and grateful to Rome, to a surly, defiant youth despising its Holy Father. The kingdom wanted to mature and felt its growth was being held back by an overbearing and corrupt web of bishoprics and monasteries.

Into this volatile situation came a new order of friars preaching the vow of poverty, and emulating the life and teachings of Jesus. Exactly the kind of message that no bejewelled bishop in Portugal wanted to hear at that moment. Martinho Rodrigues was still Bishop of Porto, despite his bitter clash with King Sancho, and dire relations with his son. His response to the Franciscans was to run them out of town and burn down their friary. Yet again, the people revolted against their own bishop who sheepishly permitted the newcomers to return. As with the Templars, the Franciscans encountered jealousy and resentment from other sections of the Church who believed that bequests that would once have come to them were now going to the poverty-advocating friars. Another new order of friars entering Portugal at around the same time were the Dominicans who put more of an emphasis on teaching the correct version of the faith than the Franciscan preoccupation with visible poverty. The Dominicans were the scourge of heresy and would play a leading role in the Spanish and Portuguese Inquisitions.

The discord between Church and State steadily worsened. Bishop Rodrigues sent the Pope a long list of accusations against the king. Bishop Soeiro claimed priests were being blackmailed by royal officials who kicked down their doors, found them in bed with concubines, and then demanded hush money. Worse, Jews were being favoured for official posts. In fact, this was nothing new. King Afonso Henriques and his successor, Sancho, appointed Jews to very senior positions, with the latter choosing a learned scholar, José Ben Yahia, to be high steward of the kingdom.[11] Portugal still had large Jewish and Muslim populations throughout the thirteenth and fourteenth centuries and their talents could not be ignored.

Yet the bishops weaponised this, whispering in the Pope's ear that inter-faith marriage and other heretical associations were being actively encouraged. Only they could ensure Portugal would unite around one faith, Roman Catholicism, as the kings were surrounded by clever Jews and fake converts to Christianity. And to really rile the Pope, the bishops repeated their usual gripes about priests being forced into military service or – horror of horrors – being dragged before the secular courts to account for their crimes. But the Pope also heard the king's side of the story. Afonso countered that the bishops were spreading lies and gross calumnies. As an example of their unethical behaviour, the king claimed they cynically ordained friends and associates into the priesthood who wanted to weasel out of army service or avoid a criminal conviction in the courts. Literally tonsuring their buddies as royal officials approached.

After Afonso II succumbed to his leprosy, his son was crowned as Sancho II (1207–1248). Despite his popular nickname, The Pious (*O Piedoso*), Sancho continued the now firmly established Portuguese royal tradition of bust ups with the papacy. In one incident, he became embroiled in the election of a new bishop of Lisbon by burning down the house of a candidate he did not favour and murdering several priests who complained. This alleged conduct led to his excommunication by Pope Innocent IV (*c.*1195–1254) who then incited the king's brother, Afonso, the Count of Boulogne, to invade and take the throne. The usurper succeeded but if the Pope expected the new king to be a compliant tool, he was soon to be disappointed.

Afonso III (1210–1279) desperately wanted the throne and grovelled before the Portuguese bishops promising to be 'ever obedient to the Roman church, his mother, as befitted a Catholic prince, no doubt nor deceit being admissible in this promise'. Everything would return to the way it had been under Portugal's first king, Dom Afonso Henriques. With the death of Sancho in the Castilian city of Toledo, Afonso mopped up all opposition. In the years that followed, with the help of the Templars, he extended Portugal to the southern coastline.

It should have been a moment to celebrate but Afonso was set on the same collision course with the Church experienced by his father and grandfather. He craved a steady flow of revenue, more financial transparency, and less corruption. Yet the Church stood in his way. For example, it rankled that Porto, the kingdom's second city, was in effect governed by its bishop with little accountability to the monarch.

Pushing ahead with reforms, Afonso provoked the Archbishop of Braga and bishops of Porto, Coimbra, Guarda, and Viseu to head for Rome with a familiar litany of complaints. The death of Pope Clement IV (1190–1268) gave Afonso a brief breathing space but the new head of the Church, Gregory X (*c.*1210–1276) resolved to put the king in his place. The Dominicans were ordered to file reports on the king's conduct. In September 1275, Gregory issued a bull fulminating against fifty years of conflict between Rome and Portugal. The pontiff demanded total submission – nothing less. All the rights and privileges of the Church were to be restored or else the consequences would be dire. But Afonso now revealed a rare talent for procrastination, fobbing off Rome for years. Pope Gregory died followed to the grave by Pope Innocent V (1225–1276) and Pope Adrian V (*c.*1210–1276), while Afonso continued to waffle. Then, in an apparent stroke of luck, a Portuguese cardinal, Pedro Julião, was elected the new Pope, John XXI (*c.*1215–1277). His father was Julião Pais, the former chancellor to Sancho I. Afonso hoped for a more sympathetic hearing from a fellow countryman, but this papacy came to a sudden, catastrophic end.

Pope John was a trained physician and an outstanding scientist. He wrote a detailed medical treatise, the *Thesaurus Pauperum* (The Pauper's Treasury), detailing cures for mental and physical conditions from baldness to insomnia, gallstones to impotence.[12] He had a special study built in the papal palace to conduct his scientific enquiries, but it was constructed far too hastily. While poring over his books one evening, the ceiling collapsed on the Pope, killing him.

The dead pontiff's critics murmured that he had been engaged in necromancy – the conjuring up and controlling of evil spirits.[13] Obviously God had then punished him by literally bringing the roof down. Ironic that a Pope of the same name, John XXII, would set up a papal commission just over forty years later to investigate the growing threat posed by necromancers. This was an especially unhappy accident for Afonso who insisted to papal representatives that John XXI had been about to scrap the bull of Pope Gregory demanding he make huge concessions, which the king described as 'the diabolic ordination'. However, he could produce no written evidence that this was the case and in October 1277, Afonso was excommunicated. This sparked a civil war in Portugal, which wrecked his health. The king breathed his last in January 1279.

While relations with Rome were dire, those military orders directly answerable to the Pope had, by and large, cordial relations with the kings of Portugal. On occasions, the only thing that restrained a Pope from excommunicating the Portuguese king was the need to maintain morale in the ongoing crusade by the monarchy, the Templars, and the Hospitallers against the Moorish foe to the south.

The Reconquista had been a 500-year struggle by the time Afonso III died. Back in 711 CE, Muslim forces had flooded across the Strait of Gibraltar and conquered almost the entire Iberian Peninsula. This ended the rule of the Visigoths – originally regarded as 'barbarians' from the north who had ruled the entire land mass since the closing years of the western Roman Empire in the fifth century CE. They had established a flourishing Christian civilisation stretching from the Algarve to the Pyrenees. But their rule ended in a conflict between rivals for the throne where one of the parties, rather unwisely, called on the Muslim Umayyads in north Africa to assist his claim. They crossed the Strait of Gibraltar, liked the fertile land they saw, and invaded the entire peninsula.

However, within a hundred years, the Moors (a term used to describe the Muslim invaders derived from Latin word 'Maurus', a native of the province of Mauretania) were pushed out of the north-west of the peninsula. An area covering Galicia in modern Spain and northern Portugal became the first rebel crusader kingdom. In the centuries that followed, more Christian realms emerged such as Castile, León, Navarre, and Aragon, pushing the once invincible Muslim caliphate to the southern half of the peninsula. This effort was further aided by the creation of Portugal, which essentially split off from León. As early as 1128, the Templars were granted a castle at Soure and to the country's first king, Afonso Henriques, they were an essential part of his strategy to create a realm ruling the entire Atlantic coastline.

As the frontier moved south from the River Douro to the Mondego and then the Tagus, it was the Knights Templars who were entrusted with holding the frontline against the Muslim rulers of Al-Andalus. To the Moors, cities like Lisbon and Silves were as much part of their world as Fez, Cairo, and Baghdad. They had no intention of surrendering them. Yet in 1147, an international crusader army, alongside the Templars, took Lisbon and other nearby cities. In 1157, Gualdim Pais (1118–1195) became the Portuguese Templar grand master and created the order's formidable citadel at Tomar in 1160. Much of it is still standing today including the octagonal 'charola' tower, modelled on the Holy Sepulchre in Jerusalem. An attempt by the Almohads to take Tomar was repelled in 1190. After that, the city became the nerve centre of Templar activity in Portugal and a place where the Jewish community thrived under the order's protection.

Much has been written about the Templars being the shock troops of Portugal defending the line between the crusader north and Moorish south. But they were in other parts of the country – and the signs can still be seen. The north-easternmost province of Portugal is the inland territory of Trás-os-Montes, which translates as 'behind the mountains'. Isolated and poor, it is geographically closer to the medieval Spanish kingdoms of Galicia and León than to Portuguese cities like Lisbon, Porto, and Coimbra, where there is still a tendency to look down their noses at the perceived rednecks of Trás-os-Montes.

It is a region that has retained pre-Christian traditions such as the annual hellraising by demonically attired figures known as 'Caretos' who run amok in local villages wearing leather or wooden masks and a bizarre fluffy costume in yellow, red, and green. They jingle cowbells tied to their waists as they dance around and grab at young women. Younger boys follow them, given the rather grim name of 'Facanitos', or little knives. This normally takes place on Shrove Tuesday marking the final day before the period of fasting in Lent, ahead of Easter. It's believed that the antics of the Caretos derive from a pagan celebration of the end of winter and the beginning of spring.

The mainstream view is that Trás-os-Montes was ignored by the Moors, when they invaded Spain and Portugal in 711 CE, as they preferred warmer climes and the urbanised south to the rugged mountainous terrain of the north-east. But this ignores Moorish power in the Iberian Peninsula at its height which extended far into the north and seemed boundless in ambition. Conquering northern Portugal was facilitated by the old Roman road network and for about 150 years, Trás-os-Montes fell to the Islamic caliphate. It was only the emergence of the Asturian Christian kingdom far to the north in modern Spain that eventually saw the Moors pushed back in the ninth century CE.

Even if there were no significant Moorish strongholds in Trás-os-Montes, its cultural influence was undoubtedly felt. Legends about magical Moors continued for centuries. More significant in the region was the presence of Jewish communities, which grew during the Middle Ages as Jews fled the Inquisition to areas where they felt safer. Today in the city of Bragança, the Sephardic Jewish influence on the region is documented at the Centro de Interpretação da Cultura Sefardita do Nordeste Transmontano (Interpretation Centre for the Sephardic Culture of the Nordeste Transmontano).

So, what were the Knights Templar doing in a political and economic backwater of the kingdom of Portugal? From the year 1160, they constructed a castle, parts of which are still standing today including the tower, squatting on a volcanic boulder. The land was donated to the order by a local noble, Fernão Mendes. Moorish power was by no means dead on the Iberian Peninsula with battles still being fought to the south and east against various emirs. But there was also the threat posed to the new kingdom of Portugal by its Spanish neighbours in the kingdoms of León and Castile. They were by no means reconciled to the idea of Portugal effectively breaking away from León and declaring itself an independent kingdom with its own monarch. Portugal had been a mere county of León and from their perspective, that was the way things should remain.

This meant that, not for the first or last time, the Templars were caught up in Christian dynastic politics, which must have imposed strains on the organisation as Portuguese and Spanish Templars clashed at chapter meetings over which side to support. Nevertheless, we never see Templars fighting each other so the order's internal strength must have overcome all divisions. The castle at Mogadouro was one of several sturdy fortifications including others at Algoso, Mirando do Douro, Outeiro de Miranda, and Vimioso. Initially holding the line for Christendom against Islam in the north-east of the Iberian Peninsula but increasingly facing fellow Christians in León and Castile.

When the Templars were crushed in the first decades of the fourteenth century, the castle was peacefully transferred to the new Order of Christ – the successor organisation to the Templars in Portugal – in the year 1319. This was in marked contrast to other parts of Europe where Templar property was handed over to the rival Knights Hospitaller or taken back by the local nobility.

After 200 years of fighting the Moors on the Iberian Peninsula, in 1307 the Knights Templar in Portugal were faced with the prospect of imprisonment, torture, and execution. King Philip of France had turned on the French knights, determined to terminate the order entirely. Pope Clement V, running the Catholic Church from Avignon in modern France, issued a string of papal bulls to the crowned heads of Europe ordering them to follow the French example and annihilate the Templars. Clement informed the Archbishop of Braga and the Bishop of Porto that they were to be the administrators of the Templar assets in Portugal, while on 3 January 1308, the Pope demanded that Diniz begin arresting all the knights. He should jail them, extract confessions by whatever means necessary, and send the evidence on to Avignon.

Among Europe's monarchs, there was a ripple of unease. What were the French doing? Why were the Templars being singled out for this treatment? On 4 December 1307, barely a month after the French began mass arrests, Edward II of England (1284–1327) wrote to the kings of Portugal, Castile, Aragon, and Sicily outlining his reservations about the accusations being levelled at the knights. Candidly, Edward told Diniz that he did not see a quest for justice on the part of the French king and the Pope, but cupidity and envy.[14]

It's somewhat ironic that twenty years later, Edward faced very similar accusations to those levelled at the Templars with regards to indecent behaviour and inappropriate relationships. Indeed, the English bishop who took the lead in prosecuting Edward, Adam Orleton (died 1345), honed his legal skills working at the papal court in Avignon during the Templar trials. As with the knights, Edward was similarly accused by Orleton of the crime of sodomy, alongside his other misdemeanours.[15]

Three of the recipients of Edward's letter, the kings of Portugal, Castile, and Aragon, joined together to resist any attempt by the Church to take over Templar properties in their respective realms. There would be no change in legal title without their royal assent. If the bishops and Hospitallers on the Iberian Peninsula were expecting an imminent Templar windfall, it was never going to materialise. Their snouts were kept well away from the trough.

Any resulting tensions rarely exploded into open conflict, with the notable exception of Estêvão Miguéis, the king's confessor, who became bishop of Porto, then Lisbon, and was appointed by Pope Clement to be Portugal's lead inquisitor, taking personal control of torturing the kingdom's Templars. Relations with the king soured, leading to Diniz accusing the bishop's nephews of murder and sentencing them to death. With this dramatic move, the king made it very clear that he alone would decide policy on the Templars and not the bishop, who wisely climbed down.

So, what motivated the Portuguese king to adopt a benign stance towards the Templars? Some see Diniz as the saviour of the order. In this rosy scenario, he appreciated that the knights had fought bravely to create the kingdom of Portugal, pushing back the boundaries of the Islamic caliphate. Even the very shape of the country was like a downwards thrusting dagger into the heart of the Moorish realms. Diniz could not permit the Templars, the shock troops deployed by his ancestors, to be so appallingly treated. He had inherited his father's gift for prevarication and played for time, while devising a cunning exit strategy for the knights. Something that would not involve throwing them in dungeons, subjecting them to inquisitors and burning their leaders in public squares.

Like Portugal's first king, Afonso Henriques, Diniz felt a strong connection to the Templars and believed his kingdom had been the fulfilment of their crusading mission. He would fob off the Pope for as long as possible, while bringing the order under his protection. It took years to realise his plan, creating a brand-new order into which they were subsumed. It took some tough diplomacy with the Pope, but it happened. A new entity called the Order of Christ was initiated and the Templars were simply re-branded and able to continue their mission.

However, the king's actions can be interpreted more negatively. Like his father and grandfather, his primary motive was to extend royal control over the whole of Portugal and roll back ecclesiastical power. The Templars were, in the final analysis, an armed wing of the papacy. Philip in France resented having an armed body of men on his soil who were not fully accountable to him, and so did Diniz.

But what really seems to have irked the Portuguese king was Templar ownership of so many estates given to them by Portugal's first king, Afonso Henriques, and his mother, Teresa. Two months before the arrest warrants were served on the Templars in France, in October 1307, Diniz was already questioning the legal title that the knights had on certain parts of the country. The royal procurator to the king, Domingo Martins, argued that the Templar's legal titles to the towns of Soure and Idanha-a-Velha were not sound. This was an astonishing assertion as Soure had been gifted to the Templars by Teresa back in the year 1128, while Idanha-a-Velha was dominated by a sturdy Templar castle thrown up on the remains of a Roman temple to Jupiter in the previous century.[16]

What was the king doing? Maybe, having observed the Templar retreat from the Holy Land, Diniz reasoned along similar lines to King Philip in France. The opportunity now arose for the Portuguese king to achieve what his father and grandfather had craved, to take back properties granted to the Church in the early days of Portugal's history. Therefore, far from protecting the Templars, Diniz was moving in for the kill.[17]

A special commission was set up to investigate the Templar ownership of Soure and Idanha-a-Vehla, before which the Portuguese grand master,

Vasco Fernandes, was ordered to appear. He questioned the authority of this commission but when that was brushed aside, pleaded for more time to build the order's case. He needed to consult with Jacques de Molay, the overall grand master of the Templars, and source ancient property deeds. However, in June 1308, Fernandes failed to show up at a hearing and the Crown took what it wanted on 19 January 1310. Diniz grabbed just under a fifth of Templar assets in Portugal. Admittedly, these assets were later transferred to the new Order of Christ, but this was hardly done in a cordial manner. First, the king seized the property, and then, years later, placed these estates in the new order.

This confiscation of Templar property was not exclusive to Diniz. Other Iberian monarchs were acting in a similar manner. The King of Castile pawned two Templar castles in the Badajoz region of Castile to Diniz in return for 3600 marks to fund his war against the emirate of Granada in his bid to retake Gibraltar from Muslim control. The castles were at Burguillos del Cerro and Alconchel. Diniz had no qualms about this transaction. Throughout the Iberian Peninsula, Templar properties were now treated as assets of the Crown that could be used as collateral for a loan. Fortresses that had once held the line against Muslim emirs became part of the property portfolio of Christian monarchs.

Veering back towards a more positive analysis of Diniz, maybe the king realised that optics are everything in politics. Appearance is just as important as reality. He was going through the motions of publicly beating up the Templars to throw the Pope a bone while ringfencing their assets under royal protection to let them re-emerge under new branding a few years later. It displayed a certain cunning and an ability to think several moves ahead. Unlike his ancestors, Diniz had no appetite for being excommunicated, nor did he want to provoke hostility from his bishops. The latter found it difficult to hide their annoyance at not being able to snap up Templar assets for their bishoprics and found themselves in a difficult position between loyalty to the king and obedience to the Pope.

Of lesser importance but worth noting was medieval public opinion in Portugal. How did the average person in Porto or Lisbon view the Knights Templar and this proposed persecution? On the Iberian Peninsula, the mainstream image of the Templars was different to perceptions in England, France, or the Holy Roman Empire. In those northern European countries, interface with the order involved Templar sergeants and retainers herding sheep, selling dairy products in the market, and issuing loans. They were more likely to be seen milking a cow than swinging a sword. Fully-fledged knights were drafted to the frontline in the Holy Land while the commanderies back home literally churned out the wealth to fund the crusades.

But on the Iberian Peninsula, there was a crusade on the doorstep against the Islamic realms to the south. The sight of armed knights on horseback charging to the battlefield was not alien, but familiar. The landscape was dotted with forbidding fortresses intended to keep out the Moors and rival Iberian kingdoms. In Portugal, the Templars also patrolled the coastline to ward off pirate attacks on villages where the inhabitants ran the risk of being carried off into slavery. It's fair to imagine then that feelings towards the knights were very positive in what is now modern Spain and Portugal compared to northern Europe, where they were often viewed simply as landlords, bankers, and royal advisers, part of the hated elite.

How did the Templars themselves in Portugal react to the threat of arrest? Whether Diniz shared his thoughts with the Templar leadership is something lost in the mists of time. His strategy may also have evolved from one year to the next, feeling his way to a workable solution. It seems unlikely the king had everything figured out from the moment he heard about the French arrests. But the core idea of national control over Church assets had been a theme of his dynasty since the first king, Afonso Henriques, died. Could the Templars read his mind? Were they reassured? They had to wait a long time for Diniz to set up the replacement organisation, the Order of Christ, into which all Templar assets were poured. From the year the Pope ordered arrests, in 1307, to the year another Pope agreed to the setting up of the Order of Christ, in 1319, there must have been many nail-biting moments.[18]

This has led to some confusion about the movement of leading Templars during this period. Take for example, the Portuguese Templar master, Vasco Fernandes. He would be the last person to hold that role – the regional equivalent of Jacques de Molay. Only Fernandes would fade into obscurity as opposed to being tied to a stake and burned to death. However, on 13 February 1312, the king of Castile and León, Fernando IV (1285–1312), wrote a letter to the master of the Order of Alcántara (*Orde de Alcántara),* Gonzalo Perez, informing him that he had Fernandes in custody, apprehended on Castilian soil with 50,000 livres tournois (an eye watering sum of money) on his person. Had he been caught in the act of fleeing Portugal?

An alternative account is that it shows Fernandes enjoyed freedom of movement and he was simply in Castile on business arranging a loan with Templar money. There is further evidence of Portuguese Templars moving across the border in documents from 1317 and 1319 and that they may have ended up under lock and key in neighbouring Castile. All of which suggests that in the years between Pope Clement's initial crackdown on the Templars in 1307 until the founding of the Order of Christ in 1319, many knights were not convinced that Diniz was going to save their skins.[19] The Templars could have been in two minds about the Portuguese king, hoping he would guarantee their survival while having a Plan B in reserve.

The backdrop to King Philip of France cracking down on the Templars was the loss of the Holy Land. How could all that Templar wealth, land, and personnel be justified when they had lost their raison d'être? But this was not the case in Portugal. There was still an ongoing crusade with an enemy at the door.

Diniz became king in 1279, and he was still consolidating his grip on the Algarve, only recently taken from Moorish control. In addition, the emirate of Granada and its north African allies posed a threat to Portugal and Castile. Nevertheless, there is a hint of institutional instability within the Portuguese Templars that points to a problematic relationship with the king. From his coronation in 1279, Dinis presided over a rapid succession of six Templar regional grand masters: Beltrão de Valverde, João Escritor, João Fernandes, Afonso Pais-Gomes, Lourenço Martins, and then the last master, Vasco Fernandes. This kind of turnover at the top of any organisation throws into question its internal morale and sense of purpose. Some Portuguese historians believe that whereas previous kings left the Templars to their own devices and trusted their judgement, Diniz was more interventionist from the start of his reign. As a natural born administrator, he could not leave the Templars alone. Did this lead to masters burning out with the stress of it all?

While the Knights Templar in Portugal were not put on trial, there was a commission of inquiry set up under the auspices of the Bishop of Lisbon, João Martins de Soalhães (*c*.1253–1325) who interrogated twenty-eight Templars at a hearing in the Galician town of Orense, which is over the border from Portugal in what is now Spain. The reason for why the Bishop of Lisbon was conducting his business on Castilian soil comes down to the complex organisation of the Catholic Church in Iberia and rivalries between the Archbishop of Braga, in Portugal, and the Archbishop of Santiago de Compostela – the site of a major shrine to Saint James the apostle. The latter prelate still believed he should have authority over Portugal – an argument that went back to when Portugal was just a county within the kingdom of León. In the centuries-long turf war between Spanish and Portuguese clerics, the border was often ignored.[20]

The commission heard nothing but pledges of loyalty to the Crown from the Templars interrogated, and a recounting of their long and proud history fighting the Muslim enemy and helping to create the kingdom of Portugal. They had received lands from the kings to 'plough and improve' and the income derived from this activity had gone towards the crusade against the Moors. The monarchy often built castles and villas for members of the royal family on Templar land, but this had never been a bone of contention – neither was the collecting of rents by State officials for the king's treasury. The Portuguese Templar master's movements were always conveyed to the king, which was why the bizarre appearance of Fernandes in Spain carrying sacks of money was reported back to Portugal. In short, the Templars had done nothing in Portugal that merited being flung into dungeons, tortured without mercy, and burned at the stake. News of what was happening to their French brothers must have caused inconceivable levels of anxiety.

So, was Diniz a friend or enemy of the Templars? On balance the evidence points to an underlying desire to prevent the Pope getting his way. Like his ancestors, Diniz wanted to clip the wings of the Church and all its various agencies. But unlike them, he avoided unnecessary conflict. His strategy was to play for time; wait for the trials in France to run their course and then propose a solution for Portugal that would best serve the Crown's interests. However, from early on the Pope knew Diniz was prevaricating, along with his fellow Iberian monarchs. He demanded action in January 1308 and in December of the same year issued yet another bull, furious in tone, that insisted on arrests and inquisitorial procedures in Portugal, by which he meant torture. Over three years later, on 18 March 1311, Pope Clement was writing to the King of Aragon demanding to know if confessions were ever going to be forcibly extracted from the knights in his realm. At around the same time, there is evidence that a benefactor called Afonso Pires Ribeiro made a sizeable donation to the Portuguese Templars, revealing that they continued to exist as a functioning entity.[21] At the end of 1311, the Pope ordered the Archbishop of Braga and the bishops of Porto, Lamego, and other Portuguese clerics to join him in Avignon at the Council of Vienne which, on 22 March 1312, officially outlawed the Templars.

Diniz responded with some more property seizures and light-touch commissions of inquiry, but no arrests, torture, or executions. Then in April 1314, the king received some welcome news: Pope Clement was dead. The architect of Templar destruction had passed away. It took two years to find a replacement but, in his place, came Pope John XXII, whose abiding interest was the prevalence of witches and sorcerers. The mood music between Lisbon and Avignon changed. Diniz accelerated his plans to create a new organisation: the Order of Christ. When Pope John attempted to give Tomar away to an Italian cardinal, who may also have been the Pope's 'nephew', Diniz slapped this down in 1317.[22] All Templar property was coming into his hands only.

On 14 March 1319, Pope John XXII issued the bull *Ad Ea Quibus Cultus Augeatur* that created the *Ordo Militie Jesu Christie* (Order of Jesus Christ) in Portugal.[23] He declared the new order would be 'the fist of Christ' (*pugillum Christi).* Its headquarters would be at Castro Marim, at the mouth of the Guadiana River in the Algarve, and not Tomar – the Templar base of operations in central

Portugal. Why this location? Based in the south-eastern corner of the Algarve, it bordered Castile and was well positioned for anticipating any aggressive moves from the Moors in Granada or across the Strait of Gibraltar in Morocco. The castle, on top of a hill, was deemed to be impregnable. However, in 1357, the order was relocated to Tomar. All the towns seized from the Templars in the preceding years, like Soure and Idanha-a-Nova, were rolled into the new order.

Two years before, Pope John created the Order of Montesa in the kingdom of Aragon, also on the Iberian Peninsula, which absorbed Templar assets in that country. But there was a subtle difference between that new body of knights and the Order of Christ. Because the Order of Montesa effectively amalgamated Hospitaller and Templar assets into one new order, while the Order of Christ was a de facto continuation of the Templars under a new branding.[24] This may seem a hair-splitting point, but it was critical to how the Portuguese order perceived itself and operated, as well as how it was viewed by others, including the papacy.[25] This deft manoeuvre by Diniz meant that no Templars in Portugal were arrested, tortured, put on trial, or executed. Instead, the Knights Templar quietly slid into a new framework and, for the moment, continued in the usual manner.

Dinis nationalised other military orders in Portugal, getting permission from the Pope to split off the Portuguese knights who were members of the Castilian-run Order of Santiago into a new body and similarly, to obtain total independence for the Military Order of Saint Benedict of Aviz (*Ordem Militar de São Bento de Avis)*, which had been beholden to the Castilian Knights of Calatrava. After this, only the Knights Hospitaller remained a truly international order operating in Portugal. All other knights were now under royal control.[26]

For those who believe that the Templars spirited vast treasure out of the Holy Land, the question remains: where was it taken after the arrest warrants were served on the knights throughout France and then the rest of Christendom? Scotland is the widely favoured destination, especially among Masonic historians, but the other is Portugal. The reason given is that the Templars were afforded protection by the king and their properties were effectively returned to them within the new Order of Christ. They were then able to settle back in and bury their priceless artefacts in a familiar setting.

One hypothesis has the Templar treasure going from Paris to the Castle of Gisors, in northern France, and from there to the island of Mont-Saint-Michel in Normandy. This island is still home to an idyllic medieval abbey, accessible at low tide and then cut off as the sea rises.[27] From there, a Portuguese Templar fleet loaded the treasure, setting sail for the Templar port of Serra d'El-Rei, near the town of Peniche, north of Lisbon in Portugal. The ships arrived with gold, silver, and objects of importance in clandestine initiation rituals practised by the knights. There were also ancient documents, mostly found in Jerusalem, that proved the veracity of an older form of Christianity, differing substantially from Roman Catholicism. They also had maps from the Arab world, and older civilisations, that would facilitate Portugal's so-called Age of Discovery when a small kingdom on the fringes of western Europe set sail for new worlds previously unknown, such as Brazil, southern Africa, and Japan.[28]

Whereas the order had been snuffed out completely in France and England, it endured in Portugal, though under new branding. So, if the Templars were looking to squirrel away sacred relics, why not at Tomar or one of their other fortresses in that kingdom? In 2018, historians Garth Baldwin and Mikey Kay investigated the possibility of buried Templar treasure at Tomar in the documentary series *Buried: Knights Templar and the Holy Grail* but after examining several tunnels, found nothing.[29] Nevertheless, stories about secret tunnels criss-crossing Tomar, linking key landmarks, have endured alongside the notion that in those subterranean depths lies the undisturbed treasure of the Templars.

The Order of Christ was relocated back to Tomar in 1357, in the same year that the king of Portugal, Pedro I (1320–1367), had an illegitimate son named João (John in English). His life might have been uneventful and unrecorded but for the fact he was propelled on to the throne in 1385 during a dynastic crisis. As a boy, João (1357–1433) had been appointed grand master of the Order of Avis, a Templar-type body of warriors founded by the first Portuguese king, Afonso Henriques, in 1162. When he became king, he established a new dynasty giving it the name: The House of Aviz. After seeing off an attempted invasion by neighbouring Castile, which refused to recognise a king they unpleasantly referred to as 'the bastard', he married the daughter of a very powerful English prince, John of Gaunt (1340–1399). This English queen, Philippa of Lancaster (1360–1415), would give birth to an ambitious brood later termed the 'illustrious generation'. Among them was a Portuguese prince who became widely known by his English nickname – Henry the Navigator (1394–1460) – though in Portugal he is remembered as Infante Dom Henrique.

Henry, like his father, headed up an order of holy warriors, though in his case it was the Order of Christ, successors to the Templars. This led to both the Order of Aviz and Order of Christ being fully integrated into the monarchy and led only by princes of royal blood. The king and Henry set Portugal on an expansionist path, laying the foundations for its future seaborne empire that stretched around the world. The nickname 'navigator' was given to Henry as he organised a series of expeditions to explore the west African coastline in search of trade routes, precious minerals, and spices.

A leap forward in late medieval shipbuilding technology led to the development of the caravel, a sturdy vessel capable of both sea travel and negotiating shallower waters. Sailors were able to plot their course using the Arab-influenced astrolabe to calculate latitude, the ballastella to measure the altitude of celestial bodies, the quadrant to confirm their location in relation to the pole star, and the magnetic compass. Meanwhile, fluttering above, were the white sails of the caravel emblazoned not with the Portuguese royal insignia, but the cross of the Order of Christ. That distinctive logo combined the cross pattée, with arms narrow at the centre and then flaring out, with the cross potent, that placed cross bars at each of the four ends.

The cross of the Order of Christ became the symbol of Portuguese expansion, leading some to question whether this indicated the continuation of the Templar mission, only now to new continents never seen before. If so, what was that mission? To advance Christianity on the point of a sword? Or for those who believe the Templars had discovered the 'true' account of Jesus, was it to take this version of Christianity to the blank slate of the New World – to peoples who knew nothing of popes and inquisitors?

Whatever the reason, all over the world, one can find the distinctive logo of the Order of Christ in the most surprising places. In Cape Verde, west Africa, a Portuguese stone pillory stands in the town square of Cidade Velha. The area is a UNESCO World Heritage site. The white marble pillar is typical of pillories, or 'pelourinhos' in Portuguese, found in village and town squares across the Portuguese mainland. They are contentious objects because in the colonies, rebellious slaves, the majority of whom were black Africans, would be chained to the pelourinho to be beaten for insubordination. The Cape Verde pelourinho dates to around 1512 or 1520 and was restored in the 1960s when the country was still under Portuguese rule. It was constructed in the Manueline style and made of marble. It is surmounted by that unmistakable symbol of the Portuguese navigators, the armillary sphere, and above that, the cross of the Order of Christ.[30]

In the town of Safi, Morocco, there are the underground remains of a Roman Catholic cathedral crypt, later converted under Muslim rule to a hammam – a bath house. The impressive structure with Gothic arches was built in 1519 when the Portuguese held various enclaves in Morocco. They pointedly located the cathedral on top of an Almohad era mosque, converting its minaret into a bell tower. To those undertaking this project, it was a statement of complete revenge against the Almohads who centuries before had terrorised the kingdom of Portugal and fought the Knights Templar. The cathedral at Safi was the first Gothic edifice in Africa and in the roof of the surviving crypt is a cross of the Order of Christ. The rest of the cathedral was destroyed by the departing Portuguese as they were driven out by a Muslim army.[31]

Much further south, in Mozambique, we find the chapel of Nossa Senhora de Baluarte, located on the easternmost tip of the Island of Mozambique, from which the entire country takes its name. The chapel is attached to the fortress of São Sebastião, built by the Portuguese in 1522. It's believed to be the oldest European building in the southern hemisphere. Again, one sees clear evidence of Manueline architecture while in the ceiling of the chapel, the cross of the Order of Christ is very visible.[32]

In 1500, Pedro Álvares Cabral (*c.*1467–1520) was the first European to set foot in Brazil, although the Spanish subsequently disputed the fact. Three years later, another Portuguese expedition erected a stone monument in the settlement of Porto Seguro, laying claim to land occupied up until that moment by indigenous tribes. The landmark can still be seen today surrounded by a protective screen. Yet again, it features the cross, as well as other Portuguese insignia. It marked the beginning of a process of aggressive colonisation by Portugal in Brazil that would change the country's demographics through a combination of immigration and the import of a huge number of slaves from Africa.

The cross can also be seen in former Portuguese colonies and trading posts across Asia, including a fantastic example near the town of Palghar, Maharashtra state, India. About forty-five kilometres from Palghar, amidst dense foliage, one finds the ruined Portuguese fortress of Vasai, dedicated to Saint Sebastian. It was second only to Goa in importance to the colonial governors of Portuguese-held India in the sixteenth century. The ramparts stretch from west to east with ten bastions and several watchtowers and staircases in a remarkable state of preservation. On the entrance to the citadel is the cross of the Order of Christ.

Everywhere one looks in the Lusitanian world, that image is omnipresent. A cross deliberately designed to resemble that of the Knights Templar with minor modifications.

The prominence of the Order of Christ in the Portuguese age of discovery has led to the hypothesis that there was a link between Christopher Columbus and the inheritors of the Templar mantle. One version of this theory rejects the claimed Italian roots of Columbus. He was not the son of a wool dealer from Genoa but the scion of a Portuguese noble family, hence his marriage to a high-born woman from Madeira, Filipa Moniz Perestrelo (*c.*1455–1478 or 1484), whose father was a knight in the Order of Santiago.[33] Another version has Columbus restored to being Italian, only now he is a secret Knight Templar aiming to found a 'New Jerusalem' in the New World where Christians, Muslims, and Jews could live in peace.[34] This Columbus is the illegitimate son of pope Innocent VIII (1432–1492) who, along with the Medici banking family, funds his voyages. It turns out that Innocent was committed to this project because he had both Jewish and Muslim ancestry, which he was forced to keep secret.

Another variation on the Templar link to Columbus centres on the expedition led by an Italian, Giovanni da Verrazzano (1485–1528), in 1524 to chart the Atlantic coastline of America for his patron, the French king, Francis I (1494–1547). But was his true mission to contact a Templar colony in the New World established at Newport, Rhode Island at the end of the fourteenth century by the Scottish noble, Henry Sinclair? This remains the site of a centuries old structure that some claim is a Templar fortification while others dismiss it as the remains of a seventeenth-century windmill. This narrative continues with Columbus marrying a woman who is Sinclair's great-granddaughter and through that family connection, he accesses the Sinclair family archive of ancient maps, which imparts to him the knowledge of a continent on the other side of the Atlantic.[35]

In 2006, the southern Portuguese town of Cuba, in the Alentejo region, unveiled a statue of Columbus in the main square announcing that it was beyond any doubt the great explorer was born there. Furthermore, he had named a large island in the Caribbean after his hometown. The seven-foot statue on a granite pedestal faces the palace of Duke Fernando of Beja who is another candidate for being the father of Columbus. Local historians insist Columbus was Portuguese of mixed aristocratic and Jewish blood and operated as a double agent taking money from both the king of Portugal and the joint monarchs of Spain: Ferdinand and Isabella.[36] Whether or not Columbus was truly Italian, or a covert Templar remains a lively bone of contention among historians in Portugal.

A great deal of ink has been expended in Portugal over the last three centuries or more to prove that the country was set up to fulfil a greater purpose, even something divinely ordained. The story begins with the Knights Templar helping Portugal's first king to forge a Christian nation on the western fringes of Europe. It continues with Diniz protecting the knights and regrouping them in a new order that will continue their mission. Then we come to the messianic figure of Sebastian (1554–1578), the tempestuous sixteenth-century king of Portugal who disappeared into the deserts of Morocco after losing the disastrous Battle of Alcácer Quibir in 1578.

Also known as the Battle of Three Kings, it was a misguided attempt to reinstate a Portuguese-friendly sultan, Abu Abdallah Mohammed II, on the throne and depose his usurping uncle, Abu Marwan Abd al-Malik I. Both sultans and Sebastian were killed in the battle, though a myth endured that the Portuguese king had not died but disappeared. At a moment of his choosing, when his country needed him the most, Sebastian would reappear to lead his kingdom again to global domination. This Arthurian-influenced millenarianism proved very seductive to generations of Portuguese.[37]

From the fifteenth century, the Portuguese were instructed by the papacy to conquer the new worlds in Africa, Asia, and the Americas, bringing the 'heathens' and 'infidels' to Christ. In 1455, this was proclaimed in a papal bull: *Romanus Pontifex*. Henry the Navigator had conquered the Moroccan city of Ceuta forty years earlier and now Pope Nicholas V (1397–1455) told the prince that Portugal had a religious obligation to do the following:

> *... invade, search out, capture, vanquish, and subdue all Saracens and pagans whatsoever, and other enemies of Christ wheresoever placed, and the kingdoms, dukedoms, principalities, dominions, possessions, and all movable and immovable goods whatsoever held and possessed by them and to reduce their persons to perpetual slavery, and to apply and appropriate to himself and his successors the kingdoms, dukedoms, counties, principalities, dominions, possessions, and goods, and to convert them to his and their use and profit...*[38]

With permission from the Pope, the Order of Christ took to the task with gusto. In the seventeenth century, it got further ideological backing with a new concept developed by a Jesuit priest, António Vieira (1608–1697). He came up with the idea that Portugal was destined to found 'the fifth empire'. The first empires had been the Assyrians followed by the Persians then the Greeks and Romans. Reinterpreting a prophecy in the biblical book of Daniel, Vieira predicted that Portugal would bring the entire globe under its dominion, planting the cross of Christ in all lands. This was very much interwoven with the Knights Templar, Order of Christ, and the imminent return of King Sebastian, which failed to materialise.[39]

In the twentieth century, the poet and writer Fernando Pessoa (1888–1935) revived interest in Portugal's alleged divine mission and the notion of the fifth empire. Pessoa was a complex figure who dabbled in mysticism, theosophy, the occult and Freemasonry. Politically conservative and elitist, he failed to hit it off with Portugal's fascist dictatorship of António de Oliveira Salazar (1889–1970) who banned several of his works. Nevertheless, Salazar also tapped into the Templar traditions and imagery of Portugal's history to create an ultra-nationalist narrative. Today, as a democracy, interest in the Templars endures with a proliferation of medieval festivals across the country imbued with a sense that Portugal and the knights had the most special of relationships.

Chapter Seven

A Secret Line of Grand Masters

After centuries of silence, the Knights Templar burst into the open in Napoleonic France, during the early years of the nineteenth century. Evidence was suddenly produced of an unbroken line of grand masters with the current leader of the Templars revealing his identity.

This living and breathing Templar grand master was Bernard-Raymond Fabré-Palaprat (1773–1838), a priest turned doctor, heavily involved in France's turbulent politics throughout his life and a friend of Napoleon Bonaparte (1769–1821). He brandished an ancient charter listing the names of twenty-two Templar grand masters going right back to Jacques de Molay. Palaprat's name was the most recent addition. Having dropped this bombshell, Palaprat set up a new church with its own Bible and sacraments to rival the Roman Catholic Church and assumed an additional title: Sovereign Pontiff.

Palaprat endured some derision, but he attracted a surprising number of adherents from the highest echelons of society. This was a period of revolutionary upheaval, profound societal change, and a strong appetite for new belief systems. In addition, there was a proliferation of secret societies, such as the rapidly expanding Freemasons, but also clandestine groups catering for dabblers in the occult, lovers of debauchery, the intellectually curious, and revivers of ancient belief systems. All were eager to circumvent the dead hand of censorship from Church and State. In this febrile environment, the appeal of the Knights Templar grew, cast now as warriors for the truth who had fallen foul of brutal kings and popes. The intellectually curious of the eighteenth century believed they shared the same enemies as the Templars: the forces of royal and clerical reaction.

Times were indeed changing. The king of France, Louis XVI, the descendant of the royal tyrant who hunted the Templars to extinction, had been tried and decapitated in 1793. The Roman Catholic Church was on the back foot as its abbeys and monasteries were despoiled by revolutionaries. So, when Palaprat stepped forward to proclaim the return of the Templars, emerging from their dark hiding places, there were plenty prepared to listen and join.

Palaprat flourished an astonishing medieval document that proved the Templars had survived. This *Carta Transmissionis* (Charter of Transmission) had allegedly been drafted by the first grand master to assume the role after the execution of Jacques de Molay – a knight called Johannes Marcus Larmenius. He was a Templar born in Outremer, chosen by De Molay from his prison cell to lead the order after his death.

After Jacques de Molay was burned at the stake, near to Notre-Dame Cathedral in Paris, Larmenius took over. Ten years later, aged over 70, he was ready to pass on the baton to another Templar, the Prior of Alexandria, and it was at this moment that Larmenius decided to create a written record. The Larmenius Charter, as it came to be known, was drafted in a Templar secret code but once that was cracked, the Latin text revealed an unbroken line of grand masters proving the Templars had not gone away.[1]

What Palaprat unleashed with this charter was a vibrant, neo-Templar movement that proved to be very resilient and is still operating today. However, it has been prone to bitter schisms. Several organisations at present claim to be the continuation of both Jacques de Molay and Palaprat, each one convinced that they alone are the true voice of the Knights Templar.

Let's take Palaprat's neo-Templarism at face value for now and assume that every word of what he said in 1804, and afterwards, was true. So, what exactly happened to the Knights Templar after the burning of Jacques de Molay in 1314? The neo-Templars stated that Marcus (or Jean Marc) Larmenius, a Templar born in Outremer, found a new home in the Knights Hospitaller, along with hundreds or even thousands of other Templars. They were dejected and frightened people. However, there was a gritty determination to carry on the Templar mission but in conditions of strict secrecy.

Under instruction from the Pope, the Hospitallers had swallowed up much of the assets of the Templars as they were wound down between 1307 and 1314. That meant absorbing people and property. Those Templars who trooped into the Hospitallers covertly strove to retain a separate identity in the hope that one day the true order would be able to emerge again. Below the radar, and out of sight of the Hospitaller leadership, the role of Templar grand master was still passed on from one brother to the next. Larmenius, the first grand master after Jacques de Molay, occupied that position until 1324 when it was transferred to another brother, Thomas Theobaldus Alexandrinus. After stepping down, Larmenius retired to what had been the Templar headquarters in Paris – the impressive fortress that dominated the skyline in the Marais district but was now in Hospitaller hands. At this point, the Charter of Transmission was drafted to record this event and all subsequent grand master appointments.

It included a blistering attack on the Hospitallers:

> *I declare … the brethren of Saint John of Jerusalem, upon whom may God have mercy, as spoilators of the domains of our soldiery and are now and hereafter to be considered beyond the pale of the Temple. I have therefore established signs, unknown to our false brethren, and not to be known by them, to be orally communicated to our fellow soldiers…*[2]

The Vatican was not unaware of all this furtive Templar activity. Neo-Templars assert that in 1326, Pope John XXII issued a decree, *Concilium Avenionense* (Councils of Avignon), directly referencing brotherhoods that swore oaths to masters, used secret signs, and wore distinctive uniforms. The Pope forbade it. He had those Templars lurking within the Hospitallers in mind. Not all knights had joined the Hospitallers – some had fled from France. Those that fled to Scotland were viewed with contempt and hatred by the Larmenius-led Templars:

> *Finally, on consequence of a decree of a Supreme Convention of the brethren, and by the supreme authority to me committed, I will, declare, and command that the Scottish exemplars, as deserters from the Order, are to be accursed.*

Therefore, any Templars claiming a lineage from these knights could never be regarded as legitimate. It's a curious and random attack unless one puts it in the context of Palaprat's own time. Then, it comes across as an unsubtle dig at Freemasonry. From the early eighteenth century, Masonic writings developed an origin myth for their movement linking Freemasonry directly to those knights who fled France for Scotland, concealing themselves among Scottish stonemasons. Over time, the knights and masons had effectively merged, resulting in Freemason degrees, rites and traditions. If one regards the Larmenius Charter as a more recent forgery, and not medieval at all, this is a broadside fired by the new neo-Templars at Freemasonry. The message being back off, we are the real Templars.

As with secret organisations, like the Priory of Sion, reputed to be the shadowy puppet masters of the Knights Templar, the charter features an illustrious line of grand masters. This includes Robert de Lenoncourt, Archbishop of Reims (died 1532) and Philippe Chabot, Count of Charny and Buzançois (died 1543), a trusted companion of King Francis I of France (1494–1547). Under the 'Sun King' Louis XIV (1638–1715), arguably the most powerful monarch in French history, the Templar grand master was Jacques Henri de Durfort (1625–1704), first Duke of Duras and Marshal of France. After him, came Philippe II, Duke of Orléans (1674–1723), who ruled as Regent of France when the five-year-old son of the previous dead monarch was crowned king. According to the neo-Templars, Philippe was elected by the Convent General of the Templar order at Versailles in 1705 and his elevation to grand master brought the order briefly into the public gaze.

If Philippe was indeed the new Templar grand master, then he was clearly unaware about the vow of chastity. His debauched parties were the talk of high society, popularising champagne drinking accompanied by copious amounts of food and sex.[3] Among those regularly attending his orgies was another Philippe, the Duke of Vendôme (1655–1727), who was the Grand Prior of the Knights of Malta in France, the successor organisation to the Knights Hospitaller. The two Philippes, one a Templar and the other a Hospitaller, frequented the sex workers around the Palais Royal and the dancers at the nearby opera house. In 1719, bored of being Grand Prior, the Duke of Vendôme sold the post to somebody else. Meanwhile at the age of 20, the Duke of Orléans was married to the illegitimate daughter of the king and his mistress, nicknaming his new wife 'Madame Lucifer'.[4]

Between orgies, Philippe indulged his interest in chivalric orders and was keen to burnish his Templar credentials. In a bold move, he sent two envoys to King John V of Portugal asking if he would recognise the Order of the Temple. Why did he do this? One theory is that a century before Palaprat's stunning revelation, Philippe had commissioned a Jesuit priest, known as Father Bonani, to forge an earlier version of the Larmenius Charter, proving that the Societé d'Aloyau (Society of the Sirloin) was the successor organisation to the Knights Templar. To stack this up, Philippe thought the Portuguese king's seal of approval would help. Portugal had, after all, allowed the Templars to continue under the guise of the Order of Christ with the monarch as protector. But the Portuguese were not about to go along with Philippe's plan.

King John was an absolute monarch, very much in the mould of Louis XIV, and dubbed the Portuguese Sun King (*o Rei-Sol Português*). He was a pious Catholic who spent hours in prayer every day and as Portuguese king, he oversaw the successor organisation to the Templars, the Order of Christ, still based in Tomar. When confronted by Philippe's Templars, he took advice from his ambassador to Paris and promptly ordered their arrest. One of the envoys escaped to Gibraltar while the other was less fortunate and found himself shipped out to the Portuguese colony of Angola, in west Africa, where he later died.

During Philippe's tenure as grand master of the Order of the Temple, a Scotsman was enrolled who would be instrumental in forging the Templar-Freemason link that would soon be rejected by neo-Templars around Palaprat. Sir Andrew Michael Ramsay (1686–1743) was a low-born Scot with aristocratic pretensions who never saw a secret society he did not want to join. Striving for spiritual truth, he moved from Scottish Presbyterianism to Roman Catholicism and then on to Freemasonry. His politics were dangerous. Ramsay plotted with other 'Jacobites' in France to overthrow the Protestant Hanoverian kings of Britain but then, somehow, returned to London to become a Fellow of the Royal Society, possibly after being pardoned by King George II (1683–1760). Singlehandedly, but maybe not intentionally, he diverted Freemasonry towards the Knights Templar impacting both the Masonic and neo-Templar worlds.[5] His shadow looms large in the run up to the Larmenius Charter being revealed and it may even be thanks to Ramsay that the Catholic Church decided to excommunicate all Freemasons.

Ramsay was a very prayerful and studious young man attracted to mysticism and a school of thought, Quietism, that advocated cutting oneself off entirely from the material world to achieve a spiritual union with God. He had a strong aversion to organised religion and rigid, dogmatic thinking but at the same time, wanted to be part of a big club. This led him to the door of François Fénelon, Archbishop of Cambrai (1651–1715) who despite his senior position in the Catholic Church was a leading advocate of Quietism, even though it had been condemned by the Pope as heretical. He converted Ramsay to Roman Catholicism, networked him into elite French circles, and shared with the Scot his own ongoing crisis of faith. In May 1723, Ramsay was inducted by Philippe, the Templar grand master, into the Order of Saint Lazarus, another sacred military order with medieval roots, making him a 'chevalier'.[6] This undoubtedly helped to awaken in Ramsay an interest in the crusader brotherhoods like the Templars and Hospitallers.

In 1727, he wrote the bestselling book *A New Cyropaedia, or the Travels of Cyrus* where he put forward his ideas on how a virtuous ruler governs his subjects, taking the Persian king Cyrus the Great (*c.*600–530 BC) as the prime example.[7] This was a king who tolerated the different views of the peoples covered by his vast empire and most notably, ended the Babylonian captivity of the Jews, allowing them to return to Israel. As Ramsay's public profile rose, he was called to Rome to tutor the Stuart claimant to the thrones of England, Scotland, and Ireland, Prince Charles Edward Stuart (1720–1788) – better known to history as 'Bonnie Prince Charlie'.[8] In the 1740s, Bonnie Prince Charlie attempted an invasion from Scotland to restore the Stuart monarchy, which ended in abject defeat. Years before, in 1724, Ramsay schooled Britain's greatest enemy in his childhood and yet by 1729, the hyperactive Scot had no problem visiting London where he became a Fellow of the Royal Society and in March 1730 was initiated as a Freemason in the Horn Lodge.[9] Some believe that Ramsay was either a spy or a double agent working for both the Stuarts and Hanoverians. Possibly he was pardoned by the Hanoverian king, George II, because His Majesty did not view Ramsay as a serious threat.

When Ramsay returned to Paris in 1731, his new patron was the Comte d'Evreux, part of the De Bouillon family that produced the first crusader ruler of Jerusalem in the year 1099, Godfrey de Bouillon. His involvement with the Masonic scene continued and in 1737, he delivered an 'oration' to the Grand Lodge in Paris. Much of it was concerned with the values and practices of Freemasonry, as well as a justification of secret signs and signals, but the small section that had the biggest impact was the connection he made between the Masons of his own time and the crusading orders. This was music to the ears of his French Masonic audience who, unlike English Freemasons, preferred their lodges to be more socially exclusive. The idea of being latter-day knights, as opposed to medieval stonemasons, had enormous appeal. Ramsay explained:

> *Our ancestors, the crusaders, gathered together from all parts of Christendom in the Holy Land, desired thus to reunite into one sole fraternity the individuals of all nations … our ancestors, the crusaders, must not be considered a revival of the Bacchanals, but as an order founded in remote antiquity, renewed in the Holy Land by our ancestors in order to recall the memory of the most sublime truths amidst the pleasures of society.*

Ever since, it's been assumed Ramsay meant the Templars, though they were not mentioned by name. The day before he was due to speak, he submitted his oration for approval to Cardinal André-Hercule de Fleury (1653–1743), chief minister to the French king and de facto chief censor. Not only was his oration forbidden, but Fleury flew into a rage banning Masonic meetings, while in the following year, Pope Clement XII (1652–1740) went a step further.[10] Clement wrote in an encyclical titled *In Eminentis:*

> *Now it has come to Our ears, and common gossip has made clear, that certain Societies, Companies, Assemblies, Meetings, Congregations or Conventicles called in the popular tongue Liberi Muratori or Francs Massons or by other names according to the various languages, are spreading far and wide and daily growing in strength…*

Clement warned that if 'they were not doing evil they would not have so great a hatred of the light'. It was not only against the Pope's will to join the

Freemasons, but even to be seen with them or allow them to rent a premises for their meetings. All contact had to cease. And Clement unleashed the Inquisition, which was still functioning in Europe in the eighteenth century, to suppress the Masons. His words were chilling and reminiscent of the fate of the Templars four hundred years before:

> *Moreover, We desire and command that both Bishops and prelates, and other local ordinaries, as well as inquisitors for heresy, shall investigate and proceed against transgressors of whatever state, grade, condition, order dignity or pre-eminence they may be; and they are to pursue and punish them with condign penalties as being most suspect of heresy.*

Incredibly, Ramsay had given the Catholic Church all the ammunition it needed to shut down the Masons.[11] It seems plausible that Ramsay hoped to reconcile the Catholic Church to Freemasonry by portraying Masons as crusaders – those faithful sons of the Church who had taken up the sword for Christ. But sadly, for Ramsay, the Church did not picture the Knights Templar in their glorious years but instead, as those wretched, criminals condemned for heresy and sodomy. The Pope was alarmed by a covert network of secretive lodges over which he had no control. And he was unnerved by reports of not only freethinking but even alleged occult practices within Freemasonry. In that sense, the Masons had a great deal in common with the Templars.

Even though Ramsay seems to have been scared off Freemasonry after Fleury's furious disapproval, followed by the blistering papal encyclical, his oration sent shockwaves through the Masonic lodges for decades afterwards. He may have been articulating an already existing story about the Templar origins of the Masons and it now spread and was further embellished. One popular Masonic legend had the fleeing Templars in Scotland forming the first lodges with their stonemason protectors and local nobility.[12] The Mother Lodge of Scotland in Kilwinning even claimed to be the oldest Masonic lodge in the world indicated by its number: zero. Faced with a choice between English or Scottish versions of Freemasonry, French masons enthusiastically adopted the Scottish Rite, which eventually spread to other European countries and the United States.[13]

The last but one Templar grand master before Palaprat, according to the Larmenius Charter, was Louis Hercule Timoléon de Cossé, 8th Duke of Brissac (1734–1792). Among his titles was the position of Grand Panetier of France, essentially in charge of bread. A curious medieval role that originally involved a noble overseeing table settings and washing up at the king's meals. Like many royal roles, it was purely ceremonial by the time De Cossé-Brissac became the final panetier. He was also a knight in several chivalric orders and most notoriously, a lover of Madame du Barry (1743–1793), the mistress of France's last but one king, Louis XV (1710–1774). On 9 September 1792, he was torn to pieces by a mob at the height of revolutionary fervour in France.

The revolution had begun in 1789 with King Louis XVI (1754–1793) deprived of absolute power. By 1792, due in large part to the king's own treacherous actions, more radical voices moved into the ascendancy. In August 1792, the king was imprisoned in what had been the Paris Temple, headquarters of the French Templar knights. In September, he was stripped of all titles, referred to simply as Citizen Louis Capet. That same month, over a thousand political prisoners were massacred including De Cossé-Brissac whose head was placed on a pike and paraded around before being tossed through the window of Du Barry's apartment. She apparently fainted at the sight of her lover's lifeless eyes staring up at her, though she would soon face the guillotine and loss of her own head.[14]

In January 1793, Louis XVI was executed on the guillotine. There is an account of somebody dipping a cloth in his blood and shouting, 'Jacques de Molay, you are avenged!'[15] This story was told by Charles Louis Cadet de Gassicourt (1769–1821), whose mother allegedly became pregnant with Charles because of a fling with King Louis XV. His father never forgave the libidinous monarch, and his son grew up to be a convinced revolutionary. He was also a Freemason. However, the revolution's 'Reign of Terror', which saw a wave of mass executions, made him more conservative and by 1795, when he wrote an account of the king's beheading, De Gassicourt was blaming undercover Templars for infiltrating Masonic lodges, united by an oath to 'exterminate all kings' and to 'destroy the power of the pope'. He viewed these Masonic Templars as a malign force:

> *The true Templar Freemasons are eight hundred lodges about the Earth bent on vengeance, ambition and their system and have sworn to massacre kings for the independence of the world.*

In the years between the French Revolution and Palaprat's announcement, Freemasons and Catholics accused each other of working with underground

Templars. The Freemason De Gassicourt believed that neo-Templars, allied to the Illuminati, had sneaked into Masonic lodges to subvert them. The French Jesuit priest Augustin Barruel (1741–1820) argued something similar from a Catholic perspective. He believed the French Revolution had been orchestrated by an Illuminati-Templar-Freemason plot. While the radical Freemason, Nicholas Bonneville (1760–1828) was convinced that Jesuits were infiltrating Masonic lodges, and they were responsible for the outbreak of Templarism within Freemasonry. What is clear from all this is that some Masons were irked by the growing neo-Templar influence in their lodges. Possibly they viewed this as a Christian straitjacket being imposed on their rationalist Enlightenment beliefs. As for the neo-Templars, they wished to be much more than just a sub-set within Freemasonry. After centuries in hiding, they yearned for an independent existence, free of Roman Catholicism and Freemasonry.

On 4 November 1804, Palaprat revealed the Larmenius Charter with its list of Templar grand masters stretching back to Jacques de Molay. He also produced De Molay's sword, four fragments of his burned bones and ashes from the execution site in 1314, original seals of the Templars as well as other relics that together were termed 'The Sacred Treasure of the Order of the Temple'. Also in his possession were the 1705 statutes drafted by Philippe, the former Templar grand master. The treasure was publicly displayed in 1808 at Saint Paul's Church in Paris on the anniversary of De Molay's execution.

The Larmenius Charter and Philippe's statues still exist but all other items have since gone missing. How the charter was passed on from the grand master decapitated in 1792, De Cossé-Brissac, to Palaprat is a little murky. In one version, the murdered grand master was able to hand over his Templar archive to Dr Jacques-Phillipe Ledru (1754–1832) before his untimely death at the hands of the Parisian mob. Ledru's father, Nicolas-Philippe Ledru (1731–1807), had been a physician to De Cossé-Brissac as well as a scientist who enjoyed tricks of illusion. This included a naked female robot that got dressed when instructed. His son was also a physician but of more relevance, the Masonic grand master of the lodge of the Knights of the Cross, based in Paris, which in turn came under the Grand Orient of France – the mother lodge of European Freemasonry. Ledru effectively 'transmitted' the role of Templar grand master to Palaprat. There's another account where Ledru bought some of De Cossé-

Brissac's furniture, when it was being auctioned, and found the charter hidden in a drawer and then shared it with Palaprat.

Then came two major ruptures. In 1811, Palaprat's Order of the Temple parted company with Freemasonry. When the Grand Orient of France attempted to assert its dominance over the neo-Templars, they declared their independence. For decades, Freemasons had come to assume that the newly resurgent Templars were part of the Masonic world. But Palaprat and his followers reasoned differently. It was true that the knights had indeed been sheltered by medieval stonemasons and owed them a debt of gratitude. But that did not mean they had to be subordinate to the heirs of stonecutters and chisellers. The Knights Templar could once more stand on their own two feet without Masonic assistance. Palaprat announced that the Order of the Temple would be faithful sons of the Church and only admit Roman Catholics from now on. Freemasons could stay away. That position lasted barely a year. Palaprat, an ex-priest, then broke with Rome and set up a new church: The Johannite Church of Primitive Christians (l'Église Johannite des Chrétiens Primitifs). Drawing heavily on the Gospel of John, he adopted a Gnostic theology and even published his own version of the Bible with all the non-Gnostic bits taken out. That made Palaprat a heretic in the eyes of the Roman Catholic Church.

Daring to edit the Bible was not unprecedented. This was the Age of Enlightenment after all, and Palaprat was in France, the beating heart of revolutionary thinking. Over in the United States, a new nation heavily influenced by French ideas, the founding father and political philosopher Thomas Jefferson (1743–1826) published *The Philosophy of Jesus of Nazareth* in 1804 – the same year Palaprat revealed the charter – and later went on to issue an edited version of the Bible with all the miracles and supernatural stuff removed.[16] Palaprat's Bible was titled the *Evangelikon* with a companion text, the *Lévitikon*. There was a rather implausible yarn that these texts were based on ancient manuscripts Palaprat chanced upon at an antiquarian bookstall on New Year's Day in 1814. In Palaprat's Bible there was no resurrection of the bodily Christ. Instead, the Messiah seems to have been initiated into the cult of Osiris, learning truths that were passed on to his favourite disciple, John, and from him down to the Knights Templar.

Palaprat's elevation to supreme pontiff of a new church to rival Rome led to a split in the Order of the Temple. He was being viewed increasingly as a megalomaniac. It was one thing to be the inheritor of De Molay's white mantle but quite another to be Christ's vicar on earth. The Italian branch of Palaprat's order seceded in 1815 resolving to remain loyal to the Pope. In Paris, a General Convent met on 15 May 1812 and removed Palaprat as grand master, replacing him with Charles Louis David Le Peletier de Rosanbo d'Aunay (1750–1831). The Peletier family were bigwigs in Paris and up until the revolution in 1789, the city's parliament had always been presided over by a Le Peletier. They were renowned for their command of jurisprudence. But that did not stop Palaprat launching a desperate bid to keep his position by hastily rewriting the order's statues, assuming absolute power. His opponents spurned this manoeuvre, resulting in two competing grand masters. In 1814, Claude Antoine Gabriel, Duc de Choiseul-Stainville took over as grand master with Palaprat still maintaining he had never left the role.

This drama being played out in the world of neo-Templarism was somewhat overshadowed by the arrival of the armies of Russia, Austria, and Prussia into the suburbs of Paris, bent on removing Napoleon as Emperor and forcing him into exile. This was the final act of Napoleon's dream of creating a European empire centred on Paris. Palaprat threw himself into the defence of his city for which he received the Legion of Honour. But as for the Emperor, he was defeated, and after one last attempt to regain power, spent his last days on the remote island of Saint Helena.

The attitude of Napoleon and France's revolutionaries to the legacy of the Knights Templar was complex. On the one hand, the knights had been the loyal servants of the Roman Catholic Church whose power the revolution set out to break, even establishing its own state-run religion in 1794, the Cult of the Supreme Being (Culte de l'Être Supreme), though Napoleon banned the cult in 1802. The knights, then, could be characterised as the military wing of the papal power so detested by the anti-clerical revolutionaries. On the other hand, the Templars had been crushed by the king of France. Maybe, therefore, the revolution should extend some empathy towards those imprisoned, tortured, and executed by the 'ancien regime'. Any enemy of the king of France was surely a friend of the revolution. In October 1793, revolutionaries burst into the Basilica of Saint-Denis, the burial place of France's monarchs for centuries, and desecrated their tombs. During this act of sacrilege, the bones of King Philip IV were brought up and dumped in a common grave. An ignominious end for the man who had annihilated the Knights Templar.

Napoleon was a child of the revolution, imbued with its values. But he was also the champion of a new form of monarchic rule, styling himself as an emperor instead of a king. Before assuming this imperial mantle, he led French military forces into Egypt and Syria in 1798 to open new trade routes and seek a line of attack against British-ruled India. This audacious invasion of a Middle Eastern, Muslim majority country was conducted in his role as a general reporting to the five-member committee, The Directory, that ruled France from 1795 to 1799. It was the first such military venture in modern times. To commentators on both sides, the memory of the saint king, Louis IX, and his crusade to Egypt, aided by the Knights Templar and Hospitaller, came to mind. A positive recollection for Europeans but viewed very negatively by the Muslim rulers of Egypt.[17]

Fighting his battles in Egypt, Napoleon could be viewed as a latter-day crusader. But while planting the French tricolour in the shadow of the pyramids, Napoleon also dealt the death blow to the last remaining legacy of the original crusades. In the same year, 1798, he destroyed what was left of the Knights Hospitaller. Unlike the Templars, they had survived the loss of the Holy Land and, in 1310, seized the island of Rhodes from the Byzantine Empire to be their new base of operations. They also constructed a fortress at Halicarnassus (modern Bodrum in Turkey), stripping the ancient mausoleum, which had been one of the Seven Wonders of the Ancient World, for building materials. The order was reorganised into eight 'langues', or 'tongues', representing the different geographies of the knights: Aragon, Auvergne, Castile, England, France, Holy Roman Empire, Italy, and Provence. They would spend the next centuries fighting the Ottoman Turks and Barbary pirates for control of the Mediterranean.[18]

By 1530, they had been forced to flee Rhodes and relocate to another island in the Mediterranean – Malta. The transfer of this territory to the knights was negotiated with the Holy Roman Emperor, Charles V (1500–1558), by Pope Clement VII (1478–1534) who had been a Hospitaller himself in his younger days. The price exacted by Charles from the order was the annual gift of a peregrine falcon on All Soul's Day.[19] This strange tribute captured the imagination of the twentieth century American detective novel writer Dashiell Hammett (1894–1961), who in 1930 penned the crime blockbuster *The Maltese Falcon*.[20] Hammett's main character was a private detective, Sam Spade, who is drawn into the search for the missing Maltese Falcon, which was no longer a living bird of prey but a gold and jewel-encrusted statuette, covered in an ugly black enamel to conceal its true value.

Long ago, the Hospitallers had lost the priceless artefact to pirates and now it was being sought by ruthless art thieves who would stop at nothing to obtain it. Hollywood adapted the novel twice, with the second movie version, starring the legendary actor Humphrey Bogart (1899–1957), becoming one of the most iconic examples of the 'film noir' genre, popular in the 1940s. Very noticeably, in the opening credits of the movie, the Hospitallers are replaced by the Templars, presumably because of their greater name recognition with cinema audiences. This was the (historically inaccurate) text that appeared in the title sequence:

In 1539, the Knight Templars (sic) of Malta, paid tribute to Charles V of Spain, by sending him a Golden Falcon encrusted from beak to claw with rarest jewels – but pirates seized the galley carrying this priceless token and the fate of the Maltese Falcon remains a mystery to this day.[21]

In 1565, the knights withstood a four-month 'great siege' imposed by an enormous Ottoman Turkish army, which correctly viewed Malta as the gateway to Christian Europe. Queen Elizabeth I of England reflected the fear felt across the continent, writing that 'if the Turks should prevail against the Isle of Malta, it is uncertain what further peril might follow to the rest of Christendom'.[22] In what has to be one of the most stunning victories by any army in the sixteenth century, the Hospitallers under grand master Jean de Valette (1495–1568) emerged victorious but at great cost. At one point, the Ottomans overran Fort Saint Elmo, slaughtering its occupants with only nine defenders surviving by diving into the sea and swimming to safety.

De Valette's valour and success was rewarded by huge donations to the order with which he built the new capital of the island named after him: Valetta. However, this was the high point of their post-crusades' history because in the centuries that followed, they struggled for relevance. They came to rely hugely on support from France which, in the seventeenth century, under Louis XIV, encouraged Frenchmen to join the order and offered commissions in the armed forces to those who were knights. Many of the leading families in France were proud to have sons in the Hospitallers. They even reserved a place in the order for younger sons on the day of their birth.[23]

But the French Revolution in 1789 changed all of this. The order's assets and property in France were seized and tithes paid to the knights were abolished. Two Hospitaller castles in south-east France, at Manosque and Puimoisson, built in the thirteenth century, were razed to the ground after the revolution. When Manosque was destroyed, the bones of the founder of the Hospitaller order, Blessed Gérard Sasso (*c.*1040–1120) were scattered, although a humerus and vertebra were subsequently recovered.

Then in 1798, as part of a broader military strategy, Napoleon took Malta and, displaying utter contempt for this old and venerable order, consigned them to the dustbin of history at the stroke of a pen. They were a relic of the medieval world and, as he had done across Europe, Napoleon ushered in a new political and social order in Malta, under which the Knights Hospitaller had no role to play. Unfortunately for Napoleon, this unleashed the forces of Maltese nationalism, leading to a rejection of both the knights and French occupation. The Maltese eventually acquiesced to the protective embrace of the British Empire, becoming a Crown colony from 1814 to 1964.[24] The Knights

Hospitaller would never re-establish control of the island, leaving behind the grand remains of castles and palaces that enthral tourists today.

After Napoleon was defeated, exiled, and passed away in 1821, aged just 51, France reverted to the Bourbon monarchy until 1830 when a second revolution swept the ancient regime away yet again. Palaprat threw himself into this uprising, which saw the absolutist monarchy of King Charles X (1757–1836) replaced with the constitutional monarchy of Louis Philippe I (1773–1850). For his action during the 'three glorious days' of the 1830 revolution, Palaprat received the July Medal, awarded to 3763 of Louis Philippe's most loyal supporters. It was in the aftermath of this major political shift in France that he attempted to pull the neo-Templar movement into his new Johannite church with its own version of the Bible, the *Evangelikon*, and a rejection of both papal supremacy and Masonic interference.[25] Palaprat also teamed up with a renegade cleric, Ferdinand François Châtel (1795–1857), who broke with the Roman Catholic Church during the 1830 revolution, declaring himself 'primate of the Gauls' and announcing that he would only say the holy mass in French, and not Latin.[26] Cast out of the Catholic Church, he was ordained by Palaprat into the Johannite Church and became its spiritual leader. Châtel's cathedral was a shabby shop premises in Montmartre bestowed with the impressive title: the Apostolic Court of the Temple. Its religious proclamations were dated from the 'magistratopolis', when the Knights Templar were founded in the year 1118. So, the year 1830 was written in documents as the year 712 in the era of the magisterium. In the shop window was a bust of King Louis Philippe to affirm the new church's loyalty to the recently installed French head of state.

The activities of the neo-Templars excited some interest in Britain judging by contemporary newspaper coverage. In 1833, the *Aberdeen Journal* reported on a major event in Paris:

> *M. Fabre Palaprat, a doctor who is their Grand Master and High Priest, took solemn possession of their new Metropolitan Convent, in the Cour Damiette, on Sunday evening, amidst an immense crowd. The whole brotherhood performed in the costumes of the old knights of the Temple, mass was said, bread and wine consecrated, and M. Barginet, a well-known political writer of Grenoble, delivered a sermon.*[27]

In 1837, *The Caledonian Mercury* published a long article on the revival of the Knights Templar and the Larmenius Charter. 'The charter by which the supreme authority has been transmitted is judicial and conclusive evidence of the Order's continued existence.' It reported that Palaprat had established 'colleges in England and in many of the chief cities of Europe'. There could be little doubt, in the newspaper's view, that 'the very ancient and sovereign Order of the Temple is now in full and chivalric existence'.[28]

But not all publicity was positive. In 1835, *The Examiner* commented on a lawsuit in Brussels over the last will and testament of a certain Abbé Grégoire, Bishop of Blois, who had died a few years before. His body was exhumed over allegations that a silver-gilt cross he wore habitually had been replaced with a copper one. The article then alleged that 'the real episcopal cross of Gregoire now adorns the neck of M. Fabre Palaprat, Grand Master of the Order of the Templars'.[29] The inference being that Palaprat had obtained the late bishop's cross dishonestly. The deceased, now wearing a cheap cross in his grave, was Henri Jean-Baptiste Grégoire (1750–1831) whose greatest claim to fame was coining the word 'vandalism' to refer to reckless destruction.

He first used the term in relation to the attacks on religious and royal works of art after the French Revolution. Despite his opposition to revolutionary excess, Grégoire was radical on the issue of slavery, supporting abolition, and even advocating racial equality.[30] He campaigned for the rights of France's black subjects in the colony of Haiti and called for an end to discrimination against the Jews. A Catholic bishop who took unorthodox positions, he also endorsed the veracity of the Larmenius Charter.[31] The allegation that Palaprat stole Grégoire's ecclesiastical cross can be seen in one of two ways: either Palaprat was genuinely light-fingered and stole the item, or this claim, appearing in the English newspapers, was a Masonic-originated slur against the French leader of the breakaway neo-Templar movement.

Palaprat's new church provoked a civil war among the neo-Templars. In France, the Duc de Choiseul led a coup, unseating him for a period as grand master. In Belgium, an offshoot under the leadership of the Marquis Albert François du Chasteler (1794–1836) split into pro-Catholic and pro-Masonic factions. The Italians swore off Palaprat and declared their loyalty to the Vatican. While in England, Admiral Sir William Sidney Smith (1764–1840) became the neo-Templar grand prior. Among those he recruited to the brotherhood was Charles Tennyson d'Eyncourt (1784–1861), uncle of the poet Alfred Lord Tennyson (1809–1892).

Earlier in his life, Smith had been a naval commander in the English wars against revolutionary France and was captured and briefly detained in the Templar fortress in Paris. In a curious twist of fate, he now found himself a modern-day Templar, adopting the role of conciliator between Palaprat and his opponents. But Smith provoked negative reactions from French neo-Templars over his Masonic connections, adherence to the Church of England, and the fact that he was English. Palaprat's health took a serious turn for the worse as he saw his Johannite church rejected by the neo-Templar movement he had brought into existence, after revealing the Larmenius Charter. His death in 1838 torpedoed the new church but the neo-Templars lived on, although becoming ever more fractious.

The appointment of Palaprat's successor earned some column inches in the French and British newspapers. A very plush ceremony was held 'in a richly ornamented apartment' at 16 Rue Notre Dame des Victoires in Paris attended by several 'knights'.[32] At some point, the ashes and bones of Jacques de Molay, his sword, and the original seals of the Knights Templar disappeared. The Larmenius Charter also vanished. Many of these items were reportedly deposited in the French National Archives, an institution created in 1790 after the revolution but then seem to have gone adrift. There were reportedly other documents proving the unbroken line from De Molay to Palaprat and refuting claims that the charter was a forgery by a Jesuit priest or that it had originated among the Freemasons. However, all this was hearsay as Palaprat's 'archive' melted into the ether.[33]

It also transpired that on two separate occasions, disgruntled members of the order burned key documents, presumably to spite Palaprat. After Palaprat's death, at his memorial service, a story was told about a magistral secretary of the order, Francois-Louis Foraisse (also known as Louis of Sundgaw), who was deposed by the grand master. In a fit of pique, Foraisse lit a brazier and grabbed some of the ancient Templar parchments. Acting on instinct, Palaprat dashed to where he knew Foraisse was located and caught him in the act, just before the sacred papers were consumed by the flames.

The Larmenius Charter was not deposited in the National Archives and remained out of sight for the rest of the nineteenth century. Three decades after Palaprat's death, Freemasons had not forgotten or forgiven the neo-Templar grand master's split with the Masonic world. Aware that the charter was still out there somewhere, they took pot shots at its credibility. A newspaper article in 1868, in the United States, published in the *National Freemason* newspaper, did not pull its punches:

> *The 'Charter of Transmission' preserved at Paris is a forgery and the 'memorials' ludicrously worthless. The list of successive Grand Masters is utterly apocryphal.*

When Palaprat invented 'The Order of the Temple' at Paris, he invented the charter and other documents. We have the complete history of this 'Order', and intend, someday, to publish it.[34]

The charter popped up at auction in the early twentieth century, wrongly listed as a 'Masonic Diploma from 1812'. By this stage, three seals once attached to the bottom had gone, including what was alleged to be the seal of Larmenius himself. Clearly this would have done a great deal to authenticate the charter.[35] It was bought by a leading Freemason, Frederick Crowe (1862–1931) – also an expert organist, astronomer, and billiards player – who handed it over to the Great Priory of England and Wales, one of several Masonic organisations run from Mark Mason's Hall in London, which is where the charter has been kept ever since. Palaprat's document ended up in the hands of those Masonic Templars he had spurned as grand master of the Ordre du Temple.

In 1892, the order of the Temple acquired a flamboyant and over-the-top grand master. Joséphin Péladan (1858–1918) was immersed in the occult, declaring himself a Rosicrucian and a Martinist. But he was also something of a fashion icon. 'A new Oscar Wilde' thundered one American newspaper in 1891, who 'poses in ruffles and velvets' and 'indulges in twenty-five different perfumes at once'. His disregard for gender norms speaks to our own times and horrified Victorian opinion.

Everybody in Paris has heard of the Sâr Josephine (sic) Peladan. Everyone in Paris connected, in near or remote fashion, with that life of Bohemia that recruits from its ranks les jeunes in literature and art has seen him. What Oscar Wilde was to London and New York ten years ago, he today is to Paris.[36]

Readers were asked to picture 'a small being in a velvet blouse belted to the waist, with cuffs of old lace turned up from the wrists' with his face surmounted by 'a penthouse roof of tangled black hair, curling in a bush to the eyebrows, and met by a sable beard, vaguely and Vandykely (*sic*) pointed'. On a more flattering note, the newspaper conceded that he was a deeply original thinker 'whom the common herd of men may despise, but who holds himself serenely far beyond the reach of sordid ridicule' dressed in 'purple velvet, knee-breeches and feathered hat, spinning magnificently in the space above the head of the crude modern man'. It was to this controversial figure that the neo-Templars turned to save them from their declining fortunes.

His answer was to blend neo-Templarism with the occult and esoteric schools of thought that were very modish in the late nineteenth century. He claimed that the title adopted ahead of his name, *Sâr*, was a result of being initiated into magical arts practised in the temples of Zoroaster while his style of dress reflected his worship of the sun god.[37]

In 1890, Péladan founded the Ordre de la Rose-Croix du Temple, a split-off from the Rosicrucians, an occult movement with its roots in the seventeenth century that combined Christianity, alchemy, Hermeticism, and the Jewish mystical Kabbalah. Péladan and his associates mixed and matched esoteric belief systems, dropping one idea and adopting another in the time it took to drink a coffee. From 1892, he moved away from any Masonic connection veering towards Roman Catholicism while still promoting Rosicrucianism and neo-Templarism. The result was some great art shows in Paris with a modern take on medieval religious beliefs that gave rise to the short-lived Symbolist movement. But for the dwindling band of neo-Templars, there was very little return on this activity.

The running of the order was taken up by the grand priory of Belgium, founded by Palaprat. But it was riven with disputes between Catholics and Masons. From Péladan's resignation in 1894, the neo-Templars just about survived until their relaunch in 1932 as The Sovereign Military Order of the Temple of Jerusalem, translated into French as the Ordre Souverain et Militaire du Temple de Jérusalem (OSMTJ), integrating priories in Belgium, Portugal, Italy, and Switzerland.

In 1942, the grand prior of Belgium, Emile Clément Joseph Isaac Vandenberg (1895–1943), transferred the archives of the OSMTJ to Porto in Portugal, entrusting them to António Campelo Pinto de Sousa Fontes (1878–1960). Belgium was being overrun by the Nazis, Vandenberg was Jewish and so at risk of arrest, and Portugal was neutral in the Second World War so relatively safe. After Vandenberg's death in a car crash, Sousa Fontes became the new grand master. He then appointed his son, Fernando Pinto Pereira de Sousa Fontes (1929–2018), to succeed him, which he did in 1960 when his father died, adopting the role of 'regent'.

In 1970, Sousa Fontes called a special 'Convent General' to meet in Paris and confirm him as the new grand master but unexpectedly, the knights elected a 70-year-old Second World War Polish general, Antoine (originally Andrzej) Josef Zdrojewski (1900–1989) to lead the order. This led to a major split among the post-war neo-Templars.

Those recognising Zdrojewski's election continued in the OSMTJ while the defeated Sousa Fontes led a breakaway group that adopted the Latin translation of the order's title, becoming the Ordo Supremus Militaris Templi

Hierosolymitani (OSMTH). Further splits have led to four OSMTH and five OSMTJ organisations. On the OSMTH side, a Swiss registered body has enjoyed a high level of recognition with special consultative status at the United Nations. Neo-Templars today include Roman Catholics, Freemasons, other Christians, and those who simply wish to continue the traditions of the original Knights Templar.

Chapter Eight

The Priory of Sion

The downfall of the Templars in 1307, and the burning of Jacques de Molay in 1314, marked the end of two centuries of crusading by these holy warriors. But some believe there was a hidden hand that brought the Templars into existence and continued after their demise. A secret network with its own grand master and a history stretching back over millennia. This has proven to be a very seductive line of argument.

The origin story of the Knights Templar outlined by the medieval chroniclers has not satisfied many Templar theorists and enthusiasts down the centuries, but especially in recent decades. Nine knights coming together to form a security service for pilgrims journeying to the Holy Land hardly explains the super-wealthy and powerful order that emerged and which Pope Clement and King Philip of France felt the need to crush so bloodily. Many prefer to envisage some kind of covert, dangerous organisation that conjured the knights into existence to fulfil a dark agenda. But what was the name and purpose of that secret society operating in the shadows? A legal case that rumbled on through 2006 and 2007 provided some clues.

In March 2007, two authors failed in their attempt to prove a breach of copyright by the publisher of the bestselling novel, *The Da Vinci Code*, authored by Dan Brown (born 1964).[1] In what was an extraordinary case, Michael Baigent (1948–2013) and Richard Leigh (1943–2007) – two of the three authors of the 1980s blockbuster *The Holy Blood and the Holy Grail*[2] – ran up a multi-million pound legal bill trying to prove that they owned the copyright to the idea about the Holy Grail that lies at the centre of Brown's novel.[3] A further twist in the case was that due to various mergers and acquisitions, the two books were under the same publisher, Random House, which issued a statement deeply regretting the situation.

The Holy Blood and the Holy Grail put forward the theory that the holy grail was not a sacred chalice but the bloodline of Jesus Christ and Mary Magdalene – from a child whose descendants the Church sought to eliminate. The mission of the Knights Templar was to stop that happening. The Templars were created by a shadowy organisation called the Priory of Sion that protects the bloodline of Jesus and is plotting to create a pan-European Christian monarchy based on the Merovingian dynasty that ruled much of modern France and Germany from the fifth century CE until its downfall in 751 CE.

Sadly, for Baigent and Leigh, the High Court in 2006, and Appeals Court in 2007, ruled that while *The Da Vinci Code* was certainly influenced by the 1980s book, it had not infringed any copyright. This was a devastating decision for the losing side. It's very telling that the two authors who sued Brown's publisher, Baigent and Leigh, died in their mid-sixties while their third co-author, Henry Lincoln (1930–2022) – who sat out the court battle – lived to the ripe old age of 92. The main weakness in the case against Brown's publisher was that *The Holy Blood and the Holy Grail* had in turn been influenced by the controversial writings of a group of eccentric French conspiracy theorists who, from the 1950s onwards, concocted an origin account for the Knights Templar that was completely discredited just before *The Holy Blood and the Holy Grail* was published. That included the existence of the mysterious Priory of Sion.

The Priory of Sion hoax began with one man: Pierre Plantard (1920–2000). Or as he preferred to style himself, Pierre Plantard de Saint-Clair, Grand Master of the Prieuré de Sion.[4] There are two ways of looking at this curious figure. Either he was a fantasist, or his life was some kind of surrealist manifesto. Two of his key collaborators certainly regarded themselves as bona fide surrealists. During the Second World War, Paris-born Plantard dabbled with xenophobic and ultra-nationalist politics at a time when France was divided between a Nazi-occupied half and the pro-Nazi Vichy regime in the south-east of the country. Plantard founded associations and groups repeatedly, only to wind them up after a few months. Between 1939 and 1945, he set up the Alpha-Galates, the Knights of Light, and the Latin Academy. At one point, he tried to curry favour with the president of Vichy France, Marshal Philippe Pétain (1856–1951), by denouncing an imaginary 'Judeo-Masonic plot'. This led to a short official investigation of Plantard with the Vichy authorities writing him off as a 'crank'.[5] After the war, he became a Freemason and in 1956, registered an association called the Priory of Sion.[6]

Quite what the Priory of Sion was originally intended to be is difficult to define. At the outset there were no overt claims to being anything to do with the Knights Templar. Its main objectives seemed to be advocating for low-cost housing and airing Plantard's political views via a journal titled *CIRCUIT.* However, its articles of association submitted to the French authorities in

May 1956 declared it was a Catholic association dedicated to restoring ancient chivalry, a portent of how it would evolve.

CIRCUIT was an acronym for Chevalerie d'Institutions et Règles Catholiques d'Union Indépendante et Traditionaliste (Chivalry of Catholic Rules and Institutions of Independent and Traditionalist Union). Plantard would go on to explain that the 'Sion' in question was in the Holy Land, but in 1956 it was just the name of a nearby hill in the Haute-Savoie region of France. Oddly, for an organisation campaigning for better housing, it had nine degrees of membership, named using Templar and Freemason terminology. Plantard, the association's Secretary, was to be referred to as 'Chyren', a character mentioned in the predictions of Nostradamus.

In the early 1960s, Plantard ditched the housing agenda and began transforming the Priory of Sion into the mythological beast that would go on to influence *The Holy Blood and the Holy Grail* and *The Da Vinci Code*. Three news stories, covered extensively in the French media, pushed Plantard in this direction. The writer Jean-Luc Chaumeil (born 1944) knew Plantard very well and was convinced that the discovery of the Dead Sea Scrolls between 1946 and 1956 excited his imagination. Especially the Copper Scroll which the archaeologist John Marco Allegro (1923–1988), argued was an inventory, made by the secretive Essenes cult 2000 years ago, of treasure taken from the second temple in Jerusalem and hidden before its destruction by the Romans after the failure of the First Jewish Revolt in 70 CE.[7] If Chaumeil is correct then Plantard now wanted to create his own ancient treasure story into which he could insert the Priory of Sion.

Initially, Plantard alighted on a long running story about hidden Templar treasure underneath Gisors castle. This old fortress was situated between Paris and Rouen. After the mass arrest of the Templars in France in 1307, several knights, including the grand master Jacques de Molay, had been imprisoned within its forbidding walls. Fast forward to the 1940s and a caretaker at Gisors, Roger Lhomoy (1904–1974), maintained he had come across a Roman chapel underneath the dungeon stuffed with statues, several sarcophagi, and coffers full of Templar treasure.

His successor as caretaker, Robert Canu, told a newspaper in 1970 that Lhomoy worked 'like a madman' to excavate this secret crypt, even though this was during the Nazi occupation of northern France and German soldiers were billeted in the castle.[8] 'He dug a well some seventy feet deep with his naked hands during the night', Canu said. Getting wind of what Lhomoy was up to, the local council sent the fire brigade chief, Emile Beyne, to have a look and he 'crept into the black depths – but never reached the bottom', instead, throwing stones into the murky gloom, which 'echoed eerily'. He reported back that there had been 'strange sounds', but the townsfolk of Gisors remained sceptical and the whole matter was forgotten.

In 1961, a middle-aged aristocrat who claimed descent through one of his great-grandmothers from Pope Clement V – Géraud-Marie de Sède, Baron de Liéoux (1921–2004) – employed Lhomoy on his estate and got to hear his story of Templar riches.[9] De Sède had fought with the French Resistance in the Second World War, been imprisoned by the Germans, flirted with Trotskyism and corresponded with the celebrated surrealist, André Breton (1896–1966). He wrote a magazine article, taking Lhomoy's story at face value. Plantard was so excited by the article that he reached out to De Sède and the two men worked on a book titled *Les Templiers sont parmi nous, ou, L'Enigme de Gisors* (The Templars are Amongst Us, or The Enigma of Gisors). The book, which featured a mention of the Priory of Sion, reignited interest in the alleged treasure trove at Gisors.

In October 1962, the local council at Gisors ordered a fresh dig to solve the mystery once and for all. New shafts were sunk and Lhomoy was summoned to help with the excavation. The workers hacked away but no secret chapel emerged. Officials from the Ministry for Cultural Affairs came over from Paris to take a closer look and concluded there was nothing there. Canu observed that Lhomoy 'crept away in despair, crying like a kid'.

In 1964, the minister of cultural affairs, André Malraux (1901–1976), commissioned one more dig but when that proved fruitless, concrete was poured into the various holes that Lhomoy had dug. The old ex-caretaker became a figure of fun. For Plantard, this was merely a momentary setback. He was still determined to have his very own treasure tale. Gisors had not delivered, but a village hundreds of miles away showed more potential.

In the late nineteenth century, Rennes-le-Château was a sleepy hamlet, located close to the Pyrenees. The area had been disputed in the Middle Ages between French barons and the kings of Aragon, in what is now Spain. From the twelfth century, this part of modern France became a hotbed of Cathar activity, attracting the full force of the Albigensian crusade launched by the papacy to crush the dangerous heresy. When the Templars were arrested in 1307 by order of the French king, the knights in the vicinity of Rennes-le-Château were left largely unmolested. This exception fuelled a slew of theories centred on supposed Templar treasure lying underneath the village and this speculation focused on a rogue priest at the turn of the twentieth century.

In 1885, François-Bérenger Saunière (1852–1917) became the parish priest at Rennes-le-Château with a small congregation, meagre income, and little hope for advancement. Yet somehow, he acquired huge sums to renovate the dilapidated eleventh-century church dedicated to Mary Magdalene. His taste in interior décor was a little eccentric, featuring a devilish figure at the entrance to the church that still stares menacingly at visitors. Some have argued it is the Talmudic demon, Asmodeus, who helped King Solomon build the original temple in Jerusalem. Somehow, this provincial priest was able to embellish his church with weird figures, and even commission an impressive medieval-style tower and a sumptuous villa with an orangery. None of this tallied with his social position as a parish priest in a rural backwater.

By the 1960s, long after his death in 1917, Saunière was said to have discovered ancient parchments and Templar treasure. But from the man himself and contemporary records, we get none of these details. The ancient parchments, allegedly found within a Visigothic pillar, were lodged with the local town hall but then lost when it was consumed by fire, an event that proved to be very beneficial to a small group of French conspiracy theorists.

Like many Catholic clerics of the time, Saunière held pro-royalist views and despised the French Republic as an agent of liberalism and anti-clericalism. For sharing these views from his pulpit, Saunière was suspended for a while from his duties by order of the Minister of Worship, René Goblet (1828–1905). But the outspoken priest was shielded by his bishop and was soon back in place. It's clear that he used his position to sell masses, which is the ecclesiastical crime of simony. Priests could accept cash for a specially dedicated mass to a dead loved one, but not actively solicit payments. A new bishop investigated Saunière in 1910 and decided that was the source of his mysterious income. In addition, villagers complained that under cover of darkness, and using the excuse of his endless renovations, Saunière had been pillaging old graves for whatever he could find of value.

That should have been the end of Saunière and rumours about his wealth being derived from Templar treasure, unearthed and kept for himself. But a good story does not die so easily – even when confronted with the facts. The disgraced priest died in 1917 leaving his property portfolio to his loyal housekeeper, Marie Dénarnaud. In 1953, Marie passed away having sold the estate to a local businessman, Noël Corbu (1912–1968), who turned Saunière's villa into a restaurant. In what was undoubtedly a ruse to drum up business, the entrepreneurial Corbu teamed up with a local journalist to pen three articles in the newspaper *La Dépêche du Midi* resurrecting the memory of Saunière and suggesting that under his church lay a multi-billion-dollar fortune buried by Blanche of Castile (1188–1252), queen of France through her marriage to King

Louis VIII (1187–1226). French television broadcast a documentary on the story in 1961 and the journalist Robert Charroux (1909–1978) – famous for his promotion of ancient astronaut theory – further popularised the story. This put the village firmly on the map and did wonders for Corbu's restaurant trade.

It also attracted the attention of Plantard, who instinctively recognised the opportunity to insert the Priory of Sion into the Rennes-le-Château treasure tale. He began paying visits to the village and met Corbu. To reshape the Priory of Sion into something more significant than a housing charity, Plantard teamed up with yet another bored French aristocrat, Philippe Louis Henri Marie de Chérisey (1923–1985), the ninth marquis of his name. Like De Sède, he had also dabbled in surrealism – in his case as a member of the so-called College of Pataphysics, a group founded by the absurdist and champion of the avant-garde, Alfred Jarry (1873–1907). Jarry's fast and loose approach to accepted truths and the evidence-based approach of modern science may go some way to explaining the conscious abandonment of facts by De Chérisey, and De Sède. As Chaumeil explained, it was all part of a 'surrealist game'.

De Sède published a book on the mystery of Rennes-le-Château that set out the familiar story of a priest suddenly becoming rich after he discovers buried Templar treasure. But he then added the notion of a curse that would befall anybody who asked too many questions. Right back to the fourteenth century, those who investigated or tried to find the riches under the village, supposedly suffered horrific deaths.

In May 1968, Corbu was killed in a car accident between Castelnaudary and Carcassone. De Sède believed his curiosity about the treasure cost him his life. 'The fact remains that M. Corbu was dragged, unrecognisable, from the shapeless debris of his Renault 16.'[10] A year before, documents were lodged at the Bibliothèque Nationale de France – the National Library in Paris – under the title: *Dossiers Secrets d'Henri Lobineau* (Secret Dossiers of Henri Lobineau). These were supposedly compiled by a man called Philippe Toscan du Plantier and claimed to be copies of the far older documents discovered by Saunière in his church then handed over to the local town hall, which then burned down. This meant that there were no originals of these allegedly ancient scraps of paper penned in Latin.

The dossiers featured a list of the grand masters of the Priory of Sion. The names included Johannes Valentinus Andreae (1586–1654) who wrote one of the foundational works of the Rosicrucian movement, a secret society advocating a new world order. Also on the list of former grand masters were Leonardo da Vinci (1452–1519), Isaac Newton (1642–1727), the French novelist Victor Hugo (1802–1885), the composer Claude Debussy (1862–1918), the artist Jean Cocteau (1889–1963) and finally, Pierre Plantard.

The dossiers revealed that the Priory of Sion's objective was to reinstate the Merovingian dynasty of Frankish kings that had ruled modern France and a large chunk of modern Germany from the fifth century CE to their overthrow in the eighth century. Plantard now claimed to be of Merovingian descent. Chaumeil sarcastically noted that this meant Plantard could face down his aristocratic buddies by exclaiming he was not a mere marquis, but a king!

The storytelling efforts of Plantard, De Sède, and De Chérisey were highly effective. By the end of the 1960s, Rennes-le-Château had been overrun by treasure hunters. One such group was the International Treasure Seekers Club based in Montmartre, Paris, with twenty-nine British members. A 1962 report in a UK newspaper, *The Sunday People*, revealed that the club was on its way to unearth treasure at Rennes-le-Château which they valued at a mere six million pounds.[11] In 1965, the village council forbade the digging of any more holes by unauthorised people. This measure had limited impact. 'The witches and water diviners, archaeologists and simple amateurs, armed with divining rods and maps, spades and pickaxes, still come, but in reduced numbers.'[12] However, in 1968 the brief calm was shattered with the exhuming of a farm labourer known simply as Rouge who had reputedly found a 110-pound gold bar back in 1860. Quite why Rouge needed to be dug up is unclear, but it renewed interest in the alleged Templar treasure still to be found.

It was at the dawn of the 1970s that the paths of Plantard and one of the authors of *The Holy Blood and the Holy Grail* crossed. Henry Soskin (1930–2022) was better known under his pen name, Henry Lincoln. He was the only one of the three authors of *The Holy Blood and the Holy Grail* who wisely decided not to get involved in suing Dan Brown. In the 1960s, he had worked in the television industry as an actor, presenter, and scriptwriter. His main claim to fame was the scripting of three Doctor Who series for the BBC when actor Patrick Troughton (1920–1987) played the intrepid time lord: *The Abominable Snowmen* (1967), *The Web of Fear* (1968), and *The Dominators* (1968).

While on holiday in the south of France in 1969, Lincoln picked up a copy of De Sède's book and was hooked. What was not to like? Treasure that possibly dated back to the original Temple of Solomon in Jerusalem had been found in a remote French church. Evidence for this was the Secret Dossiers in France's national library that also proved the existence of a secret society dedicated to putting the Merovingian dynasty back on the throne. One of the Merovingian kings, Dagobert II (died 679 CE), had owned said treasure at some point and the Knights Templar, who had been based in Jerusalem, were heavily involved in guarding these riches.

Lincoln knew a good story when he saw one. The result was a meeting with Plantard, arranged by Chaumeil, and three documentaries for the BBC's regular *Chronicles* strand: *The Lost Treasure of Jerusalem* (1972), *The Priest, The Painter, and the Devil* (1974), and *The Shadow of the Templars* (1979). However, Lincoln's storyline took on a life of its own. The Merovingian connection needed a punchier rationale. Otherwise, why should anybody care about a dynasty of Dark Ages kings with little name recognition outside of France? Something heart-stopping had to link the Merovingians to the Priory of Sion and its creation, the Knights Templar. The answer was not to be found in the works of Plantard, De Sède, and De Chérisey.

Lincoln incorporated a theory re-popularised in the 1970s that Jesus had been married. The French author, Robert Ambelain (1907–1997), asserted in 1970 that the biblical character Salome was in fact the 'concubine' of Jesus.[13] But Lincoln found that unsatisfying. Instead, he favoured Mary Magdalene as the wife of Jesus for two compelling reasons. One was that since the Middle Ages, stories had circulated that Mary Magdalene had journeyed to southern France and established a Christian community. Moreover, these medieval legends described Mary Magdalene in the company of other leading Christians including Joseph of Arimathea, who went on to Roman-controlled Britannia in the aftermath of the crucifixion.

Lincoln now had her arriving in France with Jesus, her husband still very much alive, plus children. These offspring are often referred to as the 'Desposyni' or bloodline of Christ. The French connection to Mary Magdalene was further strengthened by the presence of a major shrine at Vézelay. Back in the ninth century CE, Benedictine monks brought the relics of Mary Magdalene to their new monastery there, which became one of the most popular pilgrimage sites of the medieval period. This was mixed into the emerging tale as proof of her presence in the region nearly 2000 years ago. The other compelling reason, for Lincoln, was that Saunière's church in Rennes-le-Château was dedicated to Mary Magdalene.[14] Surely that was evidence of her missionary work in France?

The Merovingians now became the descendants of the children of Jesus and Mary Magdalene, which meant that Plantard was also a descendant of Christ. Lincoln agreed with the newly sanctified Plantard that the Priory of Sion was a secret society set up by the first crusader ruler of the kingdom of Jerusalem, Godfrey de Bouillon (1060–1100) at the Abbey of Our Lady of Mount Zion in the holy city. He also concurred that the Priory of Sion was trying to re-instal the Merovingians as a new global Christian monarchy. But Lincoln was not interested in Plantard's reactionary, monarchist politics. For him, the

Priory was dedicated to protecting the bloodline of Jesus from a hostile Roman Catholic Church. Why? Because its very existence undermined the authority of the papacy and the version of the Christ story imposed by the first Christian Roman Emperor, Constantine.

By the end of the 1970s, Lincoln had teamed up with a photographer, Michael Baigent, and a science fiction novel writer, Richard Leigh, to begin work on what would become a global bestseller: *The Holy Blood and the Holy Grail.* The Knights Templar were transformed into the military arm of the Priory of Sion, providing the required muscle to protect the bloodline of Christ from the Church.

The Secret Dossiers were presented in *The Holy Blood and the Holy Grail* as entirely legitimate, containing six 'indisputable historical facts' summarised excellently by the judge in the Dan Brown legal case mentioned:

1. The Priory of Sion was a secret order behind the creation of the Knights Templar.
2. The Priory of Sion was led by some of the greatest names in history like Leonardo da Vinci and Isaac Newton.
3. Although the Knights Templar were destroyed between 1307 and 1314, the Priory of Sion continued unscathed, orchestrating events in western history.
4. The Priory of Sion still exists today operating at the highest levels of global politics.
5. The objective of the Priory of Sion is to restore the Merovingian dynasty and thereby the bloodline of Christ to the thrones of Europe.
6. The bloodline continued through the Merovingian dynasty to Godfrey de Bouillon and other European royal families.

After the crusaders invaded Jerusalem in 1099 during the First Crusade, the Priory of Sion engineered the takeover by Godfrey de Bouillon, who became the protector of the city while not assuming the title of king. Twenty years later, the Priory – now based at Mount Zion – formed the Knights Templars as their military wing while also pulling the strings of Saint Bernard of Clairvaux, the main propagandist for the new order. However, in 1188, the Templars and Priory of Sion fell out during the disastrous leadership of the Templar grand master Gerard de Ridefort (1141–1189) who presided over military defeats at the Springs of Cresson and the Horns of Hattin.

This parting of the ways between the knights and the priory is described as 'the cutting of the elm'. Confusingly, there was a universally accepted event that took place that year by the same name involving a spat between the Angevin king of England, Henry II (1133–1189), and Philip II of France (1165–1223), also known as Philip Augustus. The two met at Gisors following the fall of Jerusalem to Muslim forces, and while Henry and his advisers enjoyed the shade of an elm tree, Philip and his entourage were forced to swelter in the sun. An incensed French monarch hacked down the elm afterwards. One event happened, while the other has a shakier evidential base.

The Holy Blood and the Holy Grail details the meetings between the authors and Plantard who confirmed that the Priory of Sion had obtained the long-lost treasure of King Solomon's temple in Jerusalem. But that treasure was spiritual. So, what was it? This is where Lincoln, Baigent, and Leigh parted company with Plantard, instead directing their readers' attention to Mary Magdalene, a woman wrongly trashed by the Church as a prostitute. Not only did she establish a sacred bloodline, but that is what defines the Holy Grail. Early accounts of the Grail called it the 'Sangreal' or 'Sangraal' and that very likely meant 'Sang Real', which translates as royal blood. The Grail was the bloodline, brought to France by Mary Magdalene. She was the wife of Jesus, and their wedding was the marriage feast at Cana, mentioned in the New Testament.

Initially the early Christian Church tried to develop a *modus vivendi* with the bloodline but then resolved to annihilate them. They were an inconvenient truth. Especially after the Emperor Constantine strongarmed the ecclesiastical Council of Nicaea to declare that Jesus was not a mortal prophet, but a god. Or more exactly, one of three 'persons' with God: father, son, and holy spirit. To achieve this, Constantine fused Christianity with elements of pagan religions like the cult of Sol Invictus (the invincible sun) and the worship of the bull god, Mithras. Once the big lie was established, the bloodline had to go. They were proof that Jesus was a human being. Down the centuries, the Church took out any Desposyni who posed a threat, hence the assassination of the Merovingian king and descendant of Jesus, Dagobert.

Not only were the Templars ordered to defend the bloodline, but by proving Jesus was mortal they intended to force a reconciliation between the conflicting Abrahamic faiths of Christianity, Judaism, and Islam. Once Jesus was re-established as human, the theological barriers would disappear. One might argue this explains why the Templars were often accused by contemporary chroniclers of being on far too friendly terms with the Saracens in Outremer – they really were engaging in some kind of heretical inter-faith dialogue. But it does stretch credulity to believe that the Templars believed that the crucifixion never happened or was somehow faked, which is assumed but never detailed at any length in *The Holy Blood and the Holy Grail*. If the knights had aired that view, they would not have enjoyed papal protection and privileges for two centuries.

The reaction in France to *The Holy Blood and the Holy Grail* could best be described as muted horror. Far from being flattered at his newly discovered link to Jesus, Plantard was mortified. Almost as if the 'surrealist game', as described by Chaumeil, had now spiralled out of his control. Unfortunately for Lincoln,

Baigent, and Leigh, it was just as their book headed for the printing presses, that the cracks began to appear among the original Priory of Sion theorists. Plantard declared publicly that he was not descended from Christ and could not accept the new take on the Merovingians. Chaumeil repeatedly stated that the Secret Dossiers were faked and in private conversations, De Chérisey cheerfully admitted to being the real author of these supposedly ancient parchments. Despite this, *The Holy Blood and the Holy Grail* achieved huge sales, and the trio of authors penned a sequel, *The Messianic Legacy*, in 1987.[15] Still focused on the Priory of Sion with attempts to link the Templars, through the Priory, to the CIA, KGB, Freemasonry, and Opus Dei.[16] This time, however, the authors struggled to find something new to say as their French sources ran dry. One review described the sequel as 'crushingly boring'.[17]

Meanwhile, in France, the Priory of Sion was about to face a major legal challenge. In 1989, a statement was issued by the 'Priory of Sion Secretariat-General' to the Priory's 'brethren' announcing the death of the current grand master, Roger-Patrice Pelat (1918–1989). Pelat was an old friend of the then French president, François Mitterrand (1916–1996; served as president 1981–1985). They had both been imprisoned in a German prisoner-of-war camp during the Second World War. The statement called for a minute's silence 'in memory of a person who was always a man in the shadows, perfectly honest and just', adding cryptically that Pelat had been brought down by American 'initiates'. These mysterious Americans would no longer be accepted into the Priory, which would remain 'exclusively European'.[18]

In 1981, Pelat had been photographed with Mitterrand during that year's presidential election campaign on a visit to the church in Rennes-le-Château. His name appeared in an updated list of priory grand masters between De Chérisey, who was grand master up to his death in 1985, and Plantard who resumed control in 1989.[19]

However, there was a problem. Pelat had never been grand master of the Priory of Sion. Only his death prevented him refuting the claim in the priory's statement. But there was worse. His fatal heart attack came as he was being investigated for insider trading. A French judge, Thierry Jean-Pierre (1955–2005), was digging through the financial records of the president's long-time associate.[20] This was a scandal that reached to the very top of the French political scene. The judge decided, as part of his investigations, to call in Plantard and investigate any links between Pelat and the Priory. Plantard's home was also searched for any incriminating documents. The outcome was the complete discrediting of the Priory of Sion. Plantard denied ever having attended a Priory meeting or knowing any of its members and confirmed that Pelat was never a grand master.

By way of a postscript to Plantard, who died in 2000, the church he placed at the centre of his conspiracy theory witnessed an unusual attack in the last decade. In April 2017, a Syrian woman dressed in a long white cape, a veil, and a Venetian mask on her face calmly walked into Saunière's church, dedicated to Mary Magdalene, and in front of shocked tourists, produced an axe and decapitated the devilish representation of Asmodeus. She also cut off the demon's arm and placed a copy of the Qur'an nearby. The woman then slashed the bas-relief on the altar of Mary Magdalene. When apprehended by police, she mentioned the ongoing French presidential election, 'while in Syria, the West is bombing and killing children. You are all infidels. My husband is over there'.[21] Her mission, to garner maximum publicity for her cause, led her to Rennes-le-Château, which had become a high-profile tourist trap.

The American novelist, Dan Brown, was of course aware of *The Holy Blood and the Holy Grail* as well as other esoteric histories of the Templars mentioned in *The Da Vinci Code*, for example *The Templar Revelation* by Lynn Picknett and Clive Prince.[22] Both those authors made a short, background appearance in the subsequent movie of the book while one of the main characters in Brown's book, Sir Leigh Teabing, was a backhanded compliment to the two *The Holy Blood and the Holy Grail* authors who went on to drag Brown's publisher before the courts: Richard Leigh and Michael Baigent. Leigh is obvious; Teabing is an anagram of Baigent. At one point, Teabing explicitly mentions *The Holy Blood and the Holy Grail* to the character Sophie, referring to it as 'the acclaimed international bestseller'. Brown also used the Saunière name but in a markedly different context with the book's dramatic climax happening at Rosslyn chapel in Scotland, as detailed in a previous chapter, and not in Rennes-le-Château.

Dan Brown's novel begins with a statement of 'fact'. He refers to the Priory of Sion as being a secret society founded in 1099, identified in the Secret Dossiers, and with an unbroken line of grand masters. He then weaves in the Catholic organisation Opus Dei, founded by Josemaría Escrivá de Balaguer y Albás (1902–1975) in 1928. Escrivá was a Spaniard, hostile to the anticlericalism and liberalism in 1930s Spain and so it's unsurprising that he became a good friend of the fascist dictator, General Francisco Franco (1892–1975) who seized power after a bitter civil war in 1936. Under Franco, Opus Dei thrived and grew. Its members came to occupy key posts in the government and civil service.[23] Escrivá was canonised as a saint by Pope John Paul II (1920–2005) in 2002, who described the Opus Dei founder as 'among the great witnesses of Christianity'.

In *The Da Vinci Code*, the secretive organisation is portrayed as a violent group of brainwashed monks who will resort to murder to suppress the truth about Jesus Christ. They are the Vatican's in-house assassins, determined to annihilate the bloodline of Christ and the true version of Christianity uncovered by the Templars. An Opus Dei monk named Silas is under orders to kill those seeking the meaning of the Holy Grail. In one scene, we see him mortifying his own flesh with a whip, his back streaked with blood. Around his thigh is a tightly bound cilice, a spiked belt that digs into his muscle. This corporal punishment is held to be common practice within Opus Dei – a way to experience the suffering of Jesus.

Negative portrayals of Opus Dei are nothing new. In 1981, the *Daily Mirror* newspaper in the United Kingdom ran a feature interviewing 'fugitives' from the organisation who painted 'a harrowing picture of daily life as a member of the sect'. They described accounts of the recently deceased Escrivá whipping himself 'for hours until blood streaked the walls and ceilings'. All individual thought was allegedly suppressed, and members were isolated from the real world.

> *It combines the horrors of the Middle Ages with the Big Brother regime of George Orwell's book, 1984.*[24]

When *The Da Vinci Code* movie was released in 2006, Opus Dei demanded that Sony Pictures put a disclaimer on the movie stating it was fiction and not fact. The letter to Sony shareholders, directors, and employees, written in Japanese but translated below into English, included the following:

> *As you already probably know, there are some aspects of The Da Vinci Code novel that distort the figure of Jesus Christ, and which affect the religious beliefs of Christians. Moreover, in the book it is said that the Christian Faith is founded on a lie, and that the Catholic Church has over the centuries employed criminal and violent means to keep people in ignorance.*[25]

As the months passed, Opus Dei changed tack in relation to *The Da Vinci Code*. It was even suggested in the media that the organisation was enjoying a surge in interest regarding its work and ethos because of the book and movie. Opus Dei started to put out statements using the claimed falsehoods in *The Da Vinci Code* to explain itself. Almost as if it was engaged in a dialogue with Dan Brown and others. It also linked users from its websites to other sites with titles like The Da Vinci Deception, De-Coding Da Vinci, and The Da Vinci Hoax. In one statement, Opus Dei went through a point-by-point rebuttal of Dan Brown's novel.[26] It stated:

1. Opus Dei members were presented as monks in *The Da Vinci Code* – 'or, rather, caricatures of monks' – but there are no monks in the organisation,

only lay people and diocesan priests. So-called 'numerary' members do take a vow of celibacy but do not wear strange robes and indulge in 'corporal mortification'.

2. Opus Dei members are 'falsely depicted murdering, lying, drugging people, and otherwise acting unethically, thinking that it is justified for the sake of God, the Church or Opus Dei'. This is not true, and neither is it interested in the pursuit of wealth and power.
3. Opus Dei members do not 'practice bloody mortifications'. They can make small sacrifices to emulate the suffering of Christ such as continuing to work when tired. The statement did concede, however, that some members make 'limited use of the cilice'.

Dan Brown depicted an Opus Dei operative, Silas, killing a top Priory of Sion member, Saunière, under orders from a senior Catholic prelate, Cardinal Aringarosa. What was the reason for this? Flash back to the Middle Ages and the Knights Templar unearthing ancient documents under their headquarters on the Temple Mount that proved the legitimacy of Christ's bloodline and destroyed the basis for Church power. The Templars gave the documents to the Priory of Sion. However, the papacy knew the Templars had this dangerous information and showered them with privileges in the hope of keeping the knights on side. Eventually, though, Rome rounded on the Templars in a manoeuvre 'worthy of the CIA' – assisted by the King of France. Before the king's agents could arrest them, the Templars smuggled the explosive documents found in Jerusalem out of France from the port of La Rochelle.

The Knights Templar have long been associated with the Holy Grail but in Brown's novel, it is not a sacred chalice but a woman. In the story, Leigh Teabing – a villainous Grail expert – explains all this to the heroes, Robert Langdon and Sophie Neveu, by revealing the hidden messaging contained within Leonardo Da Vinci's portrait of the Last Supper. It alludes very clearly to Mary Magdalene being the wife of Jesus and mother of his children. She may even have been pregnant when her husband, the Messiah, was crucified. Their marriage was a powerful union between the House of David and the House of Benjamin – fusing two royal Jewish bloodlines. Her bloodline was the Sang Real. But the Church has continued to try and snuff out the truth by murdering the bloodline and destroying the Priory of Sion. In Dan Brown's novel, Opus Dei is the instrument with which to achieve that objective. The real Opus Dei denies this while the Priory of Sion has fizzled out since Plantard's death in 2000. Or maybe – it has just gone underground again.

Belief in the Priory of Sion has endured despite Plantard's misadventures. However, for those who do not accept the Priory's existence but do believe a hidden hand created the Templars, then an alternative theory has emerged in recent years. There are similarities with the Priory of Sion but also marked differences. The Rex Deus theory claims that the families which produced the first founding knights of the Templar order were interlinked, serving a clandestine agenda.[27] Like the Priory of Sion, it sees the Templars as a body of warriors dedicated to protecting the sacred bloodline of Jesus Christ, threatened by the Roman Catholic Church, which is determined to protect the myth that Jesus was the son of God made human, who never married, nor had children.

To fully understand Rex Deus, it helps to start with the earliest years of Christianity. In the first decades after the crucifixion, nothing was recorded about the actual life of Jesus. The faithful saw no need for a biography of the Messiah because he was about to return at any moment to smite the Romans and usher in the kingdom of heaven on Earth. When the Romans destroyed the second Temple in Jerusalem in 70 CE, Christians were forced to realise that Jesus might not be coming back any time soon. At this point, the gospels start to emerge, beginning with the account by a writer we call Mark, followed by Matthew, Luke, and John.[28] The four evangelists transformed an apocalyptic Jewish preacher from a poverty-stricken region of the Roman Empire into a celibate, virgin-birth-created aspect of God who had very literally survived his own death and ascended miraculously into heaven.

But divisions on the true nature of Jesus emerged very early on. One group of Christians, the Ebionites, rejected the idea of Christ as divine, emphasising his humanity. They accepted he was a Messiah but in the Jewish sense predicted in the book of Deuteronomy. That was a man born of two parents, Joseph and Mary, who had come to show the true path to redemption. His followers simply needed to follow his example, including ritual ablutions, vegetarianism and rejecting the animal sacrifices so beloved of the Temple priests in Jerusalem.

As an organised and increasingly hierarchical Church evolved in the first three centuries after Christ, it imposed rigid dogmas and tore out unacceptable heresies by the roots. After the Emperor Constantine embraced Christianity, zealous bishops and monks employed the machinery of the State and violent terror at the local level to suppress unorthodox variants of the faith. For the first time in Roman history, people were executed for what we might term 'thought crime', heresy, a theological concept alien to pagan Romans. The very crime that would be the undoing of the Templars.

The Ebionites and their version of the gospel, along with tens of other gospel accounts, disappeared. But not, according to the Rex Deus theory, the truth about Jesus. That was guarded by a network of families descended from men who had once been the high priests of the second Temple, the *ma'madot*. They had exchanged their privileged hereditary positions for an ascetic life before the Romans had conquered Palestine.[29]

Far from being a humble Galilean peasant, Jesus came from a line of Temple priests stretching back to Zadok. Anybody familiar with the lyrics of *Zadok the Priest,* the coronation anthem composed by George Frideric Handel for King George II in 1727, will know that Zadok was the priest who crowned Solomon and served as high priest in the first Temple. Where is the evidence for this assertion? The proof can be found in the story of James the Just – the brother of Jesus. He became high priest in Jerusalem, before being stoned to death by order of the Pharisees. The fact he assumed this position is proof that he and Jesus were recognised as being descended from Jewish royalty, even if they provoked violent disagreement.

Just to plant a small bomb under this theory, one of the key sources for the story of James becoming high priest and the allegedly noble lineage of Jesus is the Jewish historian Josephus. In his history of the Jews,[30] written right after the destruction of the second Temple in 70 CE, there are references to Jesus and James that have long been suspected of being later inserts by Christian theologians.[31] Josephus was an orthodox Jew who had been involved in the revolt against Roman rule, then switched sides as the defeated Jews were rounded up. He was unlikely to have believed in Jesus as the Messiah let alone promoted him as such in his book, which was an extended grovel to the Romans who had spared his life. It stretches credulity that he would laud a man condemned by the Jerusalem priests and crucified for sedition by the Roman governor, Pontius Pilate.

So why do Jesus and James appear in his history of the Jews? The most likely reason is that there are so few references to Jesus in the decades after his crucifixion that later monks could not resist inserting fictitious asides into books from the first century CE. In this case, the finger of suspicion is pointed at an early Christian thinker called Origen who may have committed this act of literary fraud in the third century CE.

By the time the Knights Templar are founded, Jesus has been elevated to supernatural status, but this is opposed, covertly, by families descended from Zadok and his fellow high priests, sworn to guard the real story of Jesus and his descendants. Some of these people, the so-called Desposyni, are the direct bloodline of Christ. They pose a huge threat to Catholicism by evidencing that Christ had raised a family and possibly even never been crucified. Templar historian Tim Wallace-Murphy (1939–2019), the proponent of this theory, refers to all these families combined as *Rex Deus.*[32]

During the early medieval period, Rex Deus spread in Europe, most significantly in France. Wallace-Murphy argues that they helped the Emperor

Charlemagne create a vast Frankish empire that extended across modern France, Germany and Italy. This is a key difference between Rex Deus and the Priory of Sion. Rex Deus believes the Carolingian dynasty was the sacred line of kings while Plantard preferred the preceding Merovingians. Rex Deus presented a huge threat to the Church as it manipulated kings like puppets. A terrified Pope sent out a 'hit squad' to assassinate the son of William the Conqueror, William II (nicknamed Rufus), because he was an agent of Rex Deus, attacking clerical privilege in England.[33] The king certainly had a difficult relationship with the Church. His Archbishop of Canterbury, Anselm, fled into exile while in contrast his key advisor, the Bishop of Durham Ranulf Flambard (*c.*1060–1128), is widely believed to have been the monarch's homosexual lover.[34]

If there was a papal hit squad, it succeeded in killing the king by means of a stray arrow while he was hunting in the New Forest in 1100. One of the lords with William that day, Walter Tirel, fled to France and so implicated himself as the guilty party. It's believed Tirel was acting for William's ambitious brother, Henry, who wanted to be king and was indeed subsequently crowned. Just before William Rufus was felled by an arrow, Jerusalem was conquered by a crusader army during the First Crusade. Rex Deus now set about creating a new type of religious military order to fulfil its aims: the Knights Templar. And to advocate for this order, they had a member who had infiltrated the Church to its highest levels: Bernard of Clairvaux (1090–1153).

Wallace-Murphy argues that Bernard was engaged in a conspiracy with fellow relatives in Rex Deus, including the founders of the Knights Templar: Hugh de Payens (the first grand master) and André de Montbard (his uncle and fifth grand master). There was also a future Patriarch of Jerusalem, the St Clair and Seton families from Scotland, the Flemish royal family and Hugh, the Count of Champagne. They wanted to transform Christianity into something closer to the Ebionite vision. The persecution Jews suffered was based on a false depiction of Jesus by the Church. The Messiah had been robbed of his Jewishness and falsely turned from a human being into a god.

Rex Deus set up a revolutionary new kind of military and monastic order – the Knights Templar – and based it on the Temple Mount in Jerusalem. Bernard wrote propaganda tracts in praise of the Templars and urged young men to join without hesitation. Popes were convinced to give the order freedom from the local control of bishops and princes, making them answerable only to Rome. And Bernard wrote their rule book, based on that of his Cistercian order. The Rex Deus-affiliated Patriarch of Jerusalem obligingly installed the Knights Templar in the Temple of Solomon, from which they took their name. They shared the building with another Rex Deus member, King Baldwin. And with the protection of both the temporal and spiritual authorities, the knights got their shovels out and started to dig for secrets that would prove Jesus was a man and not a god.

So, how exactly did Templar theorist Tim Wallace-Murphy discover the whole Rex Deus story? It all began when he was asked to give a lecture on the esoteric side of the Templars to The Saunière Society. This group, founded by a man called Derek Burton in 1985, claims on its website as of 2024, to be dedicated to discovering the truth behind Rennes-le-Château as well as advancing the 'research and work carried out by the authors of *The Holy Blood and the Holy Grail*'.[35] At the end of his talk, a man called Michael Monkton approached Wallace-Murphy and talked about secret symbols under the Temple Mount. When he was asked how he knew about such things, Monkton declared:

> *It is part of the secret traditions of my family for the last 2000 years.*

Only the threat of having his throat torn out (*sic*), had kept him silent. But the publication of *The Holy Blood and the Holy Grail* gave him the courage to share the family secrets. Wallace-Murphy conducted further discussions with others present as witnesses. Not only did Monkton map out the whole Rex Deus proposition, but it turned out he was a direct descendant of the Templar founder, Hugh de Payens. Wallace-Murphy then set out in several books to detail how Rex Deus had kept the Templar spirit alive for its own ends. He argues that the original Templar order died out after the Battle of Bannockburn, having been told to go underground by Robert the Bruce. In Wallace-Murphy's view, no neo-Templar organisation today can legitimately claim to be the continuation of the original Templars.

Rex Deus families kept the military spirit of the Templars alive in bodies like the Scots Guard, Knights of Santiago, Order of the Crescent, Order of the Fleur de Lys, Order of Christ in Portugal, and Monkton told Wallace-Murphy that the Order of the Bath in England may have been a Rex Deus front when it was originally founded in 1725. Its name references a medieval ceremony where a candidate for knighthood was ritually bathed in an act of purification. Wallace-Murphy argued that anybody wanting to identify Rex Deus members should start with these bodies:

> *Therefore, it is reasonable to assume that a comparative study of the membership lists of these various orders would give great insight into the identity of members of this proud and secretive tradition that has reached out over the millennia from ancient Egypt to the present.*

Sceptics will scoff at both the Priory of Sion and Rex Deus accounts of the origins of the Knights Templar. Some 200 years ago, the Scottish novelist, Walter Scott, derided contemporary fascination with alleged secret societies. 'Rosicrucians and Illuminati, with all their properties of black cowls, caverns, daggers, electrical machines, trapdoors, and dark lanterns.'[36] So what motivates those who put these claims into print and defend them so vigorously? This was something investigated by the Italian author, Umberto Eco (1932–2016), in his 1988 novel, *Foucault's Pendulum*.[37] The plot revealed the perils of dabbling in conspiracy theories, even for fun.

In summary, three publishers who had grown weary of the mediocre conspiracy theories trumpeted by mediocre authors decide to develop their own ultimate theory. They input every crackpot theory they can think of into a very smart computer called Abulafia (after a medieval kabbalistic philosopher) that forms connections between the entries. The result is a super-conspiracy-theory codenamed 'The Plan', involving the Knights Templar and their alleged secret desire to control the naturally occurring electric currents that flow through our planet (telluric currents). By degrees, the trio are drawn into their own creation, which then assumes a life of its own and begins to kill them.[38]

Foucault's Pendulum is a warning about blurring reality and illusion. Some have seen it as an attack on post-modernism and the departure from rationalism in our own time. The phenomenon we refer to as 'post-truth'. Eco has every secret society imaginable working with the Templars on their dastardly plan: Rosicrucians, Freemasons, Jesuits, and even the Nazis. He weaves in hermetic ideas and ley lines. Most controversially, Eco also introduces anti-Semitic tropes to spice things up. Even if he did this in a puckish way, it was widely attacked when the book was published in 1989. But sadly, these elements are often added together today in online exchanges, proving that this book – intended to be satirical – has become an unintended playbook for conspiracy theorists.[39]

Chapter Nine

From the Jedi to Assassin's Creed

The Knights Templar have been on a long journey since the last grand master, Jacques de Molay, was consigned to the flames in 1314. They have become the keepers of the Holy Grail, the Ark of the Covenant, and the Shroud of Jesus. Many are convinced that they played a role in the foundation of the Freemasons and were somehow involved with the Illuminati and Rosicrucians. Their beliefs were either mainstream Roman Catholic or heretical Gnostic, according to your point of view. But this only scrapes the surface when we consider how the Templars have been depicted in historical fiction, the movies, and even in video games.

While it's easy to dismiss these depictions, they very often touch on questions about the knights that were raised during their two centuries of crusading – as well as the years between 1307 and 1314 when they were on trial for their lives. Were they a secretive cult adhering to heretical beliefs and engaging in diabolic rites? Was their downfall a grim foreshadowing of the witchcraft trials to follow? Did the knights possess treasure of incalculable value squirreled away when they realised the game was up? And most fundamentally of all, were the Templars a force for good or evil?

In an episode of the 1980s British TV series, *Robin of Sherwood*, based on the story of Robin Hood the outlaw, the Knights Templar are depicted as menacing, robotic figures on horseback, faces hidden behind their steel, sugar-loaf helmets, and bodies clad in chain mail, covered by white mantles with the famous red cross. Filing through the forest they dismount at intervals to form a circle, kneel, and pray in Latin.[1]

Their leader has a hypnotic hold over his fellow knights and very soon, they clash with Robin and his band of merry men, whom they believe have stolen one of their sacred relics. Even the Sheriff of Nottingham and Guy of Gisbourne, who have in fact got hold of the relic, fear their presence and treat the Templars with kid gloves. In one scene, we see a dead knight being cremated on a pyre, still in his white mantle and steel helmet, while all around the Templars chant in Latin, sounding more like a Satanic ritual than a Christian mass. Happily, Robin ambushes the thoroughly unpleasant Templars and, having got hold of their relic, melts it down in a blacksmith's forge with the words: 'That'll pay the village tithes and taxes'.

This rather unsympathetic portrayal contrasts with the way movie director, George Lucas (born 1944), viewed the knights when, as a young man, he developed the concept that would become *Star Wars*.

Lucas had just finished editing his 1973 hit movie *American Graffiti* and immediately began work on a project that would combine science fiction with traditional storytelling. He became a voracious reader of fairy tales, mythology, psychology, and history. He devoured the works of sci-fi author Isaac Asimov, alongside the adventurous fantasies of Edgar Rice Burroughs. Setting the action in the twenty-third century, his heroes were going to be a secretive order known as the 'Jedi-Templers' (the spelling 'Templer' was used by Lucas). These warriors of the future swore fealty to the Alliance of Independent Systems. They operated on jungle and desert planets and a gaseous world with a city suspended in the clouds.[2]

Lucas outlined his chivalrous Jedi-Templers in a short document titled *Journal of the Whills*, an imaginary account of a Jedi named Mace Windy. The story had been related to a 'padawaan' of the 'famed Jedi'; that is an apprentice to a fully-fledged Jedi, learning the tricks of the trade. The padawaan (in the original spelling) is the equivalent of a Templar novice or squire being schooled by a knight. Their inferior status early in their Jedi career was denoted by a braid of hair grown on one side of the head, but they could discard this and grow lustrous locks on qualifying as a knight.

Journal of the Whills is reminiscent of the Edgar Rice Burroughs novel, *A Fighting Man of Mars*,[3] published in 1931, where Burroughs introduced his readers to a complex universe of rival galactic civilisations with lashings of space age intrigue. Lucas also created a tangled geopolitical web in his Star Wars movies, defying his audiences to keep up with the increasingly dense plotlines. The real-life world of the Knights Templar was similarly characterised by rival empires and kingdoms with an endless stream of conspiracies and backstabbing.

Star Wars hit cinema screens in the United States in 1977 and was an instant hit, despite the studio's misgivings. It is beyond doubt the greatest movie franchise in history, generating vast revenues for all involved. Although Lucas dumped the 'Templer' word, the Jedi Knights retained much of the ethos of the Knights Templar, who had clearly influenced the storyline. In subsequent sequels and spin-offs, the underlying Templar theme has not only endured but become more obvious.[4]

Identifying Templar references and parallels in the Star Wars canon is a fun pastime for fans of both the movies and this period of history. For example, Obi-Wan Kenobi in the first Star Wars movie, which is confusingly now the fourth instalment of the saga, is the last of the Jedi and comparable to the last Templar grand master, Jacques de Molay. He is a noble figure who holds the secrets of the order. The only surviving guardian of the sacred knowledge.

An aged Obi-Wan Kenobi must impart what he knows to a young protégé, Luke Skywalker, before he dies, or is killed. Kenobi's nemesis, Darth Vader, is the evil tool of the malevolent Emperor Palpatine (AKA Darth Sidius). In the Emperor, we see King Philip of France and in Darth Vader, the king's chief minister, Guillaume de Nogaret.

In the 1977 movie, Obi-Wan Kenobi is a hermit living in a cave and we get only verbal references to a wider order of Jedi. It's in the three Star Wars prequels, made between 1999 and 2005, that we see this monastic order of all-powerful warriors seated in the Jedi high council – very clearly invoking the chapter meetings of the Templars.[5]

It's in this trilogy that Lucas depicts the dramatic reversal of fortune experienced by the Jedi that so clearly mirrors the Templars' fall from grace. They begin as a revered and ancient order of guardians pledged to uphold peace and justice in the Galactic Republic. However, some of their critics already felt that the Jedi were overreaching themselves, for which read the barbed comments by medieval chroniclers against the Templars. The republic then falls to the empire, necessitating the destruction of the Jedi. An army of clones, previously loyal to the Jedi and the republic, turn on their masters, slaughtering them in cold blood. The once almighty Jedi are annihilated. All of this echoes the arrests, torture, and executions that befell the Templars from the year 1307 until the execution of the last grand master in 1314.[6]

The Templar-esque cosmos conjured up by Lucas even has its own Jerusalem with the city-world of Coruscant. It is a hub of culture and politics where the Jedi headquarters was based, prior to being destroyed by imperial forces. The planet-wide city of Coruscant was conceptualised by science fiction author Timothy Zahn (born 1951) in the Thrawn Trilogy of Star Wars books, written in the early 1990s, intended to further develop the original storylines after a decade-long lull in creative activity after the original movies. The Jedi Temple was constructed on top of an earlier shrine built by the Sith – an ancient order that had worshipped the 'dark side of the Force' (the negative, evil version of Jedi magic). One immediately sees a parallel with the Templars choosing to base themselves on top of the Temple of Solomon that had once housed the long-lost Ark of the Covenant, a sacred chest possessing deadly power.[7]

At the heart of the Star Wars franchise is this Templar-like brotherhood of celibate and dedicated hooded warriors leading a monastic existence and sworn to follow the correct path after a gruelling period of training. The Jedi serve the Force. The Templars defended Christ. Both are referred to as knights. For a period, sympathetic rulers award the Jedi and Templars great powers and privileges, but this stokes resentment. Accusations swirl that their power is being abused for their own ends. Finally, a change in the political situation results in both groups of knights being cruelly betrayed and wiped out very rapidly. In the universe of Star Wars, the Jedi are the good guys and so, one assumes, George Lucas looked on the Templars favourably. But where the Templars have cropped up in popular culture, they have sometimes been the villains, not the heroes.

Another hugely successful Templar-related franchise is Assassin's Creed, which started as a video game in 2007, developed by Ubisoft, before spawning a very successful movie in 2016. Unlike Star Wars, the Knights Templar are thoroughly evil in the world of Assassin's Creed. It centres on the notion of an ongoing feud stretching back centuries – if not millennia – between the Templars and the Assassins. To keep users engaged with this fictional conflict, Assassin's Creed has gone through several versions, encompassing different historical periods from the Vikings to Ancient Egypt and Victorian London.

The original storyline involved a young American, Desmond Miles, brought up in a family in South Dakota who come from a long line of Assassins. He goes off to become a bartender in New York but is kidnapped by Templars and forced into a machine called the Animus. Owned by Abstergo Industries, a Templar-run enterprise, the Animus is used to harvest data from the minds of Assassins, forcing them to re-live past lives, to locate and retrieve the so-called 'Pieces of Eden', parts of an ancient but long-lost device that will allow Abstergo to control the minds of every human being on Earth. This will return the planet to the way it was during The First Civilisation, when God-like creatures of superior intelligence called the Precursors, or Isu, created humans and enjoyed their total submission.

This was eroded when humans began breeding with the Isu and then rebelled against their creators. At some point, a cosmic calamity of some description reduced humans to a few thousand and the survivors were divided between those craving a return to submission (the Templars) and those who valued liberty and free will (the Assassins). Desmond, therefore, is being manipulated by the Templars to give away the location of the Pieces of Eden while the Assassins are trying to stop that happening. The story mixes elements of Noah's flood, Greek mythology, Gnosticism, and philosophy with the medieval Templars and Assassins to create a terrifying scenario.[8]

Assassin's Creed is loosely based on the 1938 novel *Alamut*, by the Slovenian author, Vladimir Bartol (1903–1967).[9] The book takes its name from the castle conquered by the Assassins in the year 1095. The plot follows the story of Hasan-i Sabbah (*c.*1050–1124), founder of the Assassins, dubbed the Old Man of the Mountain by western medieval sources. At his castle we meet the story's two tragic heroes. Ibn Tahir is a young man sent by his family to become a fanatical assassin while Halima is a beautiful woman, trained to entice the trainee assassins in a paradisical garden where Hasan's pupils receive a taste of the pleasures that will be experienced after death through martyrdom. The two become disillusioned, leading to Halima's suicide while Ibn Tahir departs on a long journey, far away from Alamut, to try and find himself. *Alamut* was intended to be an anti-fascist satire on the dictatorship of Benito Mussolini (1883–1945) comparing the mind control of the Old Man of the Mountain with the totalitarianism of twentieth century fascism.[10]

Ever since the destruction of the Knights Templar, the question has been whether the knights were a thoroughly bad lot or the heroic victims of dark propaganda. In Star Wars, the Jedi, futuristic shadows of the Templars, are heroes betrayed, while Assassin's Creed casts them as a malign force operating to a covert agenda. In the early nineteenth century, the Scottish novelist Walter Scott (1771–1832) had no doubt what he thought about the Templars – they were not to be trusted.

In his medieval novel *Ivanhoe*, published in 1819, Scott demonises the Templars.[11] He promoted a longstanding trope whereby the Norman conquest of England in 1066 terminated a Saxon-run utopia of freedom, mutual respect, and just laws. The 'Norman Yoke' deprived the English of their liberties, reducing them to a miserable, servile status. This idea of a lost Saxon paradise that needed to be regained influenced various political movements down the centuries (the Levellers in the English Civil War for example) and Scott leant into it heavily for the plot of *Ivanhoe*.

In this tale, the Knights Templar are agents of Norman oppression, exemplified by the wicked Templar, Sir Brian de Bois-Guilbert.[12] Scott introduces us to an England, at the height of the crusades in the Holy Land, that is groaning under Norman tyranny.

Its king, Richard the Lionheart, is one of the few likeable Normans but his brother, John, is busily plotting to overthrow him while he is absent fighting Saracens in the Holy Land. Wilfred of Ivanhoe, son of Cedric the Saxon, is Scott's heroic protagonist – a chivalrous Englishman of high principles who detests the Normans. But he has been disinherited for falling in love with Rowena, a woman betrothed to another man. In what is a rather convoluted plot, Ivanhoe returns in disguise to fight in a tournament, calling himself rather unsubtly, The Disinherited Knight. He is assisted by a mysterious Black Knight. Ivanhoe wins, though sustains some very serious wounds. However, he musters enough strength to crown Rowena his Queen of Beauty and Love.

Ivanhoe leaves the tournament with Rowena, but his travelling party is intercepted by Bois-Guilbert who holds them prisoner in a castle. The evil Templar then compromises his vow of chastity by trying to seduce Rebecca, the daughter of a Jewish moneylender who has befriended Ivanhoe. They are rescued from the Templars by a group of 'Saxons' – downtrodden natives of Norman-occupied England – accompanied by Robin Hood and his band of outlaws. However, Rebecca is left behind. She is carried off to the Templar preceptory at Templestowe, where the despicable knights put her on trial for witchcraft. Rebecca demands a trial by combat and her champion is, of course, Ivanhoe. He wins the tournament, killing Bois-Guilbert. The now freed Rebecca leaves England for Spain, hoping to find more tolerance towards Jews in Moorish-ruled Granada. Ivanhoe meanwhile is married to Rowena and the mysterious Black Knight reveals himself as Richard the Lionheart – the rightful king of England.

Why does Scott give the Knights Templar such a bad press in Ivanhoe? The author was wrestling with his own political views at the time. He was a romantic Scottish nationalist who also fervently believed in the union between his native Scotland and England, to form Great Britain. This was highly contentious as for well over a century, the Scottish had been involved in a series of 'Jacobite' uprisings to place a Catholic king back on the British throne – specifically a member of the Stuart dynasty that had ruled Britain throughout the seventeenth century. In 1714, the last Stuart monarch, Queen Anne (1665–1714), died and parliament in London invited a German cousin to become King George I, his main redeeming feature being that he was totally Protestant. Under his son, the last Jacobite uprising was crushed decisively at the Battle of Culloden in 1746.

For good reason, British kings avoided Scotland for nearly 200 years until, in 1822, King George IV (1762–1830) ventured north of the border. Scott played a central role in the resulting pageantry, which included the creation of a plethora of tartan costumes that have endured to the present day but are not as traditional as many might imagine. Scott was crafting a new identity for Scotland, reconciling a love of its past with the benefits of union with Britain. And in *Ivanhoe*, he was pulling off a similar trick. On the one hand demonising the Norman aristocracy and Knights Templar as foreign invaders who had wrecked Saxon England but also hinting at a way forward for both Saxons and Normans under a wise king like Richard the Lionheart.

However, that path to the future would have no place for the Pope, Roman Catholic Church, nor the Templars, whose sole loyalty was to Rome. Scott shared the anti-Catholic prejudices of his time, stoked by those uprisings in the previous century. When *Ivanhoe* was published, Roman Catholics in Britain were even denied the vote, an iniquity only resolved with the Catholic Emancipation Act of 1829. For Scott, a future Britain – that would encompass Scotland – would reject all those like the Normans and Templars who bent the knee to the Pope.

Scott cast the Knights Templar in a bad light as agents of the Pope and enforcers for foreign, Norman invaders. In the Islamic world, popular cultural depictions of the Templars right up to the present day are negative for obvious reasons – they were the shock troops of the crusades.

In 2014, Turkish national television (TRT1) began broadcasting a long-running historical fiction drama based on the life of a thirteenth century Turkic warrior, Ertuğrul Bey. The series – *Diriliş: Ertuğrul* (Resurrection: Ertuğrul) – was distributed on Netflix from 2016 to 2023 with an eye-watering 448 episodes over five seasons. It tells the story of Ertuğrul's struggle to forge a new homeland for his people that would evolve into the Ottoman Empire. To achieve this feat, he must take on the Mongols, Knights Templar, and Byzantines while also dealing with constant betrayal within his own camp.

Described as the 'Muslim Game of Thrones', Ertuğrul depicts the main protagonist as both a pious Muslim, but also a proto-Turkish nationalist.[13] Every fight in the series is a foregone conclusion as our hero decorates the ground with the bodies of Knights Templar, whose fighting skills are portrayed as so inept, it's a mystery how they ever won a single battle. What the Templars excel at, in the Ertuğrul series, is intrigue and espionage, masterminded by a Machiavellian and imperious grand master, Petruchio Manzini. This is a reptilian figure who has imprisoned his own brother for converting to Islam while telling his nieces that he is dead. He also sends out lepers to spread that incurable disease among Ertuğrul's people. There is absolutely no depth to which this Templar will not descend. At the end of season one, Ertuğrul overwhelms the Templars and captures their castle in the Amanos mountains (which we are repeatedly told is in a top-secret location, though it's clearly in plain sight) putting Petruchio to the sword.

Interestingly, even though the series created a dashing Muslim hero, opinion in Muslim countries has been very divided. Audiences in Pakistan adored Ertuğrul, watching in huge numbers, but it encountered heavy criticism in Saudi Arabia and the United Arab Emirates where it was seen as a bid by Turkey to reassert its influence in the Middle East by rewriting history. Walter Scott used historical fiction around 200 years ago to project his political views on to the Middle Ages and similarly, modern Turkey stands accused today of reshaping history to suit its geopolitical ambitions. It is clearly a sore point that Islam's holy places were once ruled from Istanbul by the Ottoman caliph. One of Egypt's leading religious bodies was so hostile to this rendition of history that it even issued a fatwa against Ertuğrul.[14] Despite all this, few in the region disagree with the characterisation of the Templars as evil incarnate.

Depicting the Templars as the bad guys took a macabre turn with the horror movie boom of the 1970s. Spain generated a slew of so-called 'fantaterror' flicks combining fantasy and horror with a heavy dose of Catholicism. One Spanish film maker, Amando de Ossorio Rodríguez (1918–2001), was keen to differentiate the Iberian films from those being made in the United States and Britain, which were heavily reliant on Dracula, Frankenstein, Egyptian mummies, and werewolves. He created a monster with a strong Iberian flavour: the zombie Templar.

His 1972 movie, *La Noche del Terror Ciego* (Tombs of the Blind Dead), reveals a group of seemingly dead Templars buried at an abandoned monastery in a border town between Portugal and Spain, who climb out of their graves to murder passers-by. They are semi-decayed, hooded figures with no eyes, as those were pecked out by crows many centuries before. It transpires that King Philip of France was right all along and that the Templars were engaging in magical rituals, hoping to unlock the secret of eternal life. Their sorcery involved human sacrifice and the drinking of their victims' blood. When their activities were exposed, the knights were hanged, and their bodies publicly displayed on gibbets where the crows got to work.

Fast forward to the 1970s, and three Americans are on holiday in Portugal. Virginia White is with her boyfriend, Roger Whelan, when they run into Betty Turner, who was a flatmate and former lover of Virginia many years before. But

Virginia is now with a man, Roger, and is a little uncomfortable to have run into Betty. The three end up on a train journey together when Roger hits on Betty and a very miffed Virginia jumps off the moving train. Unhurt, she makes her way to the monastery as night falls, unaware of its malevolent occupants.

In the darkness, the zombie Templars burst out of their tombs and make for Virginia who attempts to escape on one of their zombie horses. The next day, Betty and Roger finally search for their mutual friend only to discover that she has been murdered. The coroner at the morgue remarks that it looks as if wild animals attacked the victim. But local people know the truth. Virginia has been slain by the knights. Betty and Roger now turn detective, discovering that the nearby town of Bouzano was the Templar headquarters where they hid treasures brought back from the east, and held Satanic rituals learned from ancient Egyptian texts. Their quest was for immortality, but instead, they turned themselves into fearful zombies.

The movie is a product of its time with a great deal of exploitative and unpleasant abuse of women, both in the present day and in flashbacks to the tortures carried out by the Templars. To make matters worse, Virginia comes back to life as a zombie. The movie climaxes with a fight scene back in the Templar graveyard involving Betty, Roger, other secondary characters, and a small army of undead knights. Betty is the only survivor, and she rushes away towards a passing train, which she manages to stop and board. Unfortunately, the Templars do likewise. While Betty hides amidst the train's coal supply, the Templars run amok through the carriages, slaughtering everybody. When the train reaches its destination, Betty emerges, her hair completely white with terror and unable to speak. She is powerless to warn new passengers who now board the train, condemned to being cannibalised by the Templars.

This movie became part of a four-part zombie Templar series with the immediate sequel, released in 1973, titled *El Ataque de los Muertos sin Ojos* (Attack of the Eyeless Dead). The set-up is like the first movie with a peasant mob lynching a group of Templar knights over fears they are engaged in sorcery. The only difference being that the blinding of the knights is done by the villagers with burning torches, as opposed to the crows pecking their eyes out. Centuries later, the zombie Templars come back to life and massacre festivalgoers in a Spanish town, only ceasing their slaughter when the sun rises. In film number three, *El Buque Maldito* (The Ghost Galleon), the undead Templars reside in coffins on a ship reminiscent of Dracula's travelling arrangements, while in the fourth movie, *La Noche de las Gaviotas* (Night of the Seagulls), the action begins with a woman back in the Middle Ages being carried off as a human sacrifice to a Templar castle. It turns out that in the twentieth century, they emerge from the sea every seven years to demand another female sacrifice.

Ossorio was directing his horror classics in the closing years of the dictatorship of General Francisco Franco (1892–1975) in Spain. This was an authoritarian regime that seized power in a civil war during the 1930s, ideologically allied to Hitler and Mussolini in Germany and Italy respectively. In at least one analysis, the Templars in Ossorio's four-part series have been seen as a satire on the dead hand of the traditionalism that was a hallmark of the Franco regime. The young American victims are modern thinking and progressive, therefore the zombie Templars must wipe them out. Put another way, the knights are a neo-fascist death squad.[15]

Possibly the most inventive retelling of the Templar story was by the French science fiction author, Claude Avice, who wrote mainly under the pseudonym, Pierre Barbet (1925–1995). Between 1972 and 1974, he penned two novels positing a link between the Knights Templar and a powerful extraterrestrial. It turns out that Baphomet was not a demon worshipped by the Templars – as alleged at their trials – but a being from outer space who formed a pact with the knights, making them incredibly rich and successful.

This incredible, if rather far-fetched tale, was recounted in *The Empire of Baphomet*, published in 1972, and a sequel, *Stellar Crusade*, which came out in 1974. The subheading for the first novel altered the war cry of the Templars from 'by this sign you shall conquer' to something more galactic: *In the Sign of the Atom – Conquer!*[16]

The year is 1118 and a spacecraft crash-lands in medieval France. A dazed but unharmed alien emerges and meets a local, penniless knight – Hugh de Payens – who believes the creature from another planet is some kind of devil. Patiently, the extraterrestrial explains that he is not a horned beast from hell but a space traveller who just needs to get his vehicle repaired. To win Hugh's confidence and loyalty, he gives the future first grand master of the Templars a gold bar and promises fame, invincibility, and a steady supply of food. It's an offer that is impossible to refuse.

The alien is as good as his word. Hugh forms the Knights Templar, becomes the first grand master, and conquers the Middle East, overwhelming Saracen and Mongol enemies. Baphomet helps the Templars by supplying them with weapons of mass destruction including nuclear-powered grenades. But this support for the knights comes with a sting in its tail. Because Baphomet is really using the Templars to achieve global domination.

Fast forward 150 years and Hugh has long gone. William de Beaujeu is now the grand master. After wiping out a numerically superior Mongol army with their nuclear grenades, the Templars interrogate the enemy leader, Kublai Khan. He astounds the knights with the revelation that they have been manipulated by Baphomet for centuries. Beaujeu meets a Tibetan monk who has used his psychic powers to read the mind of the alien. He confirms what Kublai Khan has said. An incensed Beaujeu forms a team of telepathic Tibetan monks to combat Baphomet with their combined mental power; incredibly, they manage to kill this long-lived being from another galaxy. Beaujeu seizes the crashed spacecraft – which has been rusting in a French field for well over a century – to study and understand how it works, so that the Templars can take their crusade into the cosmos.

As one review in 1972 put it: 'The story mixes horseback combat, swords, and Greek fire with radios, and atomic weapons'.[17] But the action does not stop on this planet. Realising that Baphomet's aim was to enslave humanity, Beajeau creates a heavily armed fleet of spaceships and launches an assault on the civilisation of the Baphomet located light years away. He is aided by his able spy, Marco Polo, and the Tibetan monks. Even the perfidious Knights Hospitaller agree to join his galactic crusade. These adventures are described in the 1974 sequel.

In 1977, the actor Mark Hamill (born 1951) played Luke Skywalker in the first Star Wars movie – a character mentored by the ageing Jedi knight, Obi-Wan Kenobi, played by Sir Alec Guinness (1914–2000). Fast forward four decades and, in 2019, Hamill took on the role of a grizzled old Templar knight mentoring a new generation of Templar knights in much the same way he had been trained to be a Jedi by Obi-Wan Kenobi.[18]

This was in season two of the History channel drama *Knightfall,* depicting the crushing of the Knights Templar by King Philip IV of France. In this series, the Templars were broadly cast as the good guys, if somewhat compromised on occasion. For example, the main protagonist, a handsome but impetuous Templar, Landry de Lauzon, struggles with this vow of chastity. Rather ill-advisedly, he beds the queen of France and gets her pregnant.

Knightfall begins with a tempestuous battle scene as the Templars lose control of Acre in 1291 and let the Holy Grail slip out of their hands. Landry ends up back in Paris where he is soon mired in the court politics of King Philip and his minister De Nogaret, who is an almost cartoonish villain in the series.

Mongols, Saracens, and Cathars all pop up in the fast-paced plot that eventually has the king discovering his wife is carrying a Templar baby. The Grail is found, but by this time, Landry's various sins lead to his ejection from the order, and excommunication. In an angry confrontation between the king, queen and Landry, Philip stabs his own wife to death. The Holy Grail is deployed to try and save her life, but she dies. However, her baby daughter is delivered alive.

This brings us into season two with Hamill's character, Master Talus, taking Landry to task over his many shortcomings as a knight. Intriguingly, we learn that De Nogaret is the child of Cathars burned at the stake by order of a young priest who would go on to become Pope Boniface VIII. In *Knightfall*, we are left in no doubt that De Nogaret murdered Boniface as an act of revenge for the execution of his parents as heretics. Before the Pope expires, De Nogaret reminds him of what he did all those years before.

Throughout season two, we see the Templars at war with the French king. Far from being meekly compliant, the knights hurl Greek Fire and gunpowder at royal troops, resisting all attempts to crush them. But eventually, the Templars are betrayed into the king's hands and marched through the streets of Paris in chains. Jacques de Molay has become grand master by this stage and is burned at the stake. But Landry and Talus survive, with the former getting to slay the king in a sword fight. With that, they limp – bloodied but not beaten – towards the horizon. Their future adventures remain uncertain, however, as a third season of *Knightfall* was not commissioned.

All of which leaves us wondering what exactly to make of the Knights Templar. Either they were a group of wronged holy warriors brought down on trumped up charges, or heretics and sorcerers who, for two centuries, fooled Christendom into believing they were a force for good. We still struggle to make up our minds.

A terrible darkness descended on Europe in the decades following the execution of De Molay. The continent was ravaged by the Black Death in the 1340s, a catastrophe which only served to further fuel belief in witchcraft and sorcery, with individuals put to death as plague bringers and servants of Satan. Popes and kings formalised the association of heresy and sorcery, which began with the Templar trials and would leave no social rank immune from deadly accusations.[19]

In the fifteenth century, a bible for dealing with heretics and witches – the *Malleus Maleficarum* (Hammer of Witches) – was penned by the German Dominican friar and inquisitor, Heinrich Kramer (*c.*1430–1505).[20] His morbidly detailed guidelines for dealing with sorcerers and heretics – who were evolving by degrees into the same thing – was endorsed by the same popes championing the Renaissance. While Michaelangelo was painting the Sistine Chapel, alleged witches were being rounded up by the Inquisition and executed.

In May 1310, fifty-four Templars were burned in a field just outside the city walls of Paris. Four years later, the grand master suffered the same fate. Their deaths unleashed a killing spree that endured for nearly 400 years. The trials of the Knights Templar proved to be a grisly dress rehearsal for the persecution of countless witches across Europe. Yet today, the Templars are still amongst us in different guises. Some are Freemasons while others are Roman Catholics. Thousands claim to be the inheritors of the white mantles of those enigmatic holy warriors, while millions are enraptured by tales of their heroism and courage. It seems that Jacques de Molay has indeed been avenged.

Notes

Chapter One

1. Demurger, Alain, *The Persecution of the Templars: Scandal, Torture, Trial,* Profile Books, 2018, ISBN: 978-1781257852.
2. Venning, Timothy, 'The Crusades after the loss of the Holy Land 1292–1456', in *A Chronology of the Crusades,* Routledge, ISBN: 978-1315712932.
3. Luttrell, Anthony, 'The Election of the Templar Master Jacques de Molay', in *The Debate on the Trial of the Templars (1307–1314)*, Routledge, 2010, ISBN: 978-0754665700.
4. Barber, Malcolm, *The Trial of the Templars,* Cambridge University Press, 2012, ISBN: 978-1107645769.
5. Menache, Sophie, *The Military Orders Volume II,* Routledge, 1998, ISBN: 978-1315085920.
6. Kurtz, Lester R., 'The Politics of Heresy', *American Journal of Sociology*, Vol. 88, No. 6, May 1983.
7. White, Chris, *Nineteenth-Century Writings on Homosexuality,* Routledge, 2012, ISBN: 978-0203002407.
8. Freshfield E., *A Manual of Roman Law: The Ecloga,* Cambridge, 1926, reprinted in Geanokoplos, Deno, *Byzantium: Church, Society, and Civilization Seen through Contemporary Eyes,* University of Chicago Press, 1986, ISBN: 978-0226284613.
9. Smith, Morton, *Clement of Alexandria and a Secret Gospel of Mark,* Harvard University Press, 1973, ISBN: 978-0674134904.
10. Benko, Stephen, 'The Libertine Gnostic Sect of the Phibionites According to Epiphanius', *Vigiliae Christianae*, Vol. 21, No. 2, 1967, pp. 103–119.
11. Parsons, Ben, 'Sympathy for the Devil: Gilles de Rais and His Modern Apologists', *Fifteenth Century Studies,* Vol. 37, 2012, pp. 113–138.
12. Trevor-Roper, Hugh, *The European Witch-Craze of the Sixteenth and Seventeenth Centuries,* Penguin Books, 1969, ISBN: 978-0140210095.
13. Iribarren, Isabel, 'From Black Magic to Heresy: A Doctrinal Leap in the Pontificate of John XXII', *Church History*, Vol. 76, Issue 1, March 2007, pp. 32–60.
14. Le Clerc, Victor, *Histoire Littéraire de la France au XIVe Siècle, Volume 1,* Michel Lévy Frères, 1865.
15. Hauréau, Barthélemy, *Bernard Délicieux et l'Inquisition Albigeoise: 1300–1320,* Librairie Hachette et Cie, 1877.
16. Lea, Henry Charles, *A History of the Inquisition of the Middle Ages. Vol. 1,* Harper & Brothers, 1887.
17. Vise, Melissa, 'The Women and the Inquisitor: Peacemaking in Bologna, 1299', *Speculum, The Journal of the Medieval Academy of America*, Vol. 93, No. 2, April 2018.
18. Ben-Yehuda, Nachman, 'The European Witch Craze of the 14 to 17 Centuries: A Sociologist's Perspective', *American Journal of Sociology*, Vol. 86, No. 1, July 1980.
19. Durrant, Jonathan, Dr, *Five Witchcraft Myths,* History Research Group, University of South Wales, October 31, 2023.
20. Tov Assis, Yom, 'The Papal Inquisition and Aragonese Jewry in the Early Fourteenth Century', *Medieval Studies*, Vol. 49, 1987, pp. 391–410.
21. Feuchter, Jörg, 'Europe Penetrated by Islam. The Orientalization of the Order of the Templars', essay in Mackenthun, Gesa (ed.), *Entangled Knowledge Scientific Discourses and Cultural Difference*, Waxmann, 2012, ISBN: 978-3830977292.

22. *Redemptionis Sacramentum*, Congregation for Divine Worship and the Discipline of the Sacrament, Vatican website, 2004.
23. Michelet, Jules, *History of France,* D. Appleton and Company, 1882.
24. Keightley, Thomas, *Secret Societies of the Middle Ages: The Assassins, the Templars, and the Secret Tribunals of Westphalia,* Red Wheel/Weiser, 2005, ISBN: 978-1578633340.
25. Barber, Malcolm, *The Trial of the Templars,* Cambridge University Press, 2012, ISBN: 978-1107645769.
26. Gaunt, Simon (ed.), Kay, Sarah (ed.), *The Troubadours: An Introduction,* Cambridge University Press, 1999, ISBN: 978-0521573887.
27. Jeanroy, A., 'Le troubadour Austorc d'Aurillac et son sirventés sur la septième Croisade', *Romanische Forschungen*, March 1906.
28. Partner, Peter, *The Murdered Magicians: Templars and Their Myth,* Aquarian Press, 1987, ISBN: 978-0850305340.
29. Von Hammer-Purgstall, Joseph, *Mysterium Baphometis Revelatum, Anton Schmid, 1818.*
30. Morgan, James, *Decoding the symbols on Satan's statue,* BBC News, August 1, 2015.
31. Lévi, Éliphas, *Transcendental Magic: Its Doctrine and Ritual,* George Redway, 1896.
32. 'Paris Devil Worshippers at work', *Los Angeles Herald,* August 11, 1895.
33. Fisher, Damien, 'Demonic Christmas Display at State House Destroyed', *NH Journal,* December 10, 2024.
34. Karlen, Arno, 'The Homosexual Heresy', *The Chaucer Review*, Penn State University Press, Vol. 6, No. 1, Summer 1971, pp. 44–63.
35. Strub, Whitney, 'The Lavender Scare: The Cold War Persecution of Gays and Lesbians in the Federal Government', *Journal of Cold War Studies*, The MIT Press, Vol. 11, No, 2, Spring 2009, pp. 158–160.
36. Gregorovius, Ferdinand, *History of the City of Rome in the Middle Ages,* George Bell & Sons, 1894.
37. Hart, Mother Columba, *Hildegard of Bingen: Scivias,* Paulist Press, 1990, ISBN: 978-0809131303.
38. Crawford, Katherine, *European Sexualities, 1400–1800,* Cambridge University Press, 2007, ISBN: 978-0521548403.
39. Meisami, Julie Scott (ed.), Starkey, Paul (ed.), *Encyclopedia of Arabic Literature,* Routledge, 1998, ISBN: 978-0415068086.
40. Kotis, India, 'She is a Boy, or if Not a Boy, Then a Boy resembles her: Cross-dressing, homosexuality, and enslaved sex and gender in Ummayad Iberia', *The Macksey Journal,* Vol. 1, Article 119.
41. Al-Tifashi, Ahmad, *The Delight of Hearts: Or what you will not find in any book,* Gay Sunshine Press, 1988, ISBN: 978-0940567092.
42. Al-Maghribi, Ibn Sacid, Bellamy, James A., 'The Banners of the Champions: An Anthology of Medieval Arabic Poetry from Andalusia and Beyond', *Hispanic Seminary of Medieval Studies*, 1989, ISBN: 978-0940639270.
43. Forey, Alan, 'Could Alleged Malpractices Have Remained Undetected for Decades?', essay in Burgtorf, Jochen, Crawford, Paul F., *The Debate on the Trial of the Templars (1307–1314),* Routledge, 2010, ISBN: 978-0754665700.
44. Harvey, Karen, *The Kiss in History,* Manchester University Press, 2005, ISBN: 978-0719065958.
45. Map, Walter, Tupper, Frederick (trans.), Bladen, Marbury (trans.), *De Nugis Curialium,* Chatto & Windus, 1924.

Chapter Two

1. Bilal, Muhammad, Tubbs, R. Shane., 'Popes convict dead Pope Twice! The unbelievable Cadaver Synod', *Clinical Anatomy*, Vol. 29, Issue 2, 2016, pp. 140–143.
2. Howarth, Stephen, *The Knights Templar,* Bloomsbury Continuum, 2006, ISBN: 978-0826480347.

3. Woodacre, Elena, *Joan of Navarre: Infanta, Duchess, Queen, Witch?,* Routledge, 2022, ISBN: 978-0367203481.
4. Prestwich, Michael, *Edward I,* Yale University Press, 1997, ISBN: 978-0300071573.
5. Woodacre, Elena, *The Queen Regnant of Navarre: Succession, Politics, and Partnership, 1274–1512 (Queenship and Power),* Palgrave Macmillan, 2013, ISBN: 978-1349464319.
6. Rigault, Ábel, *Le Procès De Guichard, Évêque De Troyes (1308–1313),* A. Picard et Fils, 1896.
7. Villani, Giovanni, Selfe Rose E. (trans.), *Villani's Chronicle being selections from the First Nine Books of the Croniche Fiorentine of Giovanni Villani,* Archibald Constable & Co. Ltd., 1906.
8. Salvèmini, Gaetano, 'L'Abolizione dell'ordine dei Templari: a proposito di una recente pubblicazione', *Archivo Storico Italiano,* Serie V, Vol. 15, No. 198, 1895, pp. 225–264.
9. Provost, Alain, *Domus Diaboli: Un évêque en procès au temps de Philippe le Bel,* Belin, 2010, ISBN: 978-2701148953.
10. Strayer, Joseph R., *The Reign of Philip the Fair,* Princeton University Press, 1980, ISBN: 978-0691100890.
11. De Boissy d'Anglas, François-Antoine, 'Mémoire sur le procès de Guichard, évêque de Troyes, en 1304 et années suivantes', *Institut de France,* 1822.
12. Myers, A. R., 'The captivity of a royal witch: the household accounts of Queen Joan of Navarre, 1419–21', *Bulletin of the John Rylands Library,* Vol. 24, Issue, 2, 1941.
13. Stabler Miller, Tanya, *The Beguines of Medieval Paris: Gender, Patronage, and Spiritual Authority (The Middle Ages Series),* University of Pennsylvania Press, 2014, ISBN: 978-0812246070.
14. *Council of Vienne 1311–1312 A.D.*, Papal Encyclicals Online.
15. Hokanson, Petra, 'A Severed Head and Two Plumes of Smoke: The Memory of Catherine of Siena and Marguerite Porete', *The Alexandrian,* Vol. 13, Issue 1, 2024.
16. Field, Sean L., *Courting Sanctity: Holy Women and the Capetians,* Cornell University Press, 2019, ISBN: 978-1501736193.
17. King, Peter, 'Marguerite Porete and Godfrey of Fontaines', *Oxford Studies in Medieval Philosophy,* Vol. 6, Issue 1, 2018.
18. Lea, Charles Henry, *History of the Inquisition of the Middle Ages – Volume 3,* Harper & Collins, 1888.
19. Martin, Graham, 'Did Boniface die of a subdural?', *Journal of Clinical Neuroscience,* Vol. 8, Issue 1, January 2001, pp. 8–9.
20. Denton, Jeffrey, 'The attempted trial of Boniface VIII for heresy', in Mulholland, Maureen, Pullan, Brian, Pullan, Anne, *Judicial Tribunals in England and Europe, 1200–1700,* Manchester University Press, 2003, ISBN: 978-0719063428.
21. Théry, Julien, 'A Heresy of State', *Journal of Medieval Religious Cultures,* Vol. 39, No. 2, 2013, pp. 117–148.
22. Gaposchkin, M. Cecilia, Field, Sean L., Field, Larry, F., *The Sanctity of Louis IX: Early Lives of Saint Louis by Geoffrey of Beaulieu and William of Chartres,* Cornell University Press, 2013, ISBN: 978-0801478185.
23. 'Relic of King Saint Louis', *Relics,* 2024, https://relics.es/en/products/reliquary-relic-of-king-saint-louis-louis-ix.
24. Hallam, Elizabeth, M., 'Philip the Fair and the cult of Saint Louis', *Studies in Church History,* Vol. 18, 1982, pp. 201–214.
25. Weiss-Krejci, 'Restless corpses: "secondary burial" in the Babenberg and Hapsburg dynasties', *Antiquity,* Cambridge University Press, Vol. 75, Issue 290, 2001.
26. Beaune, Colette, *Birth of an Ideology: Myths and Symbols of Nation in Late-Medieval France,* University of California Press, 1992, ISBN: 978-0520059412.
27. Strayer, A. R., 'The Laicisation of French and English Society in the Thirteenth Century', *Speculum,* Vol. 15, No. 1, 1940.
28. Kuroda, Akinobu, 'The Eurasian silver century, 1276–1359: commensurability and multiplicity', *Journal of Global History,* Cambridge University Press, Vol. 4, Issue 2, 2009.
29. Schwarzfuchs, Simon R., 'The Expulsion of the Jews from France', *The Jewish Quarterly Review,* University of Pennsylvania Press, Vol. 57, 1967, pp. 482–489.

30. De la Torre, Ignacio, 'The monetary fluctuations in Philip IV's kingdom of France and their relevance to the arrest of the Templars', in Nicholson, Helen, Crawford, Paul F., Burgtorf, Jochen, *The Debate on the Trial of the Templars*, Routledge, 2024, ISBN: 978-1032920108.
31. Strayer, Joseph R., 'Philip the Fair – a "constitutional" king', *The American Historical Review*, Oxford University Press, Vol. 62, No. 1, October 1956, pp. 18–32.

Chapter Three

1. Menache, Sophia, *Clement V*, Cambridge University Press, 1998, ISBN: 978-0511582806.
2. Coulson, C. L. H., 'Community and Fortress-Politics in France in the Lull before the Hundred Years War', *Nottingham Medieval Studies*, Vol. 40, January 1996.
3. Denton, J. H., 'Pope Clement V's Early Career as a Royal Clerk', *The English Historical Review*, Vol. 83, No. 327, April 1968, pp. 303–314.
4. Satora, Magdalena, 'The Role of Cardinals in the Templars' Affair (1307–1308)', *Ordines Militares Colloquia Torunensia Historica*, Vol. XVI, 2011.
5. Skuse, Alanna, 'Wombs, Worms, and Wolves: Constructing Cancer in Early Modern England', *Social History of Medicine*, Vol. 27, Issue 4, November 2014, pp. 632–648.
6. Tanner, Norman P., *Decrees of the Ecumenical Councils: Volumes 1 and 2: From Nicaea to Vatican II*, Georgetown University Press, 1990, ISBN: 978-0878404902.
7. Watt, John A., 'Jews and Christians in the Gregorian Decretals', *Studies in Church History*, Cambridge University Press, Vol. 29: Christianity and Judaism, 1992, pp: 93–105.
8. 'Gregory', Jewish Virtual Library.
9. Bishop, Jordan, 'Aquinas on Torture', *New Blackfriars*, Vol. 87, Issue 1009, May 2006, pp. 229–237.
10. Moore, Jill, 'Inquisition and its Organisation in Italy, 1250–1350', *Heresy and Inquisition in the Middle Ages*, York Medieval Press, Vol. 8, 2019, p. 314.
11. Baird, Joseph, Baglivi, Giuseppe, Kane, John Robert, 'The Chronicle of Salimbene de Adam', *Church History*, Vol. 57, Issue 2, June 1988, pp. 228–229.
12. Lo Bianco, Catherine, 'Dolcino: A Story of Italian Heretical Resistance', *Arena*, November 8, 2024.
13. Gallenga, Antonio Carlo Napoleone, *A Historical Memoir of Fra Dolcino and His Times: being an account of a general struggle for ecclesiastical reform and of an anti-heretical crusade in Italy, in the early part of the fourteenth century,* Longman, Brown, Green, and Longmans, 1853.
14. Maier, Christopher T., *Preaching the Crusades,* Cambridge University Press, 1994, ISBN: 0521 452465.
15. Barber, Malcolm, *The Trial of the Templars,* Cambridge University Press, 2012, ISBN: 978-1107645769.
16. Boutaric, Edgard, *Clément V, Philippe Le Bel Et Les Templiers,* Legare Street Press, 2023, ISBN: 978-1021227874.
17. Bellomo, Elena, *Colliding Perceptions,* Routledge, 2021, ISBN: 978-1003163510.
18. Finke, Heinrich, *Papsttum und Untergang des Templerordens: Vol. 1,* Wentworth Press, 2018, ISBN: 978-0274399475.
19. Théry-Astruc, Julien, 'The Pioneer of Royal Theocracy: Guillaume de Nogaret and the Conflicts between Philip the Fair and the Papacy', in Chester Jordan, William (ed.), Phillips, Jenna Rebecca, (ed.), *The Capetian Century 1214–1314,* Brepols, 2017, ISBN: 978-2503567181.
20. 'Knights Templar Absolved, 700 years late', *CBS News,* 12 October 2007.
21. Frale, Barbara, 'The Chinon Chart', *Journal of Medieval History,* 3 January 2012, Vol. 30, Issue 2, pp. 109–134.
22. Nicholson, Helen, *The Proceedings Against the Templars in the British Isles,* Routledge, 2018, ISBN: 978-1315085487.
23. Campbell, G. A., *The Knights Templar – Their Rise and Fall,* Duckworth, 1937.
24. *Council of Vienne,* Papal Encyclicals.
25. Roback, C. W., *The Mysteries of Astrology and the Wonders of Magic,* published by the author, 1854.

26. Demurger, Alain, *The Persecution of the Templars: Scandal, Torture, Trial,* Profile Books, 2018, ISBN: 978-1781257852.
27. Pullella, Philip, '*Knights Templar win heresy reprieve after 700 years*', Reuters, 12 October, 2007.

Chapter Four

1. 'Bloodlust, warped preoccupation with occult spurred Nazis says Oxy professor', *South Pasadena Review,* March 8, 1976.
2. Lusher, Adam, 'Nanteos Cup: "Holy Grail" stolen from sick woman's home', *The Independent,* July 16, 2014.
3. 'Holy grail is not in the pub, after all', *Malvern Gazette,* August 15, 2014.
4. Buckley, Julia, 'They all say they've got the Holy Grail. So who's right?', *CNN,* August 20, 2024
5. Carley, James P., 'Two pre-conquest manuscripts from Glastonbury Abbey', *Anglo-Saxon England,* Vol. 16, 1987, pp. 197–212.
6. Page, William, *A History of the County of Somerset: Volume 2,* Victoria County History, 1911.
7. Gerald of Wales (author), Bartlett, Robert (ed.), 'De Principis Instructione', *Academic*, 2018, ISBN: 978-0198738626.
8. Eschenbach, Wolfram von, *Parzival,* Penguin Classics, 1980, ISBN: 978-0140443615.
9. Jung, Emma, Von Franz, Marie-Louise, *The Grail Legend,* Coventure, 1986, ISBN: 978-0904575316.
10. Russell, Shahan, 'Otto Rahn, openly gay, secretly anti-Nazi', *War History Online,* January 10, 2016.
11. Harrington, Joel F., 'Himmler's Witch Hunt', *History Today,* Vol. 69, Issue 9, September 2019.
12. Hall, Alan, 'Madrid seeks return of Visigoth artefacts', *Daily Mail,* September 2, 2016.
13. Alonso, Francisco Gracia, 'Relations between Spanish Archaeologists and Nazi Germany (1939–1945): A preliminary examination of the influence of Das Ahnenerbe in Spain', *Bulletin of the History of Archaeology,* Vol. 18, No. 1, 2008.
14. Gongora, Montserrat Rico, *La Abadia Profanada,* Planeta Pub Corp, 2007, ISBN: 978-8408072256.
15. Heschel, Susannah, *The Aryan Jesus,* Princeton University Press, 2008, ISBN: 978-0691125312.
16. Keeley, Graham, 'Revealed: Himmler's secret quest to locate the "Aryan Holy Grail"', *The Independent,* February 6, 2007.
17. Kurlander, Eric, *Hitler's Monsters: A Supernatural History of the Third Reich,* Yale University Press, 2017, ISBN: 978-0300189452.
18. Goodrick-Clarke, Nicholas, *The Occult Roots of Nazism: Secret Aryan Cults and Their Influence on Nazi Ideology,* Taurus Parke Paperbacks, 2012, ISBN: 978-1860649738.
19. Rahn, Otto, *Crusade Against the Grail: The Struggle Between the Cathars, the Templars, and the Church of Rome,* Inner Traditions, 2006, ISBN: 978-1594771354.
20. Cavendish, Richard, 'Carcassonne falls in the Albigensian Crusade', *History Today,* Vol. 59, Issue 8, August 2009.
21. Verità, Marco, Speranza, Laura, Procinai, Simone, Angellotto, Daniele, 'The Sacro Catino in Genoa: Analytical and Technological Investigations of a Unique Glass Vessel', *Journal of Glass Studies,* Vol. 60, 2018, pp. 15–128.
22. Koch, Ariel, 'The New Crusaders: Contemporary Extreme Right Symbolism and Rhetoric', *Perspectives on Terrorism,* Vol. 11, No. 5, 2017, pp. 13–24.
23. Rhodes, James F., 'The Pardoner's "Vernycle" and his "Vera Icon"', *Modern Language Studies,* Vol. 13, No. 2, 1983, pp. 34–40.
24. Wilson, Ian, *The Turin Shroud,* Penguin Books Ltd., 1979, ISBN: 978-0140050646.
25. Segal, Judah Ben-Zion, *Edessa 'The Blessed City',* Gorgias Press, 2001, ISBN: 978-0971309715.
26. Eusebius of Caesaria, Maier, Paul J., (trans.), *The Church History,* Kregel Academic, 2007, ISBN: 978-0825433078.

27. Guscin, Mark (trans.), *The Sermon of Gregory Referendarius,* 2004.
28. Weaver, Maurice, 'And a missing link hidden in the heart of Somerset?' *The Daily Telegraph,* May 9, 1988.
29. Barber, Malcolm, 'The Templars and the Turin Shroud', *The Catholic Historical Review,* Catholic University of America Press, Vol. 68, No. 2, 1982, pp. 206–225.
30. Contamine, Philippe, 'Geoffroy de Charny', *Histoire et Société,* Vol. 2, 1992, pp. 107–121.
31. Brucker, Edward A., 'Let's take another look at the Shroud of Turin', *The Linacre Quarterly,* Catholic Medical Association, Vol. 57, Issue 1, 1990.
32. Maclellan, Alec, *Secret of the Spear: The Mystery of the Spear of Longinus,* Souvenir Books, 2004, ISBN: 978-0285636965.
33. Ravenscroft, Trevor, *The Spear of Destiny,* Neville Spearman, Publishers Ltd., 1973.
34. Ravenscroft, Trevor, 'Americans find the Spear as Hitler commits suicide', *The Daily Item,* August 30, 1973.
35. Vogel, Christian, 'Templar Runaways and Renegades before, during and after the Trial', in *The Debate on the Trial of the Templars (1307–1314),* Routledge, 2010, ISBN: 978-1315615349.
36. Tangredi, Sam J., Captain, 'The Elusive Fleet of the Knights Templar', *Naval History,* US Naval Institute, April 2023.

Chapter Five

1. Mackey, Albert G., Singleton, William R., *The History of Freemasonry,* The Masonic History Company, 1898.
2. Dunford, Barry, 'Was Pontius Pilate a Scot?', *Sacred Connections,* 2001, ISBN: 978-0954187309.
3. 'The Grail, Jesus's children, and Stone Age lasers: Scotland's madder myths', *The Scotsman,* February 14, 2005.
4. Ferguson, Robert, *The Knights Templar and Scotland,* The History Press, 2013, ISBN: 978-0752493381.
5. Lord, Evelyn, *The Knights Templar in Britain,* Routledge, 2004, ISBN: 978-1405801638.
6. Baker, Geoffrey, *Chronicon Angliae Temporibus Edwardi II Et Edwardi,* General Books LLC, 2012, ISBN: 978-1150057168.
7. 'Robert the Bruce – Essex Man', *Essex Record Office,* blog.
8. Menegakis, Juliana, 'The Mysterious Death of Margaret, Child Queen of Scotland', *Hektoen International, A Journal of Medical Humanities,* 2023.
9. Crome, Sarah, *Scotland's First War of Independence,* Auch Books, 1999, ISBN: 978-0953631605.
10. Martin-Gil, F. J., Martin-Ramos, P., Martin-Gil, J., 'Is Scotland's Coronation Stone a Measurement Standard from the Middle Bronze Age', *Laboratorio de Investigaciones sobre Conservacion del Patrimonio,* University of Valladolid.
11. Bower, Walter, *A History Book for Scots: Selections from the Scotichronicon,* John Donald, 2012, ISBN: 978-1906566593.
12. Grant, Alexander, 'The Death of John Comyn: What was going on?', *Scottish Historical Review,* Vol. 86. Issue 2, 2008, pp. 176–224.
13. Jill, Duchess of Hamilton, 'Benedict XVI should address the papacy's treatment of Robert the Bruce', *Catholic Herald,* August 13, 2010.
14. Fraser, C. M., *A History of Antony Bek, Bishop of Durham 1283–1311,* Oxford University Press.
15. Nicholson, Helen, *The Knights Templar on Trial,* The History Press, 2009, ISBN: 978-0750946810.
16. Wilkins, David, *Concilia Magnae Britanniae Et Hiberniae, Ab Anno 1268 Ad Annum 1349, Vol. 2,* Forgotten Books, ISBN: 978-0282250379.
17. Finke, Heinrich, *Papsttum und Untergang des Templerordens,* Wentworth Press, 2018, ISBN: 978-0274399475.
18. 'Order of Knights Templar', *The Berkshire Eagle,* September 17, 1995.
19. Catalan, Diego, *Gran crónica de Alfonso XI, Volume 1,* Seminario Menéndez Pidal, Universidad Complutense de Madrid, 1977, ISBN: 978-8460007968.

20. Hay, Father Richard Augustine, *Genealogie of the Sainteclaires of Rosslyn,* Thomas G. Stevenson, 1835.
21. Knight, Christopher, Lomas, Robert, *The Hiram Key: Pharaohs, Freemasons and the Discovery of the Secret Scrolls of Christ,* Arrow, 1997, ISBN: 978-0552980593.
22. Leroy, Thierry P. F., *Hugues de Payns, La Naissance des Templiers,* TheBookEdition, 2011, ISBN: 978-2746630499.
23. Watson, Fiona, 'A Longing for Peace: Putting the Declaration of Arbroath in Context', *Scottish Historical Review,* Vol. 101, Issue 3, 2022, pp. 379–394.
24. Horodowich, Elizabeth, 'Venetians in America: Nicolò Zen and the Virtual Exploration of the New World', *Renaissance Quarterly,* Vol. 67, Issue 3, 2014, pp. 841–877.
25. Di Robilant, Andrea, *Venetian Navigators: The Voyages of the Zen Brothers to the Far North,* Faber & Faber, 2011, ISBN: 978-0571243778.
26. 'Literary Notes', *The Pall Mall Gazette,* October 22, 1898.
27. Pohl, Frederick, *Prince Henry Sinclair: His Expedition to the New World in 1398,* Seafarer Books, 1951, ISBN: 978-1551091228.
28. 'Scot Newest New World Discoverer', *Albuquerque Journal,* October 30, 1974.
29. Soucoup, Dan, 'Acadia's military priest', *Times & Transcript,* October 6, 2001.
30. Payne, Libby, 'FYI', *The Boston Globe*, August 17, 2003.
31. 'Treasure hunters return to investigate Oak Island', *The North Bay Nugget,* October 18, 1993.
32. Fiske, John, *The Discovery of America: pre-Columbian voyages,* Houghton Mifflin, 1902.
33. Dickie, Douglas, Small, Alexander, 'Scotland's "creepiest" village thought to be home to Jesus Christ's mummified head', *Daily Record,* May 8, 2024.
34. Lyall, Sarah, 'A new breed of pilgrim hunts the elusive Holy Grail', *Chicago Tribune,* July 28, 2004.
35. Sinclair, Andrew, *The Sword and the Grail,* Century, 1993, ISBN: 978-0712657303.

Chapter Six

1. Lay, S., *The Reconquest Kings of Portugal: Political and Cultural Reorientation on the Medieval Frontier,* Palgrave Macmillan, 2008, ISBN: 978-0230525610.
2. De Vasconcellos, Antonio Garcia Ribeiro, *Evolucao de culto de Dona Isabel de Aragao, Esposa do Rei Lavrador,* Legare Street Press, 2023, ISBN: 978-1019708606.
3. John, Simon, 'The Papacy and the Establishment of the Kingdoms of Jerusalem, Sicily and Portugal: Twelfth Century Papal Political Thought on Incipient Kingship', *The Journal of Ecclesiastical History,* Cambridge University Press, Vol. 68, Issue 2, 2017, pp. 223–259.
4. 'Manifestis Probatum', *National Archive of the Torre do Tombo,* 1179.
5. Duggan, Anne J., Clarke, Peter D., *Pope Alexander III (1159–81): The Art of Survival (Church, Faith and Culture in the Medieval West),* Routledge, 2012, ISBN: 978-07564662884.
6. Herculano, Alexandre, *Historia de Portugal,* Kessinger Publishing, 2010, ISBN: 978-1160119155.
7. Wiedemann, Benedict G. E., 'The kingdom of Portugal, homage and papal "fiefdom" in the second half of the twelfth century', *Journal of Medieval History,* Vol. 41, Issue 4, 2015, pp. 432–445.
8. Stephens, Henry Morse, *The Story of Portugal,* Legare Street Press, 2022, ISBN: 978-1016097109.
9. Livermore, H. V., *A History of Portugal,* Cambridge University Press, 1966.
10. Valente, José, 'The New Frontier: The Role of the Knights Templar in the Establishment of Portugal as an Independent Kingdom', *Mediterranean Studies,* Penn State University Press, Vol. 7, 1998, pp. 49–65.
11. 'Portugal History', *Jewish Heritage Alliance,* website.
12. Nixon, Robert, *The Secret Pharmacopeia of Pope John XXI: Extracts from the Thesaurus Pauperum,* Hadean Press, 2024.
13. Klaassen, Frank, *The Routledge History of Medieval Magic,* Routledge, 2019, ISBN: 978-1315613192.

14. Gomes, Saul António, 'A extinção da Ordem do Templo em Portugal', *Impactum – Centro de História da Sociedade e da Cultura,* Coimbra University Press, 2011.
15. Dodd, Gwilyn (ed.), Musson, Anthony (ed.), *The Reign of Edward II,* Boydell & Brewer, 2006, ISBN: 978-1846155017.
16. 'The Templar Tower – Idanha-a-Velha', *Aldeias Historicas de Portugal,* website.
17. Porro, Clive, 'Reassessing the Dissolution of the Templars: King Dinis and their suppression in Portugal', in *The Debate on the Trial of the Templars (1307–1314),* Routledge, 2010, ISBN: 978-1315615349.
18. Oliveira, Luís Filipe, 'A Coroa, os Mestres e os Comendadores: As Ordens Militares de Avis e de Santiago, 1330–1449' *Universidade do Algarve,* 2009, ISBN: 978-9729341809.
19. 'As Gavetas da Torre do Tombo, II (Gav. III–XI)' *Centro de estudos históricos ultramarinos,* 1962.
20. Branco, Maria João, 'An archbishop and his claims: the allegations of Martinho Pires in Rome (1199) on the quarrels between Braga and Compostela', *Medieval Studies,* 2018.
21. De Gama Barros, Henrique, *Historia da administração publica em Portugal nos seculos 12 a 15; Volume 2,* Legare Street Press, 2023, ISBN: 978-1022597037.
22. Brandão, Frei Francisco, *Monarquia Lusitana VI,* INCM – Imprensa Nacional Casa da Moeda, 2010, ISBN: 978-9722716956.
23. 'Ad ea ex quibus cultus augeatur', *Archivo Nacional Torre do Tombo,* 1319, Reference code: PT/TT/GAV/7/5/2.
24. O'Callaghan, Joseph F., *A History of Medieval Spain: Memory and Power in the New Europe,* Cornell University Press, 1983, ISBN: 978-0801492648.
25. Moeller, Charles, 'Military Order of Montesa', *The Catholic Encyclopaedia,* Robert Appleton Company, 1911.
26. Dutra, Francis, A., 'Evolution of the Portuguese Order of Santiago, 1492–1600', *Mediterranean Studies,* Penn State University Press, Vol. 4, pp. 63–72.
27. Amarante, Eduardo, *Templários: da Milícia Cristã a Sociedade Secreta*, Zefiro, 2007, ISBN: 978-9728958336.
28. Baêna, Miguel Sanches, Loução, Paulo Alexandre, *Grandes Enigmas da História de Portugal,* Esquilo, 2009, ISBN: 978-9898092380.
29. 'Buried: Knights Templar and the Holy Grail', History channel, 2018.
30. Mariz, Vera, 'O restauro do pelourinho da Cidade Velha – Cabo Verde', *Africana Studia,* Universidade do Porto, No. 18, 2012, pp 225–248.
31. Racine, Matthew T., 'Service and Honour in Sixteenth-Century Portuguese North Africa', *The Sixteenth Century Journal,* The University of Chicago Press Journals, Vol. 32, No. 1, 2001.
32. Lavies, P. D., 'The São Sebastião fortress at Mozambique Island: A testimony of the variety in sixteenth century military architecture', University of Utrecht, 2012.
33. Barreto, Mascarenhas, *The Portuguese Columbus,* Palgrave Macmillan, 1992, ISBN: 978-1349219964.
34. Marino, Ruggero, *Christopher Columbus, the Last Templar,* Destiny Books, 2007, ISBN: 978-1594771903.
35. Sora, Steven, *The Lost Colony of the Templars: Verrazano's Secret Mission to America,* Destiny Books, 2004, ISBN: 978-1594770197.
36. Nash, Elizabeth, 'Portuguese village opens up new world of speculation as it lays claim to Columbus', *The Independent,* October 25, 2006.
37. Olsen, E., *The Calabrian Charlatan, 1598–1603: Messianic Nationalism in Early Modern Europe,* Palgrave Macmillan, 2002, ISBN: 978-1349508686.
38. 'Romanus Pontifex', *Papal Encyclicals Online,* website.
39. Boxer, C. R., 'Faith and Empire: The Cross and the Crown in Portuguese Expansion, Fifteenth-Eighteenth Centuries', *Terra Incognitae, The Journal for the History of Discoveries,* Vol. 8, Issue 1, 1976, pp. 73–89.

Chapter Seven

1. 'The Story of Modern Templary', *The Courier Journal,* August 27, 1901.
2. 'History of the Order', *OSMTJ,* website.
3. Dupilet, Alexandre, *Le régent: Philippe d'Orléans, l'héritier du roi-soleil,* Tallandier, 2020, ISBN: 979-1021001435.
4. Bern, Stéphane, 'The true story of the orgies of Philippe d'Orléans, the "debauched regent"', *Europe 1,* January 23, 2021.
5. Henderson, G. D., *Chevalier Ramsay,* Nelson (first edition), 1952.
6. Ashley, Maurice, *House of Stuart: its Rise and Fall,* Weidenfeld & Nicholson (first edition), 1980, ISBN: 978-0460044583.
7. Ramsay, Andrew Michael, *The Travels of Cyrus,* Nabu Press, 2012, ISBN: 978-1277939644.
8. Ahn, Doohwan, 'From Greece to Babylon: The political thought of Andrew Michael Ramsay (1686–1743)', *History of European Ideas,* Vol. 37, Issue 4, 2011, pp. 421–437.
9. Noticc in the *London Evening Post,* March 17, 1730.
10. 'In Eminenti', *Papal Encyclicals Online,* website.
11. Bernheim, Alain, *Ramsay et ses deux discours,* Telets, 2012, ISBN: 978-2906031746.
12. Robinson, John J., *Born in Blood: The Lost Secrets of Freemasonry,* M. Evans & Company (reprint edition), 2009, ISBN: 978-1590771488.
13. Leadbeater, Charles Webster, *Glimpses of Masonic History,* Zinc Read, 2023, ISBN: 978-9358945768.
14. Ozouf, Mona, 'War and Terror inFrench Revolutionary Discourse (1792–1794)', *The Journal of Modern History,* Vol. 56, No. 4.
15. De Gassicourt, Charles-Louis, *Le Tombeau de Jacques de Molay,* Books On Demand, 2020, ISBN: 978-2322255238.
16. Jefferson, Thomas, *The Jefferson Bible: The Life and Morals of Jesus of Nazareth,* A&D Books, 2009, ISBN: 978-1604591286.
17. Strathern, Paul, *Napoleon in Egypt: The Greatest Glory,* Vintage, 2008, ISBN: 978-1844139170.
18. Luttrell, Anthony, 'The Aragonese Crown and the Knights Hospitallers of Rhodes: 1291–1350', *The English Historical Review,* Oxford University Press, Vol. 76, No. 298, 1961, pp. 1–19.
19. Brown, Amelia Robertson, 'Antiquarian knights in Mediterranean island landscapes: the Hospitaller Order of St John and crusading among the ruins of classical antiquity, from medieval Rhodes to early modern Malta', *Journal of Medieval History,* Vol. 47, Issue 3, 2021, pp. 413–432.
20. Hammett, Dashiell, *The Maltese Falcon,* Alfred A. Knopf, 1930.
21. Miller, R. H., 'Hammett's Physical Falcon, or, What Exactly Did the Emperor Give?', *Studies in Popular Culture,* Popular Cultural Association in the South, Vol. 21, No. 2, pp. 45–52.
22. Pryor, Felix, *Elizabeth I: Her Life in Letters,* University of California Press (first edition), 2003, ISBN: 978-0520241060.
23. Bamford, Paul Walden, 'The Knights of Malta and the King of France', *French Historical Studies,* Vol. 3, No. 4, 1964, pp. 429–453.
24. Castillo, Dennis, 'The Knights cannot be admitted: Maltese nationalism, the Knights of St. John, and the French occupation of 1798–1800', *The Catholic Historical Review,* Catholic University of America Press, Vol. 79, No. 3, pp. 434–453.
25. 'Knights Templar and the Freemasons', *GPUSA Education Department,* Sovereign Military Order of the Temple of Jerusalem, 2023.
26. Sarrut, Germain, *Biographie De M. L'abbé Chatel,* Nabu Press, 2011, ISBN: 978-1246827866.
27. 'Foreign Intelligence', *Aberdeen Journal,* February 20, 1833.
28. 'Knights Templar', *The Caledonian Mercury,* March 27, 1837.
29. 'A Shrewd Priest', *The Examiner,* March 29, 1835.
30. Grégoire, Henri, *De la Littérature des Nègres,* BiblioBazaar, 2009, ISBN: 978-1110015412.
31. Fraissinet, Edouard, *Essai Sur L'Histoire De L'Ordre Des Templiers,* Kessinger Publishing, 2009, ISBN: 978-1120447715.
32. 'The Templars', *The Hull Packet,* November 1, 1839.

33. Lucas, Henry, *Manual of the Knights of the Order of the Temple,* Gleed Press, 2011, ISBN: 978-1446092682.
34. 'The Order of the Temple', *National Freemason* clipped in the *Memphis Daily Appeal,* June 14, 1868.
35. Clausen, Daniel J., 'The Missing Antique Archive of Fabre Palaprat's Ordre du Temple', *Sovereign and Military Order of the Temple of Jerusalem.*
36. 'A New Oscar Wilde', *Pittsburg Dispatch,* August 30, 1891.
37. 'A Russian prince at the French bar', *Evening Post,* October 24, 1891.

Chapter Eight

1. Brown, Dan, *The Da Vinci Code,* Corgi (first edition), 2009, ISBN: 978-0552159715.
2. Baigent, Michael, Leigh, Richard, Lincoln, Henry, *The Holy Blood and The Holy Grail,* Arrow Books, 1995, ISBN: 978-0099682417.
3. Rozenberg, Joshua, 'Authors lose appeal over Da Vinci Code', *The Daily Telegraph,* March 29, 2007.
4. Baigent, Michael, Leigh, Richard, Lincoln, Henry, 'The heirs to a Dark Age secret', *Evening Standard,* January 13, 1982.
5. Chaumeil, Jean-Luc, Low, Chantal, *The Priory of Sion: Shedding Light on the Treasure and Legacy of Rennes-le-Chateau and the Priory of Sion,* Avalonia, 2010, ISBN: 978-1905297412.
6. Schorn, Daniel, *The Priory of Sion,* CBS News, April 27, 2006.
7. Allegro, John Marco, *The Treasure of the Copper Scroll: The Opening and Decipherment of the most mysterious of the Dead Sea Scrolls, a unique inventory of buried treasure,* Routledge, 2023, ISBN: 978-1032664385.
8. Pullan, Patricia, 'Treasures rumoured beneath dungeon', *The Baltimore Sun,* September 20, 1970.
9. Bothezat, Tania, 'But the more Paris changes', *The Baltimore Sun,* November 2, 1962.
10. De Sede, Gerard, *The Accursed Treasure of Rennes-le-Chateau,* DEK Publishing, 2001.
11. Kahn, Henry, 'Dig this for a holiday', *The Sunday People,* September 2, 1962.
12. 'Village plagued by treasure hunters', *The Guardian Journal,* December 27, 1968.
13. Ambelain, Robert, *Jesus ou le mortel secret des Templiers,* Robert Laffont, 1977.
14. Introvigne, Massimo, 'The Da Vinci Code FAQ, or will the real Priory of Sion please stand up?', *Center for Studies on New Religions.*
15. Lincoln, Henry, Baigent, Michael, Leigh, Richard, *The Messianic Legacy,* Arrow, 1996, ISBN: 978-0099664215.
16. Otto, Marge, 'A shocking look at religion', *The Monitor,* September 4, 1988.
17. Beale, Robert, 'Crushingly boring', *Manchester Evening News,* January 22, 1987.
18. Reproduced in *Le Point,* No. 1112, January 8, 1994, p. 11.
19. Featured in *France-Soir,* November 15, 1993, and reproduced on the priory-of-sion.com website.
20. Riding, Alan, 'Judge is said to claim Mitterrand took payments', *The New York Times,* December 27, 1993.
21. 'Aude : voilée de blanc, elle invoque la Syrie et détruit la statue de l'église', *Midi Libre,* April 24, 2017.
22. Prince, Clive, Picknett, Lynn, *The Templar Revelation: Secret Guardians of the true identity of Christ,* Corgi, 2007, ISBN: 978-0552155403.
23. Cutler, B. J., 'Fascist party hopes to rule Spain', *The Cincinnati Post,* January 23, 1967.
24. Miller, Russell, 'Inside the sect of pain', *Daily Mirror,* February 26, 1981.
25. 'Open Letter to Sony', *Opus Dei (press release),* April 14, 2006.
26. 'The Da Vinci Code, the Catholic Church and Opus Dei', Opus Dei website, May 11, 2006.
27. Wallace-Murphy, Tim, Hopkins, Marilyn, *Rex Deus: The True Mystery of Rennes Le Chateau and the Dynasty of Jesus,* Element, 2000, ISBN: 978-1862044722.
28. Ehrman, Bart D., *How Jesus Became God: The Exaltation of a Jewish Preacher from Galilee,* Bravo Ltd (reprint), 2015, ISBN: 978-0061778193.

29. Wallace-Murphy, Tim, *The Knights of the Holy Grail: The Secret History of the Knights Templar,* Watkins Publishing, 2007, ISBN: 978-1905857225.
30. Josephus, Flavius, *The Antiquities of the Jews: The Unabridged Jewish History Classic,* Moncreiffe Press, 2023, ISBN: 979-8377480914.
31. Allen, Nicholas P. L., 'Josephus on James the Just? A re-evaluation of Antiquitates Judaicae 20.9.1', *Journal of Early Christian History,* Vol. 7, Issue 1, June 2017, pp. 1–27.
32. Wallace-Murphy, Tim, Hopkins, Marilyn, *Rex Deus: The True Mystery of Rennes Le Chateau and the Dynasty of Jesus,* Element (first edition), 2000, ISBN: 978-1862044722.
33. Knight, Christopher, Lomas, Robert, *The Second Messiah,* Arrow, 1998, ISBN: 978-0099227328.
34. Cripps, Thomas, *William II (Rufus),* Historic UK.
35. 'About us', Sauniere Society, website
36. Scott, Walter, *Waverley,* Penguin Classics (reprint), 2011, ISBN: 978-0140436600.
37. Eco, Umberto, *Foucault's Pendulum,* Mariner Books (first edition), 2007, ISBN: 978-0156032971.
38. Coe, Jonathan, 'The heights of lowdown', *The Guardian*, October 12, 1989.
39. Burgess, Anthony, 'A Conspiracy to Rule the World', *The New York Times*, October 15, 1989.

Chapter Nine

1. Carpenter, Richard (writer), Sharp, Ian (director), *Seven Poor Knights from Acre*, Robin of Sherwood TV series, first broadcast April 5 1984.
2. Pollock, Dale, 'American Graffiti makes Lucas a millionaire at 28', *Philadelphia Inquirer,* June 29, 1983.
3. Burroughs, Edgar Rice, *'A Fighting Man of Mars',* Ace Books Inc., 1931.
4. Pollock, Dale, *Skywalking: The Life and Films of George Lucas*, Da Capo Press, 1999 (updated edition), ISBN: 978-0306809040.
5. Masters, Patrick, 'How Star Wars' Jedi were inspired by the Knights Templar', *University of Portsmouth,* July 7, 2022.
6. Rinzler, Jonathan W., *The Making of Star Wars: The Definitive Story Behind the Original Film,* Aurum, 2013, ISBN: 978-1781311905.
7. McGrath, James, F., 'What has Coruscant to Do with Jerusalem? A Response and Reflections at the Crossroads of Hebrew Bible and Science Fiction', *Journal of Hebrew Scriptures,* Vol. 16, Issue 9, 2016, pp. 79–93.
8. McMahon, Tony, 'Assassin's Creed – so did the REAL Assassins hate the Templars that much?', *The Templar Knight,* 2010.
9. Bartol, Vladimir, *Alamut,* North Atlantic Books, 2007, ISBN: 978-1556436819.
10. Spasov, Malamir, '"Nothing is True, Everything is Permitted." Vladimir Bartol's Novel "Alamut" – Belated Entry in the Modern Balkan Context', *Études Balkaniques*, Issue 3, 2015, pp. 236–267.
11. Scott, Walter, *Ivanhoe,* Wordsworth Editions, 1995, ISBN: 978-1853262029.
12. Greenacre, Liam, '"The Norman Yoke": Uses of the past during the English Civil War', *The York Historian,* University of York, September 29, 2017.
13. Khan, Aina J, 'Ertuğrul: how an epic TV series became the "Muslim Game of Thrones"', *The Guardian,* August 12, 2020.
14. 'Egypt fatwa bans Ertugrul, Turkish soaps', *Middle East Monitor,* February 12, 2020.
15. Morales, Antonio Huertas, Moreno, Maria Bosch, 'Caballeros de la oscuridad: la Orden del Temple en el cine de Amando de Ossorio', *Romanica Silesiana,* Wydawnictwo Uniwersytetu Śląskiego, number 11, Issue 2, 2016.
16. Barbet, Pierre, *L'Empire du Baphomet,* Fleuve Noir (first edition), 1972.
17. 'Falling Meteor', *Northwest Arkansas Times,* December 29, 1972.
18. Perry, B. P., 'Jedi Knights vs. Knights Templar', *Sky History.*
19. Jones, William R., 'Political Uses of Sorcery in Medieval Europe', *The Historian*, Vol. 34, Issue 4, 1972, pp. 670–687
20. Kramer, Heinrich, *Malleus maleficarum,* 1508, 1928 edition published by J. Rodker.

Bibliography

Chapter One

Al-Tifashi, Ahmad, *The Delight of Hearts: Or what you will not find in any book,* Gay Sunshine Press, 1988, ISBN: 978-0940567092.

Al-Maghribi, Ibn Sacid, Bellamy, James A., 'The Banners of the Champions: An Anthology of Medieval Arabic Poetry from Andalusia and Beyond', *Hispanic Seminary of Medieval Studies,* 1989, ISBN: 978-0940639270.

Barber, Malcolm, *The Trial of the Templars,* Cambridge University Press, 2012, ISBN: 978-1107645769.

Crawford, Katherine, *European Sexualities, 1400–1800,* Cambridge University Press, 2007, ISBN: 978-0521548403.

Demurger, Alain, *The Persecution of the Templars: Scandal, Torture, Trial,* Profile Books, 2018, ISBN: 978-1781257852.

Feuchter, Jörg, 'Europe Penetrated by Islam. The Orientalization of the Order of the Templars', essay in Mackenthun, Gesa (ed.), *Entangled Knowledge Scientific Discourses and Cultural Difference,* Waxmann, 2012, ISBN: 978-3830977292.

Forey, Alan, 'Could Alleged Malpractices Have Remained Undetected for Decades?', essay in Burgtorf, Jochen, Crawford, Paul F., *The Debate on the Trial of the Templars (1307–1314),* Routledge, 2010, ISBN: 978-0754665700.

Freshfield E., *A Manual of Roman Law: The Ecloga,* Cambridge, 1926, reprinted in Geanokoplos, Deno, *Byzantium: Church, Society, and Civilization Seen through Contemporary Eyes,* University of Chicago Press, 1986, ISBN: 978-0226284613.

Gaunt, Simon (ed.), Kay, Sarah (ed.), *The Troubadours: An Introduction,* Cambridge University Press, 1999, ISBN: 978-0521573887.

Gregorovius, Ferdinand, *History of the City of Rome in the Middle Ages,* George Bell & Sons, 1894.

Hart, Mother Columba, *Hildegard of Bingen: Scivias,* Paulist Press, 1990, ISBN: 978-0809131303.

Harvey, Karen, *The Kiss in History,* Manchester University Press, 2005, ISBN: 978-0719065958.

Hauréau, Barthélemy, *Bernard Délicieux et l'Inquisition Albigeoise: 1300–1320,* Librairie Hachette et Cie, 1877.

Keightley, Thomas, *Secret Societies of the Middle Ages: The Assassins, the Templars, and the Secret Tribunals of Westphalia,* Red Wheel/Weiser, 2005, ISBN: 978-1578633340.

Lea, Henry Charles, *A History of the Inquisition of the Middle Ages. Vol. 1,* Harper & Brothers, 1887.

Lévi, Éliphas, *Transcendental Magic: Its Doctrine and Ritual,* George Redway, 1896.

Luttrell, Anthony, 'The Election of the Templar Master Jacques de Molay', in *The Debate on the Trial of the Templars (1307–1314),* Routledge, 2010, ISBN: 978-0754665700.

Map, Walter, Tupper, Frederick (trans.), Bladen, Marbury (trans.), *De Nugis Curialium,* Chatto & Windus, 1924.

Meisami, Julie Scott (ed.), Starkey, Paul (ed.), *Encyclopedia of Arabic Literature,* Routledge, 1998, ISBN: 978-0415068086.

Menache, Sophie, *The Military Orders Volume II,* Routledge, 1998, ISBN: 978-1315085920.

Michelet, Jules, *History of France,* D. Appleton and Company, 1882.

Partner, Peter, *The Murdered Magicians: Templars and Their Myth,* Aquarian Press, 1987, ISBN: 978-0850305340.

Smith, Morton, *Clement of Alexandria and a Secret Gospel of Mark,* Harvard University Press, 1973, ISBN: 978-0674134904.
Trevor-Roper, Hugh, *The European Witch-Craze of the Sixteenth and Seventeenth Centuries,* Penguin Books, 1969, ISBN: 978-0140210095.
Venning, Timothy, 'The Crusades after the loss of the Holy Land 1292–1456', in *A Chronology of the Crusades,* Routledge, ISBN: 978-1315712932.
Von Hammer-Purgstall, Joseph, *Mysterium Baphometis Revelatum,* Anton Schmid, 1818.
White, Chris, *Nineteenth-Century Writings on Homosexuality,* Routledge, 2012, ISBN: 978-0203002407.

Chapter Two

Beaune, Colette, *Birth of an Ideology: Myths and Symbols of Nation in Late-Medieval France,* University of California Press, 1992, ISBN: 978-0520059412.
De Boissy d'Anglas, François-Antoine, 'Mémoire sur le procès de Guichard, évêque de Troyes, en 1304 et années suivantes', *Institut de France,* 1822.
De la Torre, Ignacio, 'The monetary fluctuations in Philip IV's kingdom of France and their relevance to the arrest of the Templars', in Nicholson, Helen, Crawford, Paul F., Burgtorf, Jochen, *The Debate on the Trial of the Templars,* Routledge, 2024, ISBN: 978-1032920108
Denton, Jeffrey, 'The attempted trial of Boniface VIII for heresy', in Mulholland, Maureen, Pullan, Brian, Pullan, Anne, *Judicial Tribunals in England and Europe, 1200–1700,* Manchester University Press, 2003, ISBN: 978-0719063428.
Field, Sean L., *Courting Sanctity: Holy Women and the Capetians,* Cornell University Press, 2019, ISBN: 978-1501736193.
Gaposchkin, M. Cecilia, Field, Sean L., Field, Larry, F., *The Sanctity of Louis IX: Early Lives of Saint Louis by Geoffrey of Beaulieu and William of Chartres,* Cornell University Press, 2013, ISBN: 978-0801478185.
Howarth, Stephen, *The Knights Templar,* Bloomsbury Continuum, 2006, ISBN: 978-0826480347.
Lea, Charles Henry, *History of the Inquisition of the Middle Ages – Volume 3,* Harper & Collins, 1888.
Prestwich, Michael, *Edward I,* Yale University Press, 1997, ISBN: 978-0300071573.
Provost, Alain, *Domus Diaboli: Un évêque en procès au temps de Philippe le Bel,* Belin, 2010, ISBN: 978-2701148953.
Rigault, Abel, *Le Procès De Guichard, Évêque De Troyes (1308–1313),* A. Picard et Fils, 1896.
Stabler Miller, Tanya, *The Beguines of Medieval Paris: Gender, Patronage, and Spiritual Authority (The Middle Ages Series),* University of Pennsylvania Press, 2014, ISBN: 978-0812246070.
Strayer, Joseph R., *The Reign of Philip the Fair,* Princeton University Press, 1980, ISBN: 978-0691100890.
Villani, Giovanni, Selfe Rose E. (trans.), *Villani's Chronicle being selections from the First Nine Books of the Croniche Fiorentine of Giovanni Villani,* Archibald Constable & Co. Ltd., 1906.
Woodacre, Elena, *Joan of Navarre: Infanta, Duchess, Queen, Witch?,* Routledge, 2022, ISBN: 978-0367203481.
Woodacre, Elena, *The Queen Regnant of Navarre: Succession, Politics, and Partnership, 1274–1512 (Queenship and Power),* Palgrave Macmillan, 2013, ISBN: 978-1349464319.

Chapter Three

Barber, Malcolm, *The Trial of the Templars,* Cambridge University Press, 2012, ISBN: 978-1107645769.
Bellomo, Elena, *Colliding Perceptions,* Routledge, 2021, ISBN: 978-1003163510.
Boutaric, Edgard, *Clément V, Philippe Le Bel Et Les Templiers,* Legare Street Press, 2023, ISBN: 978-1021227874.
Campbell, G. A., *The Knights Templar – Their Rise and Fall,* Duckworth, 1937.
Demurger, Alain, *The Persecution of the Templars: Scandal, Torture, Trial,* Profile Books, 2018, ISBN: 978-1781257852.

Finke, Heinrich, *Papsttum und Untergang des Templerordens: Vol. 1,* Wentworth Press, 2018, ISBN: 978-0274399475.

Gallenga, Antonio Carlo Napoleone, *A Historical Memoir of Fra Dolcino and His Times: being an account of a general struggle for ecclesiastical reform and of an anti-heretical crusade in Italy, in the early part of the fourteenth century,* Longman, Brown, Green, and Longmans, 1853.

Maier, Christopher T., *Preaching the Crusades,* Cambridge University Press, 1994, ISBN: 0521 452465.

Menache, Sophia, *Clement V,* Cambridge University Press, 1998, ISBN: 978-0511582806.

Nicholson, Helen, *The Proceedings Against the Templars in the British Isles,* Routledge, 2018, ISBN: 978-1315085487.

Roback, C. W., *The Mysteries of Astrology and the Wonders of Magic,* published by the author, 1854.

Tanner, Norman P., *Decrees of the Ecumenical Councils: Volumes 1 and 2: From Nicaea to Vatican II,* Georgetown University Press, 1990, ISBN: 978-0878404902.

Théry-Astruc, Julien, 'The Pioneer of Royal Theocracy: Guillaume de Nogaret and the Conflicts between Philip the Fair and the Papacy', in Chester Jordan, William (ed.), Phillips, Jenna Rebecca, (ed.), *The Capetian Century 1214–1314,* Brepols, 2017, ISBN: 978-2503567181.

Chapter Four

Eschenbach, Wolfram von, *Parzival,* Penguin Classics, 1980, ISBN: 978-0140443615.

Eusebius of Caesaria, Maier, Paul J., (trans.), *The Church History,* Kregel Academic, 2007, ISBN: 978-0825433078.

Gerald of Wales (author), Bartlett, Robert (ed.), 'De Principis Instructione', *Academic,* 2018, ISBN: 978-0198738626.

Gongora, Montserrat Rico, *La Abadia Profanada,* Planeta Pub Corp, 2007, ISBN: 978-8408072256.

Goodrick-Clarke, Nicholas, *The Occult Roots of Nazism: Secret Aryan Cults and Their Influence on Nazi Ideology,* Taurus Parke Paperbacks, 2012, ISBN: 978-1860649738.

Heschel, Susannah, *The Aryan Jesus,* Princeton University Press, 2008, ISBN: 978-0691125312.

Jung, Emma, Von Franz, Marie-Louise, *The Grail Legend,* Coventure, 1986, ISBN: 978-0904575316.

Kurlander, Eric, *Hitler's Monsters: A Supernatural History of the Third Reich,* Yale University Press, 2017, ISBN: 978-0300189452.

Maclellan, Alec, *Secret of the Spear: The Mystery of the Spear of Longinus,* Souvenir Books, 2004, ISBN: 978-0285636965.

Rahn, Otto, *Crusade Against the Grail: The Struggle Between the Cathars, the Templars, and the Church of Rome,* Inner Traditions, 2006, ISBN: 978-1594771354.

Ravenscroft, Trevor, *The Spear of Destiny,* Neville Spearman, Publishers Ltd., 1973.

Segal, Judah Ben-Zion, *Edessa 'The Blessed City',* Gorgias Press, 2001, ISBN: 978-0971309715.

Vogel, Christian, 'Templar Runaways and Renegades before, during and after the Trial', in *The Debate on the Trial of the Templars (1307–1314),* Routledge, 2010, ISBN: 978-1315615349.

Wilson, Ian, *The Turin Shroud,* Penguin Books Ltd., 1979, ISBN: 978-0140050646.

Chapter Five

Baker, Geoffrey, *Chronicon Angliae Temporibus Edwardi II Et Edwardi,* General Books LLC, 2012, ISBN: 978-1150057168.

Bower, Walter, *A History Book for Scots: Selections from the Scotichronicon,* John Donald, 2012, ISBN: 978-1906566593.

Catalan, Diego, *Gran crónica de Alfonso XI, Volume 1,* Seminario Menéndez Pidal, Universidad Complutense de Madrid, 1977, ISBN: 978-8460007968.

Crome, Sarah, *Scotland's First War of Independence,* Auch Books, 1999, ISBN: 978-0953631605.

Di Robilant, Andrea, *Venetian Navigators: The Voyages of the Zen Brothers to the Far North,* Faber & Faber, 2011, ISBN: 978-0571243778.

Dunford, Barry, 'Was Pontius Pilate a Scot?', *Sacred Connections,* 2001, ISBN: 978-0954187309.

Ferguson, Robert, *The Knights Templar and Scotland,* The History Press, 2013, ISBN: 978-0752493381.

Finke, Heinrich, *Papsttum und Untergang des Templerordens,* Wentworth Press, 2018, ISBN: 978-0274399475.

Hay, Father Richard Augustine, *Genealogie of the Sainteclaires of Rosslyn,* Thomas G. Stevenson, 1835.

Knight, Christopher, Lomas, Robert, *The Hiram Key: Pharaohs, Freemasons and the Discovery of the Secret Scrolls of Christ,* Arrow, 1997, ISBN: 978-0552980593.

Leroy, Thierry P. F., *Hugues de Payns, La Naissance des Templiers,* TheBookEdition, 2011, ISBN: 978-2746630499.

Lord, Evelyn, *The Knights Templar in Britain,* Routledge, 2004, ISBN: 978-1405801638.

Mackey, Albert G., Singleton, William R., *The History of Freemasonry,* The Masonic History Company, 1898.

Nicholson, Helen, *The Knights Templar on Trial,* The History Press, 2009, ISBN: 978-0750946810.

Pohl, Frederick, *Prince Henry Sinclair: His Expedition to the New World in 1398,* Seafarer Books, 1951, ISBN: 978-1551091228.

Sinclair, Andrew, *The Sword and the Grail,* Century, 1993, ISBN: 978-0712657303.

Wilkins, David, *Concilia Magnae Britanniae Et Hiberniae, Ab Anno 1268 Ad Annum 1349, Vol. 2,* Forgotten Books, ISBN: 978-0282250379.

Chapter Six

Amarante, Eduardo, *Templários: da Milícia Cristã a Sociedade Secreta*, Zefiro, 2007, ISBN: 978-9728958336.

Baêna, Miguel Sanches, Loução, Paulo Alexandre, *Grandes Enigmas da História de Portugal,* Esquilo, 2009, ISBN: 978-9898092380.

Barreto, Mascarenhas, *The Portuguese Columbus,* Palgrave Macmillan, 1992, ISBN: 978-1349219964.

Brandão, Frei Francisco, *Monarquia Lusitana VI,* INCM – Imprensa Nacional Casa da Moeda, 2010, ISBN: 978-9722716956.

De Gama Barros, Henrique, *Historia da administração publica em Portugal nos seculos 12 a 15; Volume 2,* Legare Street Press, 2023, ISBN: 978-1022597037.

De Vasconcellos, Antonio Garcia Ribeiro, *Evolucao de culto de Dona Isabel de Aragao, Esposa do Rei Lavrador,* Legare Street Press, 2023, ISBN: 978-1019708606.

Dodd, Gwilyn (ed.), Musson, Anthony (ed.), *The Reign of Edward II,* Boydell & Brewer, 2006, ISBN: 978-1846155017.

Duggan, Anne J., Clarke, Peter D., *Pope Alexander III (1159–81): The Art of Survival (Church, Faith and Culture in the Medieval West),* Routledge, 2012, ISBN: 978-07564662884.

Herculano, Alexandre, *Historia de Portugal,* Kessinger Publishing, 2010, ISBN: 978-1160119155.

Klaassen, Frank, *The Routledge History of Medieval Magic,* Routledge, 2019, ISBN: 978-1315613192.

Lay, S., *The Reconquest Kings of Portugal: Political and Cultural Reorientation on the Medieval Frontier,* Palgrave Macmillan, 2008, ISBN: 978-0230525610.

Livermore, H. V., *A History of Portugal,* Cambridge University Press, 1966.

Marino, Ruggero, *Christopher Columbus, the Last Templar,* Destiny Books, 2007, ISBN: 978-1594771903.

Moeller, Charles, 'Military Order of Montesa', *The Catholic Encyclopaedia,* Robert Appleton Company, 1911.

O'Callaghan, Joseph F., *A History of Medieval Spain: Memory and Power in the New Europe,* Cornell University Press, 1983, ISBN: 978-0801492648.

Oliveira, Luís Filipe, 'A Coroa, os Mestres e os Comendadores: As Ordens Militares de Avis e de Santiago, 1330–1449' *Universidade do Algarve,* 2009, ISBN: 978-9729341809.

Olsen, E., *The Calabrian Charlatan, 1598–1603: Messianic Nationalism in Early Modern Europe,* Palgrave Macmillan, 2002, ISBN: 978-1349508686.

Porro, Clive, 'Reassessing the Dissolution of the Templars: King Dinis and their suppression in Portugal', in *The Debate on the Trial of the Templars (1307–1314),* Routledge, 2010, ISBN: 978-1315615349.

Sora, Steven, *The Lost Colony of the Templars: Verrazano's Secret Mission to America,* Destiny Books, 2004, ISBN: 978-1594770197.

Stephens, Henry Morse, *The Story of Portugal,* Legare Street Press, 2022, ISBN: 978-1016097109.

Chapter Seven

Ashley, Maurice, *House of Stuart: its Rise and Fall,* Weidenfeld & Nicholson (first edition), 1980, ISBN: 978-0460044583.

Bernheim, Alain, *Ramsay et ses deux discours,* Telets, 2012, ISBN: 978-2906031746.

De Gassicourt, Charles-Louis, *Le Tombeau de Jacques de Molay,* Books On Demand, 2020, ISBN: 978-2322255238.

Dupilet, Alexandre, *Le régent: Philippe d'Orléans, l'héritier du roi-soleil,* Tallandier, 2020, ISBN: 979-1021001435.

Fraissinet, Edouard, *Essai Sur L'Histoire De L'Ordre Des Templiers,* Kessinger Publishing, 2009, ISBN: 978-1120447715.

Grégoire, Henri, *De la Littérature des Nègres,* BiblioBazaar, 2009, ISBN: 978-1110015412.

Hammett, Dashiell, *The Maltese Falcon,* Alfred A. Knopf, 1930.

Henderson, G. D., *Chevalier Ramsay,* Nelson (first edition), 1952.

Jefferson, Thomas, *The Jefferson Bible: The Life and Morals of Jesus of Nazareth,* A&D Books, 2009, ISBN: 978-1604591286.

Leadbeater, Charles Webster, *Glimpses of Masonic History,* Zinc Read, 2023, ISBN: 978-9358945768.

Lucas, Henry, *Manual of the Knights of the Order of the Temple,* Gleed Press, 2011, ISBN: 978-1446092682.

Pryor, Felix, *Elizabeth I: Her Life in Letters,* University of California Press (first edition), 2003, ISBN: 978-0520241060.

Ramsay, Andrew Michael, *The Travels of Cyrus,* Nabu Press, 2012, ISBN: 978-1277939644.

Robinson, John J., *Born in Blood: The Lost Secrets of Freemasonry,* M. Evans & Company (reprint edition), 2009, ISBN: 978-1590771488.

Strathern, Paul, *Napoleon in Egypt: The Greatest Glory,* Vintage, 2008, ISBN: 978-1844139170.

Sarrut, Germain, *Biographie De M. L'abbé Chatel,* Nabu Press, 2011, ISBN: 978-1246827866.

Chapter Eight

Allegro, John Marco, *The Treasure of the Copper Scroll: The Opening and Decipherment of the most mysterious of the Dead Sea Scrolls, a unique inventory of buried treasure*, Routledge, 2023, ISBN: 978-1032664385.

Baigent, Michael, Leigh, Richard, Lincoln, Henry, *The Holy Blood and The Holy Grail,* Arrow Books, 1995, ISBN: 978-0099682417.

Brown, Dan, *The Da Vinci Code*, Corgi (first edition), 2009, ISBN: 978-0552159715.

Chaumeil, Jean-Luc, Low, Chantal, *The Priory of Sion: Shedding Light on the Treasure and Legacy of Rennes-le-Chateau and the Priory of Sion,* Avalonia, 2010, ISBN: 978-1905297412.

De Sede, Gerard, *The Accursed Treasure of Rennes-le-Chateau,* DEK Publishing, 2001.

Eco, Umberto, *Foucault's Pendulum,* Mariner Books (first edition), 2007, ISBN: 978-0156032971.

Ehrman, Bart D., *How Jesus Became God: The Exaltation of a Jewish Preacher from Galilee,* Bravo Ltd (reprint), 2015, ISBN: 978-0061778193.

Josephus, Flavius, *The Antiquities of the Jews: The Unabridged Jewish History Classic,* Moncreiffe Press, 2023, ISBN: 979-8377480914.

Knight, Christopher, Lomas, Robert, *The Second Messiah,* Arrow, 1998, ISBN: 978-0099227328.

Lincoln, Henry, Baigent, Michael, Leigh, Richard, *The Messianic Legacy,* Arrow, 1996, ISBN: 978-0099664215.

Prince, Clive, Picknett, Lynn, *The Templar Revelation: Secret Guardians of the true identity of Christ,* Corgi, 2007, ISBN: 978-0552155403.
Scott, Walter, *Waverley,* Penguin Classics (reprint), 2011, ISBN: 978-0140436600.
Wallace-Murphy, Tim, *The Knights of the Holy Grail: The Secret History of the Knights Templar,* Watkins Publishing, 2007, ISBN: 978-1905857225.
Wallace-Murphy, Tim, Hopkins, Marilyn, *Rex Deus: The True Mystery of Rennes Le Chateau and the Dynasty of Jesus,* Element, 2000, ISBN: 978-1862044722.
Wallace-Murphy, Tim, Hopkins, Marilyn, *Rex Deus: The True Mystery of Rennes Le Chateau and the Dynasty of Jesus,* Element (first edition), 2000, ISBN: 978-1862044722.

Chapter Nine

Barbet, Pierre, *L'Empire du Baphomet,* Fleuve Noir (first edition), 1972.
Bartol, Vladimir, *Alamut,* North Atlantic Books, 2007, ISBN: 978-1556436819.
Burroughs, Edgar Rice, *A Fighting Man of Mars,* Ace Books Inc., 1931.
Kramer, Heinrich, *Malleus maleficarum,* 1508, 1928 edition published by J. Rodker.
Pollock, Dale, *Skywalking: The Life and Films of George Lucas,* Da Capo Press, 1999 (updated edition), ISBN: 978-0306809040.
Rinzler, Jonathan W., *The Making of Star Wars: The Definitive Story Behind the Original Film,* Aurum, 2013, ISBN: 978-1781311905.
Scott, Walter, *Ivanhoe,* Wordsworth Editions, 1995, ISBN: 978-1853262029.

Index